Learn Algorithmic Trading

Build and deploy algorithmic trading systems and strategies
using Python and advanced data analysis

Sebastien Donadio
Sourav Ghosh

BIRMINGHAM - MUMBAI

Learn Algorithmic Trading

Copyright © 2019 Packt Publishing

Commissioning Editor: Sunith Shetty
Acquisition Editor: Ali Abidi
Content Development Editor: Nazia Shaikh
Senior Editor: Sheetal Rane
Technical Editor: Dinesh Chaudhary
Copy Editor: Safis Editing
Project Coordinator: Kirti Pisat
Proofreader: Safis Editing
Indexer: Pratik Shirodkar
Production Designer: Joshua Misquitta

First published: November 2019

Production reference: 1071119

Published by Packt Publishing Ltd.
Livery Place
35 Livery Street
Birmingham
B3 2PB, UK.

ISBN 978-1-78934-834-7

www.packt.com

Packt.com

Subscribe to our online digital library for full access to over 7,000 books and videos, as well as industry leading tools to help you plan your personal development and advance your career. For more information, please visit our website.

Why subscribe?

- Spend less time learning and more time coding with practical eBooks and videos from over 4,000 industry professionals

- Improve your learning with Skill Plans built especially for you

- Get a free eBook or video every month

- Fully searchable for easy access to vital information

- Copy and paste, print, and bookmark content

Did you know that Packt offers eBook versions of every book published, with PDF and ePub files available? You can upgrade to the eBook version at www.packt.com and, as a print book customer, you are entitled to a discount on the eBook copy. Get in touch with us at customercare@packtpub.com for more details.

At www.packt.com, you can also read a collection of free technical articles, sign up for a range of free newsletters, and receive exclusive discounts and offers on Packt books and eBooks.

Contributors

About the authors

Sebastien Donadio is the Chief Technology Officer at Tradair, responsible for leading the technology. He has a wide variety of professional experience, including being head of software engineering at HC Technologies, partner and technical director of a high-frequency FX firm, a quantitative trading strategy software developer at Sun Trading, working as project lead for the Department of Defense. He also has research experience with Bull SAS, and an IT Credit Risk Manager with Société Générale while in France. He has taught various computer science courses for the past ten years in the University of Chicago, NYU and Columbia University. His main passion is technology but he is also a scuba diving instructor and an experienced rock-climber.

Sourav Ghosh has worked in several proprietary high-frequency algorithmic trading firms over the last decade. He has built and deployed extremely low latency, high throughput automated trading systems for trading exchanges around the world, across multiple asset classes. He specializes in statistical arbitrage market-making, and pairs trading strategies for the most liquid global futures contracts. He works as a Senior Quantitative Developer at a trading firm in Chicago. He holds a Masters in Computer Science from the University of Southern California. His areas of interest include Computer Architecture, FinTech, Probability Theory and Stochastic Processes, Statistical Learning and Inference Methods, and Natural Language Processing.

About the reviewers

Nataraj Dasgupta is the VP of Advanced Analytics at RxDataScience Inc. He has been in the IT industry for more than 19 years and has worked in the technical & analytics divisions of Philip Morris, IBM, UBS Investment Bank, and Purdue Pharma. He led the Data Science team at Purdue, where he developed the company's award-winning Big Data and Machine Learning platform. Prior to Purdue, at UBS, he held the role of Associate Director, working with high-frequency & algorithmic trading technologies in the Foreign Exchange Trading group. He has authored *Practical Big Data Analytics* and co-authored *Hands-on Data Science with R*. Apart from his role at RxDataScience, and is also currently affiliated with Imperial College, London.

Ratanlal Mahanta is currently working as a quantitative analyst at bittQsrv, a global quantitative research company offering quant models for its investors. He has several years of experience in the modeling and simulation of quantitative trading. Ratanlal holds a master's degree in science in computational finance, and his research areas include quant trading, optimal execution, and high-frequency trading. He has over 9 years' work experience in the finance industry, and is gifted at solving difficult problems that lie at the intersection of the market, technology, research, and design.

Jiri Pik is an artificial intelligence architect & strategist who works with major investment banks, hedge funds, and other players. He has architected and delivered breakthrough trading, portfolio, and risk management systems, as well as decision support systems, across numerous industries.

Jiri's consulting firm, Jiri Pik—RocketEdge, provides its clients with certified expertise, judgment, and execution at the speed of light.

Packt is searching for authors like you

If you're interested in becoming an author for Packt, please visit `authors.packtpub.com` and apply today. We have worked with thousands of developers and tech professionals, just like you, to help them share their insight with the global tech community. You can make a general application, apply for a specific hot topic that we are recruiting an author for, or submit your own idea.

Table of Contents

Preface

In modern times, it is increasingly difficult to gain a significant competitive edge just by being faster than others, which means relying on sophisticated trading signals, predictive models, and strategies. In our book *Learn Algorithmic Trading*, we provide a broad audience with the knowledge and hands-on practical experience required to build a good understanding of how modern electronic trading markets and market participants operate, as well as how to go about designing, building, and operating all the components required to build a practical and profitable algorithmic trading business using Python.

You will be introduced to algorithmic trading and setting up the environment required to perform tasks throughout the book. You will learn the key components of an algorithmic trading business and the questions you need to ask before embarking on an automated trading project.

Later, you will learn how quantitative trading signals and trading strategies are developed. You will get to grips with the workings and implementation of some well-known trading strategies. You will also understand, implement, and analyze more sophisticated trading strategies, including volatility strategies, economic release strategies, and statistical arbitrage. You will learn how to build a trading bot from scratch using the algorithms built in the previous sections.

By now, you will be ready to connect to the market and start researching, implementing, evaluating, and safely operating algorithmic trading strategies in live markets.

Who this book is for

This book is for software engineers, financial traders, data analysts, entrepreneurs, and anyone who wants to begin their journey in algorithmic trading. If you want to understand how algorithmic trading works, what all the components of a trading system are, the protocols and algorithms required for black box and gray box trading, and how to build a completely automated and profitable trading business, then this book is what you need!

What this book covers

Chapter 1, *Algorithmic Trading Fundamentals*, explains what algorithmic trading is and how algorithmic trading is related to high frequency or low latency trading. We will discuss the evolution of algorithmic trading, from rule-based to AI. We will look at essential algorithmic trading concepts, asset classes, and instruments. You will learn how to set up your mind for algorithmic decisions.

Chapter 2, *Deciphering the Markets with Technical Analysis*, covers some popular technical analysis methods and shows how to apply them to the analysis of market data. We will perform basic algorithmic trading using market trends, support, and resistance.

Chapter 3, *Predicting the Markets with Basic Machine Learning*, reviews and implements a number of simple regression and classification methods and explains the advantages of applying supervised statistical learning methods to trading.

Chapter 4, *Classical Trading Strategies Driven by Human Intuition*, looks at some basic algorithmic strategies (momentum, trend, mean-reversion), and explains their workings, as well as their advantages and disadvantages.

Chapter 5, *Sophisticated Algorithmic Strategies*, consolidates the basic algorithmic strategies by looking at more advanced approaches (statistical arbitrage, pair correlation), as well as their advantages and disadvantages.

Chapter 6, *Managing Risk in Algorithmic Strategies*, explains how to measure and manage risk (market risk, operational risk, and software implementation bugs) in algorithmic strategies.

Chapter 7, *Building a Trading System in Python*, describes the functional components supporting the trading strategy based on the algorithm created in the preceding chapters. We will be using Python to build a small trading system, and will use the algorithm from the preceding chapters to build a trading system capable of trading.

Chapter 8, *Connecting to Trading Exchanges*, describes the communication components of a trading system. We will be using the quickfix library in Python to connect the trading system to a real exchange.

Chapter 9, *Creating a Backtester in Python*, explains how to improve your trading algorithm by running tests with large amounts of data to validate the performance of your trading bot. Once a model is implemented, it is necessary to test whether the trading robot behaves as expected in the trading infrastructure (by checking for implementation-related mistakes).

Chapter 10, *Adapting to Market Participants and Conditions*, discusses why strategies do not perform as expected when deployed in live trading markets and provides examples of how to address those issues in the strategies themselves or the underlying assumptions. We will also discuss why strategies that are performing well slowly deteriorate in terms of performance and provide some simple examples to explain how to address this.

To get the most out of this book

Readers should have a basic knowledge of finance and Python.

Download the example code files

You can download the example code files for this book from your account at www.packt.com. If you purchased this book elsewhere, you can visit www.packtpub.com/support and register to have the files emailed directly to you.

You can download the code files by following these steps:

1. Log in or register at www.packt.com.
2. Select the **Support** tab.
3. Click on **Code Downloads**.
4. Enter the name of the book in the **Search** box and follow the onscreen instructions.

Once the file is downloaded, please make sure that you unzip or extract the folder using the latest version of:

- WinRAR/7-Zip for Windows
- Zipeg/iZip/UnRarX for Mac
- 7-Zip/PeaZip for Linux

The code bundle for the book is also hosted on GitHub at https://github.com/PacktPublishing/Learn-Algorithmic-Trading. In case there's an update to the code, it will be updated on the existing GitHub repository.

We also have other code bundles from our rich catalog of books and videos available at https://github.com/PacktPublishing/. Check them out!

Download the color images

We also provide a PDF file that has color images of the screenshots/diagrams used in this book. You can download it here: `http://www.packtpub.com/sites/default/files/downloads/9781789348347_ColorImages.pdf`.

Conventions used

There are a number of text conventions used throughout this book.

`CodeInText`: Indicates code words in text, database table names, folder names, filenames, file extensions, pathnames, dummy URLs, user input, and Twitter handles. Here is an example: "This code will use the `DataReader` function from the `pandas_datareader` package."

A block of code is set as follows:

```
import pandas as pd
from pandas_datareader import data
```

When we wish to draw your attention to a particular part of a code block, the relevant lines or items are set in bold:

```
if order['action'] == 'to_be_sent':
        # Send order
        order['status'] = 'new'
        order['action'] = 'no_action'
        if self.ts_2_om is None:
```

Bold: Indicates a new term, an important word, or words that you see on screen. For example, words in menus or dialog boxes appear in the text like this. Here is an example: "A mean reversion strategy that relies on the **Absolute Price Oscillator (APO)** trading signal indicator."

Warnings or important notes appear like this.

Tips and tricks appear like this.

Get in touch

Feedback from our readers is always welcome.

General feedback: If you have questions about any aspect of this book, mention the book title in the subject of your message and email us at customercare@packtpub.com.

Errata: Although we have taken every care to ensure the accuracy of our content, mistakes do happen. If you have found a mistake in this book, we would be grateful if you would report this to us. Please visit www.packtpub.com/support/errata, selecting your book, clicking on the Errata Submission Form link, and entering the details.

Piracy: If you come across any illegal copies of our works in any form on the internet, we would be grateful if you would provide us with the location address or website name. Please contact us at copyright@packt.com with a link to the material.

If you are interested in becoming an author: If there is a topic that you have expertise in, and you are interested in either writing or contributing to a book, please visit authors.packtpub.com.

Reviews

Please leave a review. Once you have read and used this book, why not leave a review on the site that you purchased it from? Potential readers can then see and use your unbiased opinion to make purchase decisions, we at Packt can understand what you think about our products, and our authors can see your feedback on their book. Thank you!

For more information about Packt, please visit packt.com.

Section 1: Introduction and Environment Setup

In this section, you will be introduced to algorithmic trading and setting up the environment required to perform tasks throughout the book. You will learn the key components of trading and the questions you need to ask before embarking on a robot trading project.

This section comprises the following chapter:

- Chapter 1, *Algorithmic Trading Fundamentals*

1
Algorithmic Trading Fundamentals

Algorithmic trading, or automated trading, works with a program that contains a set of instructions for trading purposes. Compared to a human trader, this trade can generate profits and losses at a higher speed. In this chapter, this will be your first time being exposed to trading automation. We will walk you through the different steps to implement your first trading robot. You will learn the trading world and the technical trading components behind it. We will also go into detail about the tools that you will use and, by the end of this chapter, you will be capable of coding your first native trading strategy in Python. We will cover the following topics in this chapter:

- Why are we trading?
- Introducing algorithm trading and automation
- What the main trading components are
- Setting up your first programming environment
- Implementing your first native strategy

Why are we trading?

From the Roman era through to the present day, trading is an inherent part of humankind. Buying raw materials when the price is low to resell it when the price is high has been a part of many cultures. In ancient Rome, the rich Romans used the *Roman Forum* to exchange currencies, bonds, and investments. In the 14th century, traders negotiated government debts in Venice. The earliest form of the stock exchange was created in Antwerp, Belgium, in 1531. Traders used to meet regularly to exchange promissory notes and bonds. The conquests of new worlds entailed a high cost, but also a good return. The Dutch East India Company in 1602 opened their capital for investors to participate in this costly project with a high potential return. During the same time period, a well-known tulip was sold everywhere in the world, creating a profitable market for investors and sellers. A future contract was created for this reason, since many people speculated regarding the price of this flower.

A hundred years later, a French expedition to Louisiana was also attracting many investors, creating the dream of making a lot of money. The Mississippi Company was created to handle all the investments based on potential wealth in Louisiana. Many other investment opportunities arose across the centuries, including the British railroad and the conquest of Latin America.

All these events had a common root: wealthy people willing to make more money. If we want to answer the question *Why are we trading?*, the answer is to potentially make more money. However, all the previous historical examples ended pretty badly. Investments turned out to be bad investments or, most of the time, the value was over-estimated and traders ended up losing their money. This is actually a good lesson for the readers of this book. Even if trading can sound a profitable business, always keep in mind the ephemeral part of profitability (it can work sometimes, but not always) and also taking into account the inherent risk that goes with investment.

Basic concepts regarding the modern trading setup

This section will cover the basics of trading and what drives market prices, as well as supply and demand.

As we touched upon in the previous section, trading has been around since the beginning of time, when people wanted to exchange goods between one another and make profits while doing so. Modern markets are still driven by basic economic principles of supply and demand. When demand outweighs supply, prices of a commodity or service are likely to rise higher to reflect the relative shortage of the commodity or service in relation to the demand for it. Conversely, if the market is flooded with a lot of sellers for a particular product, prices are likely to drop. Hence, the market is always trying to reflect the equilibrium price between available supply and demand for a particular product. We will see later how this is the fundamental driver of price discovery in today's markets. With the evolution of modern markets and available technology, price discovery becomes increasingly efficient.

Intuitively, you may draw a parallel with the fact that with the advances in online retail businesses, prices of products have become increasingly efficient across all sellers, and the best offers are always the ones that customers are buying because the information (price discovery) is so easily accessible. The same is true for modern trading. With advances in technology and regulations, more and more market participants have access to complete market data that makes price discovery much more efficient than in the past. Of course, the speed at which participants receive information, the speed at which they react, the granularity of the data that they can receive and handle, and the sophistication with which each participant draws trading insights from the data they receive, is where the competition lies in modern trading, and we will go over these in the subsequent sections. But first, let's introduce some basic concepts regarding the modern trading setup.

Market sectors

In this section, we will briefly introduce the concepts of what different types of market sectors are and how they differ from the concept of asset classes.

Market sectors are the different kinds of underlying products that can be traded. The most popular market sectors are commodities (metals, agricultural produce), energy (oil, gas), equities (stocks of different companies), interest rate bonds (coupons you get in exchange for debt, which accrues interest, hence the name), and foreign exchange (cash exchange rates between currencies for different countries):

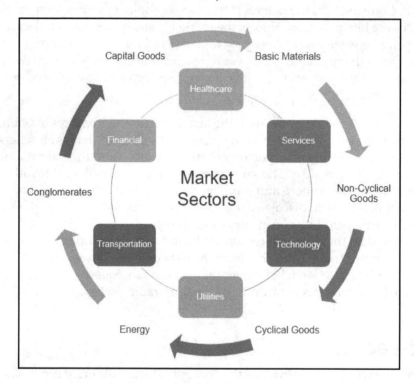

Asset classes

Asset classes are the different kinds of actual vehicles that are available for trading at different exchanges. For example, cash interest rate bonds, cash foreign exchange, and cash stock shares are what we described in the previous section, but we can have financial instruments that are derivatives of these underlying products. Derivatives are instruments that are built on top of other instruments and have some additional constraints, which we will explore in this section. The two most popular derivatives are futures and options, and are heavily traded across all derivatives electronic exchanges.

We can have future contracts pertaining to underlying commodities, energy, equities, interest rate bonds, and foreign exchanges that are tied to the prices of the underlying instruments, but have different characteristics and rules. A simple way to think of a future contract is that it is a contract between a buyer and a seller in which the seller promises to sell a certain amount of the underlying product at a certain date in the future (also known as the expiry date), and where the buyer agrees to accept the agreed-upon amount at the specific date at the specific price.

For example, a producer of butter might want to protect themselves from a potential future spike in the price of milk, on which the production costs of butter directly depend, in which case, the butter producer can enter into an agreement with a milk producer to provide them with enough milk in the future at a certain price. Conversely, a milk producer may worry about possible buyers of milk in the future and may want to reduce the risk by making an agreement with butter producers to buy at least a certain amount of milk in the future at a certain price, since milk is perishable and a lack of supply would mean a total loss for a milk producer. This is a very simple example of a future contract trade; modern future contracts are much more complex than this.

Similar to future contracts, we can have options contracts for underlying commodities, energy, equities, interest rate bonds, and foreign exchanges that are tied to the prices of the underlying instruments, but have different characteristics and rules. The difference in an options contract compared to a futures contract is that the buyer and seller of an options contract have the option of refusing to buy or sell at the specific amount, at the specific date, and at the specific price. To safeguard both counterparties involved in an options trade, we have the concept of a premium, which is the minimum amount of money that has been paid upfront to buy/sell an options contract.

A call option, or the right to buy, but not an obligation to buy at expiration, makes money if the price of the underlying product increases prior to expiration because now, such a party can exercise their option at expiration and buy the underlying product at a price lower than the current market price. Conversely, if the price of the underlying product goes down prior to expiration, such a party now has the option of backing out of exercising their option and thus, only losing the premium that they paid for. Put options are analogous, but they give the holder of a put contract the right to sell, but not an obligation to sell, at expiration.

We will not delve too deeply into different financial products and derivatives since that is not the focus of this book, but this brief introduction was meant to introduce the idea that there are a lot of different tradeable financial products out there and that they vary significantly in terms of their rules and complexity.

Basics of what a modern trading exchange looks like

Since this book is primarily designed to introduce what modern algorithmic trading looks like, we will focus on trying to understand how a modern electronic trading exchange appears. Gone are the days of people yelling at one another in the trading pits and making hand signals to convey their intentions to buy and sell products at certain prices. These remain amusing ideas for movies, but modern trading looks significantly different.

Today, most of the trading is done electronically through different software applications. Market data feed handlers process and understand market data disseminated by the trading exchanges to reflect the true state of the limit book and market prices (bids and offers). The market data is published in a specific market data protocol previously agreed upon by the exchange and the market participants (FIX/FAST, ITCH, and HSVF). Then, the same software applications can relay that information back to humans or make decisions themselves algorithmically. Those decisions are then again communicated to the exchange by a similar software application (order entry gateways) that informs the exchange of our interest in a specific product and our interest in buying or selling that product at specific prices by sending specific order types (GTDs, GTCs, IOCs, and so on). This involves understanding and communicating with the exchange in an exchange order entry protocol previously agreed upon by the exchange and participants at the exchange (FIX, OMEX, OUCH).

After a match takes place against available market participants, that match is conveyed back to the software application again via the order entry gateways and relayed back to the trading algorithm or the humans, thereby completing a transaction, often wholly electronically. The speed of this round trip varies a lot based on the market, the participant, and the algorithms themselves. This can be as low as under 10 microseconds all the way up to seconds, but we will discuss this in greater detail later.

The following diagram is a descriptive view of the flow of information from an electronic trading exchange to the market participants involved, and the flow of information back to the exchange:

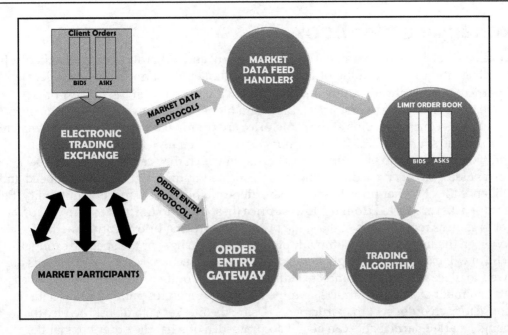

As shown in the preceding diagram, the trading exchange maintains a book of client buy orders (bids) and client ask orders (asks), and publishes market data using market data protocols to provide the state of the book to all market participants. Market data feed handlers on the client side decode the incoming market data feed and build a limit order book on their side to reflect the state of the order book as the exchange sees it. This is then propagated through the client's trading algorithm and then goes through the order entry gateway to generate an outgoing order flow. The outgoing order flow is communicated to the exchange via order entry protocols. This, in turn, will generate further market data flow, and so the trading information cycle continues.

Understanding algorithmic trading concepts

We introduced a lot of new concepts in the previous section, such as exchange order books (consisting of different kinds of orders sent by market participants), exchange matching algorithms, exchange market data protocols, and exchange order entry protocols. Let's formally discuss these in greater detail here.

Exchange order book

The exchange order book maintains all incoming buy and sell orders placed by clients. It tracks all attributes for incoming orders—prices, number of contracts/shares, order types, and participant identification. Buy orders (or bids) are sorted from the highest price (best price) to the lowest price (worst price). Bids with higher prices have a higher priority as far as matching is concerned. Bids at the same price are prioritized depending on the matching algorithm. The simplest FIFO (First In First Out) algorithm uses the intuitive rule of prioritizing orders at the same price in the order in which they came in. This will be important later on when we discuss how sophisticated trading algorithms use speed and intelligence to get higher priorities for their orders and how this impacts profitability. Sell orders (or asks) are sorted from the lowest price (best price) to the highest price (worst price). Again, as regards asks at the same price, the matching prioritization method depends on the matching algorithm adopted by the exchange for the specific product, which we will expand upon in greater detail in the next section. Market participants are allowed to place new orders, cancel existing orders, or modify order attributes such as price and the number of shares/contracts, and the exchange generates public market data in response to each order sent by participants. Using the market data distributed by the exchange, market participants can get an accurate idea of what the order book at the exchange looks like (depending on what information the exchange chooses to hide, but we ignore that nuance for now).

Exchange matching algorithm

When incoming bids are at or above the best (lowest price) ask orders, then a match occurs. Conversely, when incoming asks are at or below the best (highest price) bid orders, then a match occurs. Incoming aggressive orders continue to match against existing passive orders in the book until one of these two conditions is met. Either the new aggressive order is fully matched, or the other possibility is that the remaining orders on the opposite side have prices worse than the incoming order price and, hence, the match cannot occur. This is because of the fundamental rule that an order cannot be matched at a price worse than the limit price it was entered at. Now, as far as orders at the same price level are concerned, the order of matching is dictated by what matching algorithm rules the exchange adopts.

FIFO matching

We briefly described the FIFO algorithm previously, but let's expand on it by showing an example. Assume the following state of an order book when the exchange bid orders A, B, and C were entered at price 10.00 in that order in time. So, at the same price, order A has a higher priority than order B, which has a higher priority than order C. Bid order D is at a worse price, 9.00. Similarly, on the ask side, order X was entered at price 11.00 before order Y, also at price 11.00. Hence, order X has a higher priority than order Y, and then ask order Z was entered at a worse price, 12.00:

BIDS	ASKS
Order A: Buy 1 @ 10.00	Order X: Sell 1 @ 11.00
Order B: Buy 2 @ 10.00	Order Y: Sell 2 @ 11.00
Order C: Buy 3 @ 10.00	Order Z: Sell 2 @ 12.00
Order D: Buy 1 @ 9.00	

Assume an incoming sell order K for 4 shares @ 10.00 would match against order A for 1 share, order B for 2 shares, and order C for 1 share, in that order, under FIFO matching. At the end of the matching, order C would still have the remaining size of 2 shares at price 10.00 and will have the highest priority.

Pro-rata matching

Pro-rata matching comes in a variety of flavors and is usually implemented in slightly different ways. For the scope of this book, we provide some intuition behind this matching algorithm and provide a hypothetical matching scenario.

The underlying intuition between pro-rata matching is that it favors larger orders over smaller orders at the same price and ignores the time at which the orders were entered. This changes the market's microstructure quite a bit, and the participants are favored to enter larger orders to gain priority instead of entering orders as fast as possible:

BIDS	ASKS
Order A: Buy 100 @ 10.00	Order X: Sell 100 @ 11.00
Order B: Buy 200 @ 10.00	Order Y: Sell 200 @ 11.00
Order C: Buy 700 @ 10.00	Order Z: Sell 200 @ 12.00
Order D: Buy 100 @ 9.00	

Consider a market state as shown earlier. For the sake of this example, the hypothetical order sizes have been raised by a factor of 100. Here, bid orders A, B, and C are at the same price, 10.00. However, when an incoming sell order of size 100 comes in for price 10.00, order C gets a fill for 70 contracts, order B gets a fill for 20 contracts, and order A gets a fill for 10 contracts, proportional to how big they are at that level. This is an overly simplified example that excludes complications related to fractional match sizes and breaking ties between orders with the same size, and so on. Also, some exchanges have a mix of pro-rata and FIFO, where part of the incoming aggressor matches using pro-rata, and part matches in FIFO order. But this should serve as a good basic understanding of how different pro-rata matching is compared to FIFO matching. A detailed examination of pro-rata matching and its impact is beyond the scope of this book, so we exclude it.

Limit order book

A limit order book is very similar in spirit to the exchange order book. The only difference is that this is built by the market participants based on the market data that is being sent out by the exchange in response to market participants sending orders to it. The limit order book is a central concept in all algorithmic trading, and one often found in all other forms of trading as well. The purpose is to collect and arrange bids and offers in a meaningful way to gain insight into the market participants present at any particular time, as well as gain insight regarding what the equilibrium prices are. We will revisit these in the next chapter when we dig deeper into technical analysis. Depending on what information the exchange decides to make available to all market participants via public market data, the limit order book that the client builds can be slightly different from what the order book at the exchange matching engine looks like.

Exchange market data protocols

Exchange market data protocols are not the focus of this book, so a rigorous treatment of this topic is beyond the scope of this book. These market data protocols are outgoing communication streams from the exchange to all market participants that are well-documented for new participants to build their software applications to subscribe, receive, decode, and check for errors and network losses. These are designed with latency, throughput, error tolerance, redundancy, and many other requirements in mind.

Market data feed handlers

Market data feed handlers are software applications that market participants build with a view to interfacing with the specific exchange market data protocol. These are able to subscribe, receive, decode, and check for errors and network losses, and are designed with latency, throughput, error tolerance, redundancy, and many other requirements in mind.

Order types

Most exchanges support a variety of orders that they accept from market participants. We will discuss a few of the most common types in this section.

IOC – Immediate Or Cancel

These orders never get added to the book. They either match against existing resting orders to a maximum of the IOC order size, or the rest of the incoming order gets canceled. If no resting order is available at a price that the IOC can match against, then the IOC is canceled in its entirety. IOC orders have the benefit of not resting in the book post matching and causing additional complexity with order management in trading algorithms.

GTD – Good Till Day

These orders get added to the book. If they match fully against existing resting orders in the book, then they don't get added, otherwise the remaining quantity on the order (which can be the entire original quantity if there's no partial match) gets added to the book and sits as resting orders that the incoming aggressors can match against. The benefits of GTD orders are that they can take advantage of FIFO matching algorithms by having better priorities than orders that just showed up in the book, but require more complex order management in trading algorithms.

Stop orders

Stop orders are orders that aren't in the book until a specific price (called the stop price) is traded in the market, at which point they become regular GTD orders at a pre-specified price. These orders are great as exit orders (either to liquidate a losing position or to realize profit on a winning position). We will revisit these orders after we have explained what having a losing or winning position means and what exiting a position means.

Exchange order entry protocols

Exchange order entry protocols are how market participant software applications send order requests (new, cancels, modifies) and how the exchange replies to these requests.

Order entry gateway

Order entry gateways are the market participant client applications that communicate with the exchange matching engine over the order entry protocols. These have to deal with order flow in a reliable manner, sending orders to the exchange, modifying and canceling those orders, and getting notifications when these orders are accepted, canceled, executed, and so on. Oftentimes, market participants run a second variant of order entry gateways that simply receive order-executed notifications to check consistency against the primary order entry gateway order flow. These are called drop-copy gateways.

Positions and profit and loss (PnL) management

Orders that get executed cause market participants to have positions in the instrument that they got executed, for the amount the order executed, and at the price of the execution (limit orders can match at better prices than they were entered for, but not worse). A buy side execution is called having a long position, while a sell side execution is called having a short position. When we have no position at all, this is referred to as being flat. Long positions make money when market prices are higher than the price of the position, and lose money when market prices are lower than the price of the position. Short positions, conversely, make money when market prices go down from the price of the position and lose money when market prices go up from the price of the position, hence, the well-known ideas of buy low, sell high, and buy high, sell higher, and so on.

Multiple buy executions, or multiple sell executions for different amounts and prices, cause the overall position price to be the volume weighted average of the execution prices and quantities. This is called the **Volume Weighted Average Price (VWAP)** of the position. Open positions are marked to market to get a sense of what the unrealized **Profit and Loss (PnL)** of the position is. This means that current market prices are compared to the price of the position; a long position where market prices have gone up is considered unrealized profit, and the opposite is considered unrealized loss. Similar terms apply to short positions. Profit or loss is realized when an open position is closed, meaning you sell to close a long position and you buy to close a short position. At that point, the PnL is given the term *realized PnL*. The total PnL at any point is the total of the realized PnLs so far and the unrealized PnLs for open positions at the market price.

From intuition to algorithmic trading

Here, we will discuss how trading ideas are born and how they are turned into algorithmic trading strategies. Fundamentally, all trading ideas are driven by human intuition to a large extent. If markets have been moving up/down all the time, you might intuitively think that it will continue to move in the same direction, which is the fundamental idea behind trend-following strategies. Conversely, you might argue that if prices have moved up/down a lot, it is mispriced and likely to move in the opposite direction, which is the fundamental idea behind mean reversion strategies. Intuitively, you may also reason that instruments that are very similar to one another, or loosely dependent on one another, will move together, which is the idea behind correlation-based trading or pairs trading. Since every market participant has their own view of the market, the final market prices are a reflection of the majority of market participants. If your views are aligned with the majority of the market participants, then that particular strategy is profitable in that particular instance. Of course, no trading idea can be right all the time, and whether a strategy is profitable or not depends on how often the idea is correct versus how often it is not correct.

Why do we need to automate trading?

Historically, human traders implemented such rule-based trading to manually enter orders, take positions, and make profits or losses through the day. Over time, with advances in technology, they've moved from yelling in the pits to get orders executed with other pit traders, to calling up a broker and entering orders over the telephone, to having GUI applications that allow entering orders through point and click interfaces.

Such manual approaches have a lot of drawbacks – humans are slow to react to markets so they miss information or are slow to react to new information, they can't scale well or focus on multiple things at a time, humans are prone to making mistakes, they get distracted, and they feel a fear of losing money and a joy of making money. All of these drawbacks cause them to deviate from a planned trading strategy, severely limiting the profitability of the trading strategy.

Computers are extremely good at rule-based repetitive tasks. When designed and programmed correctly, they can execute instructions and algorithms extremely quickly, and can be scaled and deployed across a lot of instruments seamlessly. They are extremely fast at reacting to market data, and they don't get distracted or make mistakes (unless they were programmed incorrectly, which is a software bug and not a drawback of computers themselves). They don't have emotions, so don't deviate from what they are programmed to do. All of these advantages make computerized automated trading systems extremely profitable when done right, which is where algorithmic trading starts.

Evolution of algorithmic trading – from rule-based to AI

Let's take a simple example of a trend-following strategy and see how that has evolved from a manual approach all the way to a fully automated algorithmic trading strategy. Historically, human traders are used to having simple charting applications that can be used to detect when trends are starting or continuing. These can be simple rules, such as if a share rises 5% every day for a week, then it is something we should buy and hold (put on a long position), or if a share price has dropped 10% in 2 hours, then that is something we should sell short and wait for it to drop further. This would be a classic manual trading strategy in the past. As we discussed previously, computers are very good at following repetitive rule-based algorithms. Simpler rules are easier to program and require less development time, but computer software applications are only limited by the complexity that the software developer programming the computer can handle. At the end of this chapter, we will deal with a realistic trading strategy written in Python, but for now, we will continue to introduce all the ideas and concepts required prior to that.

Here is some pseudo code that implements our trend-following, human intuition trading idea. This can then be translated into whatever language of our choosing based on our application's needs.

We can use trend-following, which means, buying/selling when the price changes by 10% in 2 hours. This variable tracks our current position in the market:

```
Current_position_ = 0;
```

This is the expected profit threshold for our positions. If a position is more profitable than this threshold, we flatten the position and the unrealized profit to realized profit:

```
PROFIT_EXIT_PRICE_PERCENT = 0.2;
```

This is the maximum loss threshold for our positions. If a position is losing more than this threshold, we flatten the position and convert the unrealized loss to realized loss. Why would we close a position if it's losing money? The idea is simply to not lose all of our money on one bad position, but rather cut our losses early so that we have capital to continue trading. More on this when we dive into risk management practices in more detail. For now, we define a parameter that is the maximum allowed loss for a position in terms of the price change from the entry price for our position:

```
LOSS_EXIT_PRICE_PERCENT = -0.1;
```

Note that in the thresholds we saw, we expect to make more money on our winning/profitable positions than we expect to lose on our losing positions. This is not always symmetrical, but we will address the distributions of winning and losing positions when we look into these trading strategies in greater detail later in this book. This is a method/callback that is invoked every time the market prices change. We need to check whether our signal causes an entry and whether one of our open positions needs to be closed for PnL reasons:

```
def OnMarketPriceChange( current_price, current_time ):
```

First, check whether we are flat and prices have moved up more than 10%. This is our entry signal to go long, so we will send a buy order and update our position. Technically, we should not update our position until the exchange confirms that our order matched, but for the sake of simplicity in this first-pass pseudo code, we ignore that complexity and address it later:

```
If Current_position_ == 0 AND ( current_price - price_two_hours_ago ) /
current_price >; 10%:
  SendBuyOrderAtCurrentPrice();
  Current_position_ = Current_position_ + 1;
```

Now, check whether we are flat and prices have moved down more than 10%. This is our entry signal to go short, so we will send a sell order and update our position:

```
Else If Current_position_ == 0 AND ( current_price - price_two_hours_ago )
/ current_price < -10%:
  SendSellOrderAtCurrentPrice();
  Current_position_ = Current_position_ - 1;
```

If we are currently long, and market prices have moved in a favorable direction, check whether this position's profitability exceeds predetermined thresholds. In that case, we will send a sell order to flatten our position and convert our unrealized profit to realized profit:

```
If Current_position_ >; 0 AND current_price - position_price >;
PROFIT_EXIT_PRICE_PERCENT:
  SendSellOrderAtCurrentPrice();
  Current_position_ = Current_position_ - 1;
```

If we are currently long, and market prices have moved against us, check whether this position loss exceeds predetermined thresholds. In that case, we will send a sell order to *flatten* our position and convert our unrealized loss to realized loss.

```
Else If Current_position_ >; 0 AND current_price - position_price <
LOSS_EXIT_PRICE_PERCENT::
  SendSellOrderAtCurrentPrice();
  Current_position_ = Current_position_ - 1;
```

If we are currently short, and market prices have moved in a favorable direction, check whether this position profitability exceeds predetermined thresholds. In that case, we will send a buy order to *flatten* our position and convert our unrealized profit to realized profit:

```
Else If Current_position_ < 0 AND position_price - current_price >;
PROFIT_EXIT_PRICE_PERCENT:
  SendBuyOrderAtCurrentPrice();
  Current_position_ = Current_position_ - 1;
```

If we are currently short, and market prices have moved against us, check whether this position loss exceeds predetermined thresholds. In that case, we will send a buy order to *flatten* our position and convert our unrealized loss to realized loss:

```
Else If Current_position_ < 0 AND position_price - current_price <
LOSS_EXIT_PRICE_PERCENT:
  SendBuyOrderAtCurrentPrice();
  Current_position_ = Current_position_ - 1;
```

Components of an algorithmic trading system

In an earlier section, we provided a top-level view of the entire algorithmic trading setup and many of the different components involved. In practice, a complete algorithmic trading setup is divided into two sections, as shown in the following diagram:

- Core infrastructure deals with exchange-facing market data protocol integration, market data feed handlers, internal market data format normalization, historical data recording, instrument definition recording and dissemination, exchange order entry protocols, exchange order entry gateways, core side risk systems, broker-facing applications, back office reconciliation applications, addressing compliance requirements, and others.
- Algorithmic trading strategy components deal with using normalized market data, building order books, generating signals from incoming market data and order flow information, the aggregation of different signals, efficient execution logic built on top of statistical predictive abilities (alpha), position and PnL management inside the strategies, risk management inside the strategies, backtesting, and historical signal and trading research platforms:

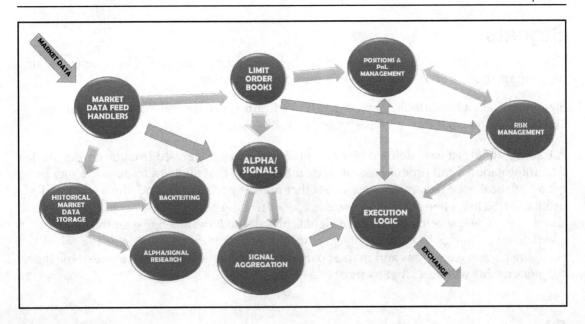

Market data subscription

These components are responsible for interacting with the feed handler components that publish normalized data. This data can be delivered over a network or locally using a variety of **Inter-Process Communication (IPC)** mechanisms from the feed handlers. We do not go into great detail about this here. Low latency delivery and scalability are the major driving design decisions in this regard.

Limit order books

Once the trading strategy gets normalized market data, it uses that data to build and maintain limit order books for each instrument. Depending on the sophistication and complexity of the limit order books, it can be simple enough such that it tells us how many participants there are on each side, or sophisticated enough to track market participant order priorities as well as track our own orders in the limit order book.

Signals

Once limit order books are built, every time they are updated due to new incoming market data information, we build signals using the new information.

Signals are called by various names—signals, indicators, predictors, calculators, features, alpha, and so on—but they all have roughly the same meaning.

A trading signal is a well-defined piece of intelligence that is derived from incoming market data information, limit order books or trade information that allows a trading strategy to get a statistical edge (advantage) vis-à-vis other market participants and, thus, increased profitability. This is one of the areas where a lot of trading teams focus much of their time and energy. The key is to build a lot of signals in order to have an edge over the competition as well as keep adapting existing signals and adding new signals to deal with changing market conditions and market participants. We will revisit this in one of the later chapters, as this will be a large focus of this book.

Signal aggregators

Often, a lot of algorithmic trading systems combine a lot of different kinds of signals in order to gain a bigger edge than individual signals provide. The approach is to essentially combine different signals that have different predictive abilities/advantages under different market conditions. There are many different ways to combine individual signals. You can use classical statistical learning methods to generate linear and non-linear combinations to output classification or regression output values that represent a combination of individual signals. Machine learning is not the focus of this book, so we avoid diving too deep into this topic, but we will revisit it briefly in a later section.

Execution logic

Another key component of algorithmic trading is quickly and efficiently managing orders based on signals in order to gain an edge over the competition. It is important to react to changing market data, changing signal values in a fast but intelligent manner. Oftentimes, speed and sophistication are two competing goals, and good execution logic will try to balance the two objectives in an optimal manner. It is also extremely important to disguise our intentions/intelligence from other market participants so that we get the best executions possible.

Remember that other market competitors can observe what orders are sent to the exchange and assess the potential impact it might have, so this component needs to be intelligent enough to not make it obvious what our trading strategy is doing. Slippage and fees are also very important factors as far as execution logic design is concerned.

Slippage is defined as the difference in the expected price of a trade and the price at which the trade is actually executed. This can happen for predominantly two reasons:

- If the order reaches the exchange later than expected (latency), then it might end up either not executing at all, or executing at a worse price than you might expect.
- If the order is very large such that it executes at multiple prices, then the VWAP of the entire execution may be significantly different from the market price observed when the order was sent.

Slippage obviously causes losses that might not have been correctly factored in, in addition to difficulty liquidating positions. As the position sizes for trading algorithms scale up, slippage becomes a larger problem.

Fees are another issue with executing orders efficiently. Typically, there are exchange fees and broker fees proportional to the size of the orders and the total volume traded.

Again, as the position sizes for trading algorithms scale up, trading volumes typically increase and fees increase along with it. Oftentimes, a good trading strategy can end up being non-profitable because it trades too much and accumulates a lot of trading fees. Again, a good execution logic seeks to minimize the fees paid.

Position and PnL management

All algorithmic trading strategies need to track and manage their positions and PnLs effectively. Depending on the actual trading strategy, this can often range in complexity.

For more sophisticated trading strategies, such as pairs trading (curve trading is another similar strategy), you have to track positions and PnLs on multiple instruments and often, these positions and PnLs offset one another and introduce complexity/uncertainty as regards determining true positions and PnLs. We will explore these issues when we talk in detail about these strategies in Chapter 4, *Classical Trading Strategies Driven by Human Intuition*, but for now, we won't discuss this in too much detail.

Risk management

Good risk management is one of the cornerstones of algorithmic trading. Bad risk management practices can turn potential profitable strategies into non-profitable ones. There is an even bigger risk of violating rules and regulations at trading exchanges that can often lead to legal actions and huge penalties. Finally, one of the biggest risks with high-speed automated algorithmic trading is that poorly programmed computer software is prone to bugs and errors. There are many instances of entire firms shutting down due to automated high-speed algorithmic trading systems that run amok. Hence, risk management systems need to be built to be extremely robust, feature rich, and have multiple layers of redundancy. There also needs to be a very high level of testing, stress testing, and strict change management to minimize the possibility of risk systems failing. In Chapter 6, *Managing the Risk of Algorithmic Strategies*, of this book, we will have an entire section dedicated to best risk management practices so as to maximize the profitability of trading strategies as well as avoid common pitfalls resulting in losses or bankruptcy.

Backtesting

When researching an automated trading strategy for expected behavior, a key component in a good algorithmic trading research system is a good backtester. A backtester is used to simulate automated trading strategy behavior and retrieve statistics on expected PnLs, expected risk exposure, and other metrics based on historically recorded market data. The basic idea is to answer the question: given historical data, what kind of performance would a specific trading strategy have? This is built by recording historical market data accurately, having a framework to replay it, having a framework that can accept simulated order flow from potential trading strategies, and mimicking how a trading exchange would match this strategy's order flow in the presence of other market participants as specified in the historical market data. It is also a good place to try out different trading strategies to see what ideas work before deploying them to market.

Building and maintaining a highly accurate backtester is one of the most complicated tasks involved in setting up an algorithmic trading research system. It has to accurately simulate things such as software latencies, network latencies, accurate FIFO priorities for orders, slippage, fees, and, in some cases, also the market impact caused by the order flow for the strategy under consideration (that is, how the other market participants may react in the presence of this strategy's order flow and trading activity). We will revisit backtesting at the end of this chapter and then again in later chapters in this book. Finally, we explain practical issues faced in setting up and calibrating a backtester, their impact on an algorithmic trading strategy, and what approaches best minimize damage caused due to inaccurate backtesting.

Why Python?

Python is the most widely used programming language in the world (one-third of new software development uses this language):

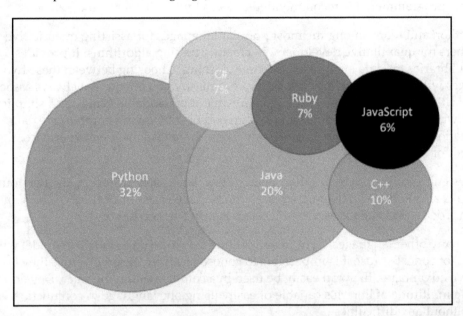

This language is very simple to learn. Python is an interpreted, high-level programming language with type inference. Unlike C/C++, where you need to focus on memory management and the hardware features of the machine you are using to code, Python takes care of the internal implementation, such as memory management. As a result, this type of language will ease the focus on coding trading algorithms. Python is versatile; it can be used in any domain for any application development. Since Python has been widely used for years, the community of programmers is large enough to get many critical libraries for your trading strategy, ranging from data analytics, machine learning, data extraction, and runtime to communication; the list of open source libraries is gigantic. Additionally, on the software engineering side, Python includes paradigms used in other languages, such as object-oriented, functional, and dynamic types. The online resources for Python are unlimited, and tons of book will drive you through any domains where you can use Python. Python is not the only language using in trading. We will preferably use Python (or eventually R) to do data analysis and to create trading models. We will use C, C++, or Java in trading for production code. These language will compile source code into executable or byte codes. Consequently, the software will be one hundred times faster than Python or R. Even if these three last languages are faster than Python, we will use all of them to create libraries. We will wrap these libraries to be used with Python (or R).

When choosing Python, we also need to choose the version of the language. While Python 2 is the most commonly used Python standard, Python 3 should take over in a few years. The Python community develops Python 3 libraries. Tech firms have started their migration toward this version. After 2020, Python 2.X will no longer be maintained. Therefore, if you are a new programmer, it is recommended to learn Python 3 over Python 2.

Both Python and R are among the most popular languages for assisting quantitative researchers (or quantitative developers) in creating trading algorithms. It provides a ton of support libraries for data analysis or machine learning. Choosing between these two languages will depend on which side of the community you are on. We always associate Python with a general-purpose language with an understandable syntax and simplicity, while R was developed with statisticians as an end user by giving emphasis to data visualization. Even if Python can also give you the same visualization experience, R was designed for this purpose.

R is not significantly more recent than Python. It was released in 1995 by the two founders, Ross Ihaka and Robert Gentleman, while Python was released in 1991 by Guido Van Rossum. Today, R is mainly used by the academic and research world.

Unlike many other languages, Python and R allows us to write a statistical model with a few lines of code. Because it is impossible to choose one over the other, since they both have their own advantages, they can easily be used in a complementary manner. Developers created a multitude of libraries capable of easily using one language in conjunction with the other without any difficulties.

Choice of IDE – Pycharm or Notebook

While RStudio became the standard **IDE** (**Integrated Development Environment**) for R, choosing between JetBrains PyCharm and Jupyter Notebook is much more challenging. To begin with, we need to talk about the features of these two different IDEs. PyCharm was developed by the Czech company JetBrains, and is a text editor providing code analysis, a graphical debugger, and an advanced unit tester. Jupyter Notebook is a non-profit organization that created a web-based interactive computational environment for the following three languages: Julia, Python, and R. This software helps you to code Python by giving you a web-based interface where you will run the Python code line by line.

The major difference between these two IDEs is that PyCharm became a reference IDE among programmers, since the version control system and the debugger are an important part of this product. Additionally, PyCharm can easily handle a large code base and has a ton of plugins.

Jupyter Notebook is a friendly choice when data analysis is the only motivation, while PyCharm doesn't have the same user-friendly interface to run code line by line for data analytics. The features that PyCharm provides are the most frequently used in the Python programming world.

Our first algorithmic trading (buy when the price is low, and sell when the price is high)

You may now feel that you are impatient to make money, and you may also be thinking *When can you start doing so?*

We have talked about what we will address in this book. In this section, we will start building our first trading strategy, called **buy low, sell high**.

Building a trading strategy takes time and goes through numerous steps:

1. You need an *original* idea. This part will use a well-known money-making strategy: we buy an asset with a price lower than the one we will use to sell it. For the purpose of illustrating this idea, we will be using Google stock.
2. Once we get the idea, we need data to validate the idea. In Python, there are many packages that we can use, to get trading data.
3. You will then need to use a large amount of historical data to backtest your trading strategy assuming this rule: what worked in the past will work in the future.

Setting up your workspace

For this book, we have picked PyCharm as the IDE. We will go through all the examples using this tool.

You can find videos on the JetBrains website: `https://blog.jetbrains.com/pycharm/` `2016/01/introducing-getting-started-with-pycharm-video-tutorials/`.

PyCharm 101

Once PyCharm is loaded, you will need to create a project and choose an interpreter. As we previously discussed, you will need to choose a version of Python 3. At the time of writing this book, the most up-to-date version is Python 3.7.0, but feel free to start with a more recent version than this one. Once the project is open, you need to create a Python file that you will call buylowsellhigh.py. This file will contain the code of your first Python implementation.

Getting the data

Many libraries can help download financial data; our choice though is to use the pandas library. This software Python library is well known for data manipulation and analysis. We will use the DataReader function, which is capable of connecting to a financial news server such as Yahoo, Google, and many others, and then downloading the data that you will need for the example of this book. DataReader takes four arguments in this example:

1. The first one is the symbol (our example uses GOOG for Google) you would like to use for analysis.
2. The second specifies the source for retrieving the data, and then you will specify the range of days to get the data.
3. The third specifies the starting data from which to fetch historical data.
4. The fourth and final argument specifies the end data for the historical data series:

```
# loading the class data from the package pandas_datareader
from pandas_datareader import data
# First day
start_date = '2014-01-01'
# Last day
end_date = '2018-01-01'
# Call the function DataReader from the class data
goog_data = data.DataReader('GOOG', 'yahoo', start_date, end_date)
```

The goog_data variable is the data frame containing the Google data from January 1, 2014 to January 1, 2018. If you print the goog_data variable, you will see the following:

```
print(goog_data)
   High Low     ... Volume Adj Close
Date                                        ...
2010-01-04  312.721039 310.103088    ... 3937800.0 311.349976
2010-01-05  311.891449 308.761810    ... 6048500.0 309.978882
2010-01-06  310.907837 301.220856    ... 8009000.0 302.164703
2010-01-07  303.029083 294.410156    ... 12912000.0 295.130463
```

If you would like to see all the columns, you should change the option of the pandas library by allowing more than four displayed columns:

```
import pandas as pd
pd.set_printoptions(max_colwidth, 1000)
pd.set_option('display.width', 1000)
                  High Low        Open Close Volume    Adj Close
Date
2010-01-04   312.721039 310.103088   311.449310 311.349976 3937800.0
311.349976
2010-01-05   311.891449 308.761810   311.563568 309.978882 6048500.0
309.978882
2010-01-06   310.907837 301.220856   310.907837 302.164703 8009000.0
302.164703
2010-01-07   303.029083 294.410156   302.731018 295.130463 12912000.0
295.130463
```

As per the previous output, there are six columns:

- High: The highest price of the stock on that trading day.
- Low: The lowest price of the stock on that trading day.
- Close: The price of the stock at closing time.
- Open: The price of the stock at the beginning of the trading day (closing price of the previous trading day).
- Volume: How many stocks were traded.
- Adj Close: The closing price of the stock that adjusts the price of the stock for corporate actions. This price takes into account the stock splits and dividends.

The adjusted close is the price we will use for this example. Indeed, since it takes into account splits and dividends, we will not need to adjust the price manually.

Preparing the data – signal

The main part of a trading strategy (or a trading algorithm) is to decide when to trade (either to buy or sell a security or other asset). The event triggering the sending of an order is called a signal. A signal can use a large variety of inputs. These inputs may be market information, news, or a social networking website. Any combination of data can be a signal.

From the section entitled *Our first algorithmic trading (buy when the price is low, and sell when the price is high)*, for the *buy low sell high* example, we will calculate the difference in the adjusted close between two consecutive days. If the value of the adjusted close is negative, this means the price on the previous day was higher than the price the following day, so we can buy since the price is lower now. If this value is positive, this means that we can sell because the price is higher.

In Python, we are building a pandas data frame getting the same dimension as the data frame containing the data. This data frame will be called goog_data_signal:

```
goog_data_signal = pd.DataFrame(index=goog_data.index)
```

Following the creation of this data frame, we will copy the data we will use to build our signal to trade. In this case, we will copy the values of the Adj Close column from the goog_data data frame:

```
goog_data_signal['price'] = goog_data['Adj Close']
```

Based on our trading strategy, we need to have a column, daily_difference, to store the difference between two consecutive days. In order to create this column, we will use the diff function from the data frame object:

```
goog_data_signal['daily_difference'] = goog_data_signal['price'].diff()
```

As a sanity check, we can use the print function to display what goog_data_signal contains:

```
print(goog_data_signal.head())
            price daily_difference
Date
2014-01-02  552.963501              NaN
2014-01-03  548.929749        -4.033752
2014-01-06  555.049927         6.120178
2014-01-07  565.750366        10.700439
2014-01-08  566.927673         1.177307
```

We can observe that the daily_difference column has a non-numerical value for January 2, since it is the first row in this data frame.

We will create the signal based on the values of the column, `daily_difference`. If the value is positive, we will give the value 1, otherwise, the value will remain 0:

```
goog_data_signal['signal'] = 0.0
goog_data_signal['signal'] = np.where(goog_data_signal['daily_difference']
>; 0, 1.0, 0.0)
                price daily_difference  signal
Date
2014-01-02  552.963501           NaN 0.0
2014-01-03  548.929749     -4.033752 0.0
2014-01-06  555.049927      6.120178 1.0
2014-01-07  565.750366     10.700439 1.0
2014-01-08  566.927673      1.177307 1.0
```

Reading the column signal, we have 0 when we need to buy, and we have 1 when we need to sell.

Since we don't want to constantly buy if the market keeps moving down, or constantly sell when the market is moving up, we will limit the number of orders by restricting ourselves to the number of positions on the market. The position is your inventory of stocks or assets that you have on the market. For instance, if you buy one Google share, this means you have a position of one share on the market. If you sell this share, you will not have any positions on the market.

To simplify our example and limit the position on the market, it will be impossible to buy or sell more than one time consecutively. Therefore, we will apply `diff()` to the column signal:

```
goog_data_signal['positions'] = goog_data_signal['signal'].diff()
                price daily_difference  signal positions
Date
2014-01-02  552.963501           NaN 0.0 NaN
2014-01-03  548.929749     -4.033752 0.0       0.0
2014-01-06  555.049927      6.120178 1.0       1.0
2014-01-07  565.750366     10.700439 1.0       0.0
2014-01-08  566.927673      1.177307 1.0       0.0
2014-01-09  561.468201     -5.459473 0.0      -1.0
2014-01-10  561.438354     -0.029846 0.0       0.0
2014-01-13  557.861633     -3.576721 0.0       0.0
```

We will buy a share of Google on January 6 for a price of `555.049927`, and then sell this share for a price of `561.468201`. The profit of this trade is `561.468201-555.049927=6.418274`.

Signal visualization

While creating signals is just the beginning of the process of building a trading strategy, we need to visualize how the strategy performs in the long term. We will plot the graph of the historical data we used by using the matplotlib library. This library is well known in the Python world for making it easy to plot charts:

1. We will start by importing this library:

   ```
   import matplotlib.pyplot as plt
   ```

2. Next, we will define a figure that will contain our chart:

   ```
   fig = plt.figure()
   ax1 = fig.add_subplot(111, ylabel='Google price in $')
   ```

3. Now, we will plot the price within the range of days we initially chose:

   ```
   goog_data_signal['price'].plot(ax=ax1, color='r', lw=2.)
   ```

4. Next, we will draw an *up* arrow when we buy one Google share:

   ```
   ax1.plot(goog_data_signal.loc[goog_data_signal.positions ==
   1.0].index,
           goog_data_signal.price[goog_data_signal.positions == 1.0],
           '^', markersize=5, color='m')
   ```

5. Next, we will draw a *down* arrow when we sell one Google share:

   ```
   ax1.plot(goog_data_signal.loc[goog_data_signal.positions ==
   -1.0].index,
           goog_data_signal.price[goog_data_signal.positions == -1.0],
           'v', markersize=5, color='k')
   plt.show()
   ```

This code will return the following output. Let's have a look at the following plot:

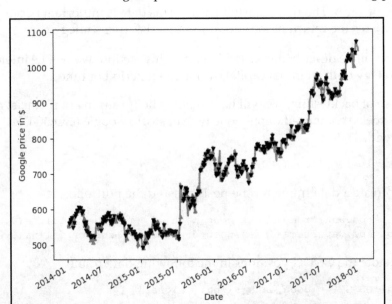

Up to this point, we introduced the trading idea, we implemented the signal triggering buy and sell orders, and we talked about the way of restricting the strategy by limiting the position to one share on the market. Once these steps are satisfactory, the following step is backtesting.

Backtesting

Backtesting is a key phase to get statistics showing how effective the trading strategy is. As we previously learned, the backtesting relies on the assumption that the past predicts the future. This phase will provide the statistics that you or your company consider important, such as the following:

- **Profit and loss (P and L)**: The money made by the strategy without transaction fees.
- **Net profit and loss (net P and L)**: The money made by the strategy with transaction fees.
- **Exposure**: The capital invested.
- **Number of trades**: The number of trades placed during a trading session.

- **Annualized return**: This is the return for a year of trading.
- **Sharpe ratio**: The risk-adjusted return. This date is important because it compares the return of the strategy with a risk-free strategy.

While this part will be described in detail later, for this section, we will be interested in testing our strategy with an initial capital over a given period of time.

For the purpose of backtesting, we will have a portfolio (grouping of financial assets such as bonds and stocks) composed of only one type of stock: Google (GOOG). We will start this portfolio with $1,000:

```
initial_capital = float(1000.0)
```

Now, we will create a data frame for the positions and the portfolio:

```
positions = pd.DataFrame(index=goog_data_signal.index).fillna(0.0)
portfolio = pd.DataFrame(index=goog_data_signal.index).fillna(0.0)
```

Next, we will store the GOOG positions in the following data frame:

```
positions['GOOG'] = goog_data_signal['signal']
```

Then, we will store the amount of the GOOG positions for the portfolio in this one:

```
portfolio['positions'] = (positions.multiply(goog_data_signal['price'],
axis=0))
```

Next, we will calculate the non-invested money (cash):

```
portfolio['cash'] = initial_capital -
(positions.diff().multiply(goog_data_signal['price'], axis=0)).cumsum()
```

The total investment will be calculated by summing the positions and the cash:

```
portfolio['total'] = portfolio['positions'] + portfolio['cash']
```

When we draw the following plot, we can easily establish that our strategy is profitable:

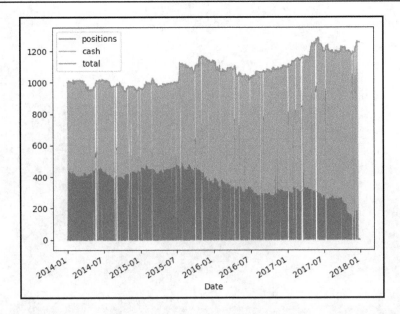

When we create a trading strategy, we have an initial amount of money (cash). We will invest this money (holdings). This holding value is based on the market value of the investment. If we own a stock and the price of this stock increases, the value of the holding will increase. When we decide to sell, we move the value of the holding corresponding to this sale to the cash amount. The sum total of the assets is the sum of the cash and the holdings. The preceding chart shows that the strategy is profitable since the amount of cash increases toward the end. The graph allows you to check whether your trading idea can generate money.

Summary

During this chapter, you were introduced to the trading world. You learned why people trade and you are capable of describing the critical actors and the trading systems with which you will interact during your life as an algorithm trading designer. You were exposed to the tools you will use in this book to build your trading robot. Finally, you encountered your first implementation of algorithmic trading by coding your first trading strategy implementing the economic idea of buying low and selling high. We observed that this strategy was far from being a profitable and safe strategy.

In the next chapter, we will address how to make a strategy more advanced, linked to more sophisticated trading ideas, while implementing these strategies in Python.

2
Section 2: Trading Signal Generation and Strategies

In this section, you will learn how quantitative trading signals and trading strategies are developed. Learning can be applied to market research and the design of algorithmic strategies.

This section comprises the following chapters:

- Chapter 2, *Deciphering the Markets with Technical Analysis*
- Chapter 3, *Predicting the Markets with Basic Machine Learning*

2

Deciphering the Markets with Technical Analysis

In this chapter, we will go through some popular methods of technical analysis and show how to apply them while analyzing market data. We will perform basic algorithmic trading using market trends, support, and resistance.

You may be thinking of how we can come up with our own strategies? And are there any naive strategies that worked in the past that we can use by way of reference?

As you read in the first chapter of this book, mankind has been trading assets for centuries. Numerous strategies have been created to increase the profit or sometimes just to keep the same profit. In this zero-sum game, the competition is considerable. It necessitates a constant innovation in terms of trading models and also in terms of technology. In this race to get the biggest part of the pie first, it is important to know the basic foundation of analysis in order to create trading strategies. When predicting the market, we mainly assume that the past repeats itself in future. In order to predict future prices and volumes, technical analysts study the historical market data. Based on behavioral economics and quantitative analysis, the market data is divided into two main areas.

First, are chart patterns. This side of technical analysis is based on recognizing trading patterns and anticipating when they will reproduce in the future. This is usually more difficult to implement.

Second, are technical indicators. This other side uses mathematical calculation to forecast the financial market direction. The list of technical indicators is sufficiently long to fill an entire book on this topic alone, but they are composed of a few different principal domains: trend, momentum, volume, volatility, and support and resistance. We will focus on the support and resistance strategy as an example to illustrate one of the most well-known technical analysis approaches.

In this chapter, we will cover the following topics:

- Designing a trading strategy based on trend-and momentum-based indicators
- Creating trading signals based on fundamental technical analysis
- Implementing advanced concepts, such as seasonality, in trading instruments

Designing a trading strategy based on trend- and momentum-based indicators

Trading strategies based on trend and momentum are pretty similar. If we can use a metaphor to illustrate the difference, the trend strategy uses speed, whereas the momentum strategy uses acceleration. With the trend strategy, we will study the price historical data. If this price keeps increasing for the last fixed amount of days, we will open a long position by assuming that the price will keep raising.

The trading strategy based on momentum is a technique where we send orders based on the strength of past behavior. The price momentum is the quantity of motion that a price has. The underlying rule is to bet that an asset price with a strong movement in a given direction will keep going in the same direction in the future. We will review a number of technical indicators expressing momentum in the market. Support and resistance are examples of indicators predicting future behavior.

Support and resistance indicators

In the first chapter, we explained the principle of the evolution of prices based on supply and demand. The price decreases when there is an increase in supply, and the price increases when demand rises. When there is a fall in price, we expect the price fall to pause due to a concentration of demands. This virtual limit will be referred to as a support line. Since the price becomes lower, it is more likely to find buyers. Inversely, when the price starts rising, we expect a pause in this increase due to a concentration of supplies. This is referred to as the resistance line. It is based on the same principle, showing that a high price leads sellers to sell. This exploits the market psychology of investors following this trend of buying when the price is low and selling when the price is high.

To illustrate an example of a technical indicator (in this part, support and resistance), we will use the Google data from the first chapter. Since you will use the data for testing many times, you should store this data frame to your disk. Doing this will help you save time when you want to replay the data. To avoid complications with stock split, we will only take dates without splits. Therefore, we will keep only 620 days. Let's have a look at the following code:

```python
import pandas as pd
from pandas_datareader import data

start_date = '2014-01-01'
end_date = '2018-01-01'
SRC_DATA_FILENAME='goog_data.pkl'

try:
    goog_data2 = pd.read_pickle(SRC_DATA_FILENAME)
except FileNotFoundError:
    goog_data2 = data.DataReader('GOOG', 'yahoo', start_date, end_date)
    goog_data2.to_pickle(SRC_DATA_FILENAME)

goog_data=goog_data2.tail(620)
lows=goog_data['Low']
highs=goog_data['High']

import matplotlib.pyplot as plt

fig = plt.figure()
ax1 = fig.add_subplot(111, ylabel='Google price in $')
highs.plot(ax=ax1, color='c', lw=2.)
lows.plot(ax=ax1, color='y', lw=2.)
plt.hlines(highs.head(200).max(),lows.index.values[0],lows.index.values[-1]
,linewidth=2, color='g')
plt.hlines(lows.head(200).min(),lows.index.values[0],lows.index.values[-1],
linewidth=2, color='r')
plt.axvline(linewidth=2,color='b',x=lows.index.values[200],linestyle=':')
plt.show()
```

In this code, the following applies:

- This retrieves the financial data from the Yahoo finance website between January 1, 2014 and January 1, 2018.

- We used the maximum and minimum values to create the support and the resistance limits, as shown in the following plot:

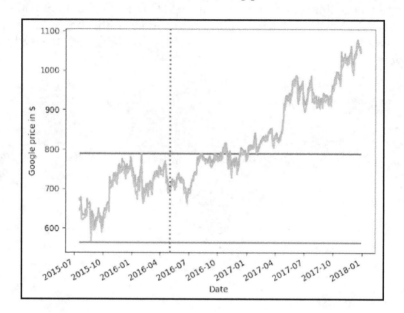

In this plot, the following applies:

- We draw the highs and lows of the GOOG price.
- The green line represents the resistance level, and the red line represents the support level.
- To build these lines, we use the maximum value of the GOOG price and the minimum value of the GOOG price stored daily.
- After the 200th day (dotted vertical blue line), we will buy when we reach the support line, and sell when we reach the resistance line. In this example, we used 200 days so that we have sufficient data points to get an estimate of the trend.
- It is observed that the GOOG price will reach the resistance line around August 2016. This means that we have a signal to enter a short position (sell).
- Once traded, we will wait to get out of this short position when the GOOG price will reach the support line.
- With this historical data, it is easily noticeable that this condition will not happen.
- This will result in carrying a short position in a rising market without having any signal to sell it, thereby resulting in a huge loss.

- This means that, even if the trading idea based on support/resistance has strong grounds in terms of economical behavior, in reality, we will need to modify this trading strategy to make it work.
- Moving the support/resistance line to adapt to the market evolution will be key to the trading strategy efficiency.

In the middle of the following chart, we show three fixed-size time windows. We took care of adding the tolerance margin that we will consider to be sufficiently close to the limits (support and resistance):

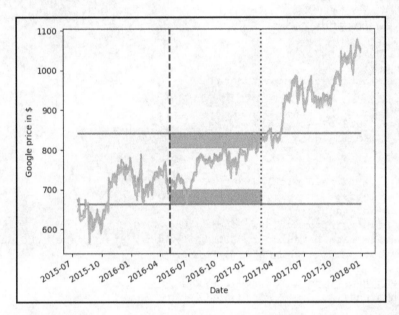

If we take a new 200-day window after the first one, the support/resistance levels will be recalculated. We observe that the trading strategy will not get rid of the GOOG position (while the market keeps raising) since the price does not go back to the support level.

Since the algorithm cannot get rid of a position, we will need to add more parameters to change the behavior in order to enter a position. The following parameters can be added to the algorithm to change its position:

- There can be a shorter rolling window.
- We can count the number of times the price reaches a support or resistance line.
- A tolerance margin can be added to consider that a support or resistance value can attain around a certain percentage of this value.

This phase is critical when creating your trading strategy. You will start by observing how your trading idea will perform using historical data, and then you will increase the number of parameters of this strategy to adjust to more realistic test cases.

In our example, we can introduce two further parameters:

- The minimum number of times that a price needs to reach the support/resistance level.
- We will define the tolerance margin of what we consider being close to the support/resistance level.

Let's now have a look at the code:

```
import pandas as pd
import numpy as np
from pandas_datareader import data

start_date = '2014-01-01'
end_date = '2018-01-01'
SRC_DATA_FILENAME='goog_data.pkl'

try:
    goog_data = pd.read_pickle(SRC_DATA_FILENAME)
    print('File data found...reading GOOG data')
except FileNotFoundError:
    print('File not found...downloading the GOOG data')
    goog_data = data.DataReader('GOOG', 'yahoo', start_date, end_date)
    goog_data.to_pickle(SRC_DATA_FILENAME)

goog_data_signal = pd.DataFrame(index=goog_data.index)
goog_data_signal['price'] = goog_data['Adj Close']
```

In the code, the data is collected by using the `pandas_datareader` library and by using the class. Now, let's have a look at the other part of the code where we will implement the trading strategy:

```
def trading_support_resistance(data, bin_width=20):
    data['sup_tolerance'] = pd.Series(np.zeros(len(data)))
    data['res_tolerance'] = pd.Series(np.zeros(len(data)))
    data['sup_count'] = pd.Series(np.zeros(len(data)))
    data['res_count'] = pd.Series(np.zeros(len(data)))
    data['sup'] = pd.Series(np.zeros(len(data)))
    data['res'] = pd.Series(np.zeros(len(data)))
    data['positions'] = pd.Series(np.zeros(len(data)))
    data['signal'] = pd.Series(np.zeros(len(data)))
    in_support=0
    in_resistance=0
```

```
for x in range((bin_width - 1) + bin_width, len(data)):
    data_section = data[x - bin_width:x + 1]
    support_level=min(data_section['price'])
    resistance_level=max(data_section['price'])
    range_level=resistance_level-support_level
    data['res'][x]=resistance_level
    data['sup'][x]=support_level
    data['sup_tolerance'][x]=support_level + 0.2 * range_level
    data['res_tolerance'][x]=resistance_level - 0.2 * range_level

    if data['price'][x]>=data['res_tolerance'][x] and\
                        data['price'][x] <= data['res'][x]:
        in_resistance+=1
        data['res_count'][x]=in_resistance
    elif data['price'][x] <= data['sup_tolerance'][x] and \
                        data['price'][x] >= data['sup'][x]:
        in_support += 1
        data['sup_count'][x] = in_support
    else:
        in_support=0
        in_resistance=0
    if in_resistance>2:
        data['signal'][x]=1
    elif in_support>2:
        data['signal'][x]=0
    else:
        data['signal'][x] = data['signal'][x-1]

data['positions']=data['signal'].diff()

trading_support_resistance(goog_data_signal)
```

In the preceding code, the following applies:

- The `trading_support_resistance` function defines the time window in the price that is used to calculate the resistance and support levels.
- The level of support and resistance is calculated by taking the maximum and minimum price and then subtracting and adding a 20% margin.
- We used `diff` to know when we place the orders.
- When the price is below/above the support/resistance, we will enter a long/short position. For that, we will have 1 for a long position and 0 for a short position.

The code will print the chart representing the time when orders go out:

```
import matplotlib.pyplot as plt

fig = plt.figure()
ax1 = fig.add_subplot(111, ylabel='Google price in $')
goog_data_signal['sup'].plot(ax=ax1, color='g', lw=2.)
goog_data_signal['res'].plot(ax=ax1, color='b', lw=2.)
goog_data_signal['price'].plot(ax=ax1, color='r', lw=2.)
ax1.plot(goog_data_signal.loc[goog_data_signal.positions == 1.0].index,
         goog_data_signal.price[goog_data_signal.positions == 1.0],
         '^', markersize=7, color='k',label='buy')
ax1.plot(goog_data_signal.loc[goog_data_signal.positions == -1.0].index,
         goog_data_signal.price[goog_data_signal.positions == -1.0],
         'v', markersize=7, color='k',label='sell')
plt.legend()
plt.show()
```

The codes will return the following output. The plot shows a 20-day rolling window calculating resistance and support:

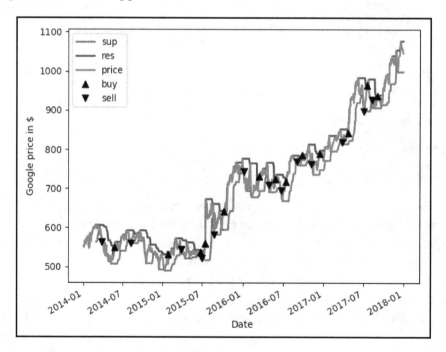

From this plot, it is observed that a buy order is sent when a price stays in the resistance tolerance margin for 2 consecutive days, and that a sell order is sent when a price stays in the support tolerance margin for 2 consecutive days.

In this section, we learned the difference between trend and momentum trading strategies, and we implemented a very well used momentum trading strategy based on support and resistance levels. We will now explore new ideas to create trading strategies by using more technical analysis.

Creating trading signals based on fundamental technical analysis

This section will show you how to use technical analysis to build trading signals. We will start with one of the most common methods, the simple moving average, and we will discuss more advanced techniques along the way. Here is a list of the signals we will cover:

- **Simple Moving Average (SMA)**
- **Exponential Moving Average (EMA)**
- **Absolute Price Oscillator (APO)**
- **Moving Average Convergence Divergence (MACD)**
- **Bollinger Bands (BBANDS)**
- **Relative Strength Indicator (RSI)**
- **Standard Deviation (STDEV)**
- **Momentum (MOM)**

Simple moving average

Simple moving average, which we will refer to as **SMA**, is a basic technical analysis indicator. The simple moving average, as you may have guessed from its name, is computed by adding up the price of an instrument over a certain period of time divided by the number of time periods. It is basically the price average over a certain time period, with equal weight being used for each price. The time period over which it is averaged is often referred to as the lookback period or history. Let's have a look at the following formula of the simple moving average:

$$SimpleMovingAverage = \frac{\sum_{i=1}^{N} Pi}{N}$$

Here, the following applies:

P_i: Price at time period i

N: Number of prices added together or the number of time periods

Let's implement a simple moving average that computes an average over a 20-day moving window. We will then compare the SMA values against daily prices, and it should be easy to observe the smoothing that SMA achieves.

Implementation of the simple moving average

In this section, the code demonstrates how you would implement a simple moving average, using a list (history) to maintain a moving window of prices and a list (SMA values) to maintain a list of SMA values:

```
import statistics as stats

time_period = 20 # number of days over which to average
history = [] # to track a history of prices
sma_values = [] # to track simple moving average values

for close_price in close:
 history.append(close_price)
 if len(history) > time_period: # we remove oldest price because we only
average over last 'time_period' prices
    del (history[0])

 sma_values.append(stats.mean(history))

goog_data = goog_data.assign(ClosePrice=pd.Series(close,
index=goog_data.index))
goog_data = goog_data.assign(Simple20DayMovingAverage=pd.Series(sma_values,
index=goog_data.index))
close_price = goog_data['ClosePrice']
sma = goog_data['Simple20DayMovingAverage']

import matplotlib.pyplot as plt

fig = plt.figure()
ax1 = fig.add_subplot(111, ylabel='Google price in $')
close_price.plot(ax=ax1, color='g', lw=2., legend=True)
sma.plot(ax=ax1, color='r', lw=2., legend=True)
plt.show()
```

In the preceding code, the following applies:

- We have used the Python statistics package to compute the mean of the values in history.
- Finally, we used matplotlib to plot the SMA against the actual prices to observe the behavior.

The following plot is an output of the code:

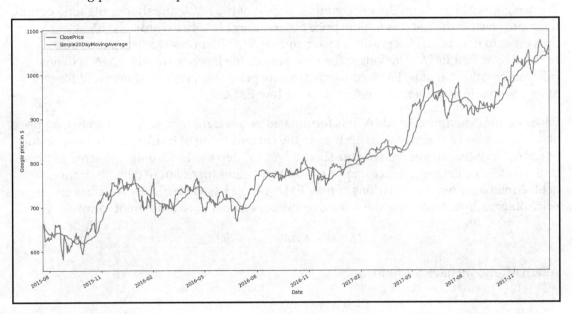

In this plot, it is easy to observe that the 20-day SMA has the intended smoothing effect and evens out the micro-volatility in the actual stock price, yielding a more stable price curve.

Exponential moving average

The **exponential moving average**, which we will refer to as the **EMA**, is the single most well-known and widely used technical analysis indicator for time series data.

The EMA is similar to the simple moving average, but, instead of weighing all prices in the history equally, it places more weight on the most recent price observation and less weight on the older price observations. This is endeavoring to capture the intuitive idea that the new price observation has more up-to-date information than prices in the past. It is also possible to place more weight on older price observations and less weight on the newer price observations. This would try to capture the idea that longer-term trends have more information than short-term volatile price movements.

The weighting depends on the selected time period of the EMA; the shorter the time period, the more reactive the EMA is to new price observations; in other words, the EMA converges to new price observations faster and forgets older observations faster, also referred to as **Fast EMA**. The longer the time period, the less reactive the EMA is to new price observations; that is, EMA converges to new price observations slower and forgets older observations slower, also referred to as **Slow EMA**.

Based on the description of EMA, it is formulated as a weight factor, μ, applied to new price observations and a weight factor applied to the current value of EMA to get the new value of EMA. Since the sum of the weights should be 1 to keep the EMA units the same as price units, that is, \$s, the weight factor applied to EMA values turns out to be $1 - \mu$. Hence, we get the following two formulations of new EMA values based on old EMA values and new price observations, which are the same definitions, written in two different forms:

$$EMA = (P - EMA_{old}) \times \mu + EMA_{old}$$

Alternatively, we have the following:

$$EMA = P \times \mu + (1 - \mu) \times EMA_{old}$$

Here, the following applies:

P: Current price of the instrument

EMA_{old}: EMA value prior to the current price observation

μ: Smoothing constant, most commonly set to $\dfrac{2}{(n + 1)}$

N: Number of time periods (similar to what we used in the simple moving average)

Implementation of the exponential moving average

Let's implement an exponential moving average with 20 days as the number of time periods to compute the average over. We will use a default smoothing factor of *2 / (n + 1)* for this implementation. Similar to SMA, EMA also achieves an evening out across normal daily prices. EMA has the advantage of allowing us to weigh recent prices with higher weights than an SMA does, which does uniform weighting.

In the following code, we will see the implementation of the exponential moving average:

```
num_periods = 20 # number of days over which to average
K = 2 / (num_periods + 1) # smoothing constant
ema_p = 0
ema_values = [] # to hold computed EMA values

for close_price in close:
  if (ema_p == 0): # first observation, EMA = current-price
    ema_p = close_price
  else:
    ema_p = (close_price - ema_p) * K + ema_p

  ema_values.append(ema_p)

goog_data = goog_data.assign(ClosePrice=pd.Series(close,
index=goog_data.index))
goog_data =
goog_data.assign(Exponential20DayMovingAverage=pd.Series(ema_values,
index=goog_data.index))
close_price = goog_data['ClosePrice']
ema = goog_data['Exponential20DayMovingAverage']

import matplotlib.pyplot as plt

fig = plt.figure()
ax1 = fig.add_subplot(111, ylabel='Google price in $')
close_price.plot(ax=ax1, color='g', lw=2., legend=True)
ema.plot(ax=ax1, color='b', lw=2., legend=True)
plt.savefig('ema.png')
plt.show()
```

In the preceding code, the following applies:

- We used a list (`ema_values`) to track EMA values computed so far.
- On each new observation of close price, we decay the difference from the old EMA value and update the old EMA value slightly to find the new EMA value.
- Finally, the matplotlib plot shows the difference between EMA and non-EMA prices.

Let's now have a look at the plot. This is the output of the code:

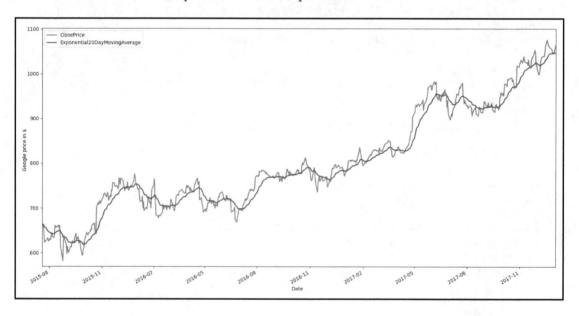

From the plot, it is observed that EMA has a very similar smoothing effect to SMA, as expected, and it reduces the noise in the raw prices. However the extra parameter, μ, available in EMA in addition to the parameter N, allows us to control the relative weight placed on the new price observation, as compared to older price observations. This allows us to build different variants of EMA by varying the μ parameter to make fast and slow EMAs, even for the same parameter, N. We will explore fast and slow EMAs more in the rest of this chapter and in later chapters.

Absolute price oscillator

The absolute price oscillator, which we will refer to as APO, is a class of indicators that builds on top of moving averages of prices to capture specific short-term deviations in prices.

The absolute price oscillator is computed by finding the difference between a fast exponential moving average and a slow exponential moving average. Intuitively, it is trying to measure how far the more reactive EMA (EMA_{fast}) is deviating from the more stable EMA (EMA_{slow}). A large difference is usually interpreted as one of two things: instrument prices are starting to trend or break out, or instrument prices are far away from their equilibrium prices, in other words, overbought or oversold:

$$AbsolutePriceOscillator = EMA_{fast} - EMA_{slow}$$

Implementation of the absolute price oscillator

Let's now implement the absolute price oscillator, with the faster EMA using a period of 10 days and a slower EMA using a period of 40 days, and default smoothing factors being 2/11 and 2/41, respectively, for the two EMAs:

```
num_periods_fast = 10 # time period for the fast EMA
K_fast = 2 / (num_periods_fast + 1) # smoothing factor for fast EMA
ema_fast = 0

num_periods_slow = 40 # time period for slow EMA
K_slow = 2 / (num_periods_slow + 1) # smoothing factor for slow EMA
ema_slow = 0

ema_fast_values = [] # we will hold fast EMA values for visualization
purposes
ema_slow_values = [] # we will hold slow EMA values for visualization
purposes
apo_values = [] # track computed absolute price oscillator values

for close_price in close:
  if (ema_fast == 0): # first observation
    ema_fast = close_price
    ema_slow = close_price
  else:
    ema_fast = (close_price - ema_fast) * K_fast + ema_fast
    ema_slow = (close_price - ema_slow) * K_slow + ema_slow

  ema_fast_values.append(ema_fast)
```

```
ema_slow_values.append(ema_slow)
apo_values.append(ema_fast - ema_slow)
```

The preceding code generates APO values that have higher positive and negative values when the prices are moving away from long-term EMA very quickly (breaking out), which can have a trend-starting interpretation or an overbought/sold interpretation. Now, let's visualize the fast and slow EMAs and visualize the APO values generated:

```
goog_data = goog_data.assign(ClosePrice=pd.Series(close,
index=goog_data.index))
goog_data =
goog_data.assign(FastExponential10DayMovingAverage=pd.Series(ema_fast_value
s, index=goog_data.index))
goog_data =
goog_data.assign(SlowExponential40DayMovingAverage=pd.Series(ema_slow_value
s, index=goog_data.index))
goog_data = goog_data.assign(AbsolutePriceOscillator=pd.Series(apo_values,
index=goog_data.index))
close_price = goog_data['ClosePrice']
ema_f = goog_data['FastExponential10DayMovingAverage']
ema_s = goog_data['SlowExponential40DayMovingAverage']
apo = goog_data['AbsolutePriceOscillator']

import matplotlib.pyplot as plt

fig = plt.figure()
ax1 = fig.add_subplot(211, ylabel='Google price in $')
close_price.plot(ax=ax1, color='g', lw=2., legend=True)
ema_f.plot(ax=ax1, color='b', lw=2., legend=True)
ema_s.plot(ax=ax1, color='r', lw=2., legend=True)
ax2 = fig.add_subplot(212, ylabel='APO')
apo.plot(ax=ax2, color='black', lw=2., legend=True)
plt.show()
```

The preceding code will return the following output. Let's have a look at the plot:

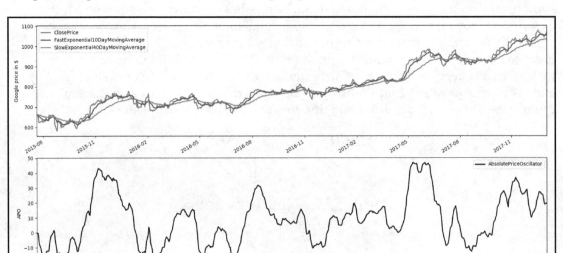

One observation here is the difference in behavior between fast and slow EMAs. The faster one is more reactive to new price observations, and the slower one is less reactive to new price observations and decays slower. The APO values are positive when prices are breaking out to the upside, and the magnitude of the APO values captures the magnitude of the breakout. The APO values are negative when prices are breaking out to the downside, and the magnitude of the APO values captures the magnitude of the breakout. In a later chapter in this book, we will use this signal in a realistic trading strategy.

Moving average convergence divergence

The moving average convergence divergence is another in the class of indicators that builds on top of moving averages of prices. We'll refer to it as MACD. This goes a step further than the APO. Let's look at it in greater detail.

The moving average convergence divergence was created by Gerald Appel. It is similar in spirit to an absolute price oscillator in that it establishes the difference between a fast exponential moving average and a slow exponential moving average. However, in the case of MACD, we apply a smoothing exponential moving average to the MACD value itself in order to get the final signal output from the MACD indicator. Optionally, you may also look at the difference between MACD values and the EMA of the MACD values (signal) and visualize it as a histogram. A properly configured MACD signal can successfully capture the direction, magnitude, and duration of a trending instrument price:

$$MACD = EMA_{Fast} - EMA_{Slow}$$

$$MACD_{Signal} = EMA_{MACD}$$

$$MACD_{Histogram} = MACD - MACD_{Signal}$$

Implementation of the moving average convergence divergence

Let's implement a moving average convergence divergence signal with a fast EMA period of 10 days, a slow EMA period of 40 days, and with default smoothing factors of 2/11 and 2/41, respectively:

```
num_periods_fast = 10 # fast EMA time period
K_fast = 2 / (num_periods_fast + 1) # fast EMA smoothing factor
ema_fast = 0

num_periods_slow = 40 # slow EMA time period
K_slow = 2 / (num_periods_slow + 1) # slow EMA smoothing factor
ema_slow = 0

num_periods_macd = 20 # MACD EMA time period
K_macd = 2 / (num_periods_macd + 1) # MACD EMA smoothing factor
ema_macd = 0

ema_fast_values = [] # track fast EMA values for visualization purposes
ema_slow_values = [] # track slow EMA values for visualization purposes
macd_values = [] # track MACD values for visualization purposes
macd_signal_values = [] # MACD EMA values tracker

macd_histogram_values = [] # MACD - MACD-EMA

for close_price in close:
  if (ema_fast == 0): # first observation
```

```
    ema_fast = close_price
    ema_slow = close_price
  else:
    ema_fast = (close_price - ema_fast) * K_fast + ema_fast
    ema_slow = (close_price - ema_slow) * K_slow + ema_slow

  ema_fast_values.append(ema_fast)
  ema_slow_values.append(ema_slow)
  macd = ema_fast - ema_slow # MACD is fast_MA - slow_EMA

  if ema_macd == 0:
    ema_macd = macd
  else:
    ema_macd = (macd - ema_macd) * K_slow + ema_macd # signal is EMA of MACD
values

  macd_values.append(macd)
  macd_signal_values.append(ema_macd)
  macd_histogram_values.append(macd - ema_macd)
```

In the preceding code, the following applies:

- The EMA_{MACD} time period used a period of 20 days and a default smoothing factor of 2/21.
- We also computed a $MACD_{Histogram}$ value ($MACD$- EMA_{MACD}).

Let's look at the code to plot and visualize the different signals and see what we can understand from it:

```
goog_data = goog_data.assign(ClosePrice=pd.Series(close,
index=goog_data.index))
goog_data =
goog_data.assign(FastExponential10DayMovingAverage=pd.Series(ema_fast_value
s, index=goog_data.index))
goog_data =
goog_data.assign(SlowExponential40DayMovingAverage=pd.Series(ema_slow_value
s, index=goog_data.index))
goog_data =
goog_data.assign(MovingAverageConvergenceDivergence=pd.Series(macd_values,
index=goog_data.index))
goog_data =
goog_data.assign(Exponential20DayMovingAverageOfMACD=pd.Series(macd_signal_
values, index=goog_data.index))
goog_data =
goog_data.assign(MACDHistorgram=pd.Series(macd_historgram_values,
index=goog_data.index))
close_price = goog_data['ClosePrice']
```

```
ema_f = goog_data['FastExponential10DayMovingAverage']
ema_s = goog_data['SlowExponential40DayMovingAverage']
macd = goog_data['MovingAverageConvergenceDivergence']
ema_macd = goog_data['Exponential20DayMovingAverageOfMACD']
macd_histogram = goog_data['MACDHistorgram']

import matplotlib.pyplot as plt

fig = plt.figure()
ax1 = fig.add_subplot(311, ylabel='Google price in $')
close_price.plot(ax=ax1, color='g', lw=2., legend=True)
ema_f.plot(ax=ax1, color='b', lw=2., legend=True)
ema_s.plot(ax=ax1, color='r', lw=2., legend=True)
ax2 = fig.add_subplot(312, ylabel='MACD')
macd.plot(ax=ax2, color='black', lw=2., legend=True)
ema_macd.plot(ax=ax2, color='g', lw=2., legend=True)s
ax3 = fig.add_subplot(313, ylabel='MACD')
macd_histogram.plot(ax=ax3, color='r', kind='bar', legend=True,
use_index=False)
plt.show()
```

The preceding code will return the following output. Let's have a look at the plot:

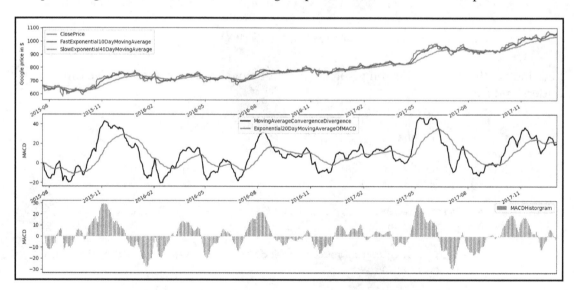

The MACD signal is very similar to the APO, as we expected, but now, in addition, the EMA_{MACD} is an additional smoothing factor on top of raw $MACD$ values to capture lasting trending periods by smoothing out the noise of raw $MACD$ values. Finally, the $MACD_{Histogram}$, which is the difference in the two series, captures (a) the time period when the trend is starting or reversion, and (b) the magnitude of lasting trends when $MACD_{Histogram}$ values stay positive or negative after reversing signs.

Bollinger bands

Bollinger bands (**BBANDS**) also builds on top of moving averages, but incorporates recent price volatility that makes the indicator more adaptive to different market conditions. Let's now discuss this in greater detail.

Bollinger bands is a well-known technical analysis indicator developed by John Bollinger. It computes a moving average of the prices (you can use the simple moving average or the exponential moving average or any other variant). In addition, it computes the standard deviation of the prices in the lookback period by treating the moving average as the mean price. It then creates an upper band that is a moving average, plus some multiple of standard price deviations, and a lower band that is a moving average minus multiple standard price deviations. This band represents the expected volatility of the prices by treating the moving average of the price as the reference price. Now, when prices move outside of these bands, that can be interpreted as a breakout/trend signal or an overbought/sold mean reversion signal.

Let's look at the equations to compute the upper Bollinger band, $BBAND_{Upper}$, and the lower Bollinger band, $BBAND_{Lower}$. Both depend, in the first instance, on the middle Bollinger band, $BBAND_{Middle}$, which is simply the simple moving average of the previous n time periods(in this case, the last n days) denoted by $SMA_{n-periods}$. The upper and lower bands are then computed by adding/subtracting $(\beta * \delta)$ to $BBAND_{Middle}$, which is the product of standard deviation, σ, which we've seen before, and β, which is a standard deviation factor of our choice. The larger the value of β chosen, the greater the Bollinger bandwidth for our signal, so it is just a parameter that controls the width in our trading signal:

$$BBAND_{Middle} = SMA_{n-periods}$$

$$BBAND_{Upper} = BBAND_{Middle} + (\beta * \delta)$$

$$BBAND_{Lower} = BBAND_{Middle} - (\beta * \delta)$$

Here, the following applies:

β: Standard deviation factor of our choice

To compute the standard deviation, first we compute the variance:

$$\sigma^2 = \frac{\sum_{i=1}^{n}(Pi - SMA)^2}{n}$$

Then, the standard deviation is simply the square root of the variance:

$$\sigma = \sqrt{\sigma^2}$$

Implementation of Bollinger bands

We will implement and visualize Bollinger bands, with 20 days as the time period for SMA ($BBAND_{Middle}$):

```
import statistics as stats
import math as math

time_period = 20 # history length for Simple Moving Average for middle band
stdev_factor = 2 # Standard Deviation Scaling factor for the upper and
lower bands

history = [] # price history for computing simple moving average
sma_values = [] # moving average of prices for visualization purposes
upper_band = [] # upper band values
lower_band = [] # lower band values

for close_price in close:
 history.append(close_price)
 if len(history) > time_period: # we only want to maintain at most
'time_period' number of price observations
   del (history[0])

 sma = stats.mean(history)
 sma_values.append(sma) # simple moving average or middle band

 variance = 0 # variance is the square of standard deviation

 for hist_price in history:
   variance = variance + ((hist_price - sma) ** 2)

 stdev = math.sqrt(variance / len(history)) # use square root to get
```

```
standard deviation
  upper_band.append(sma + stdev_factor * stdev)
  lower_band.append(sma - stdev_factor * stdev)
```

In the preceding code, we used a `stdev` factor, β, of 2 to compute the upper band and lower band from the middle band, and the standard deviation σ we compute.

Now, let's add some code to visualize the Bollinger bands and make some observations:

```
goog_data = goog_data.assign(ClosePrice=pd.Series(close,
index=goog_data.index))
goog_data =
goog_data.assign(MiddleBollingerBand20DaySMA=pd.Series(sma_values,
index=goog_data.index))
goog_data =
goog_data.assign(UpperBollingerBand20DaySMA2StdevFactor=pd.Series(upper_ban
d, index=goog_data.index))
goog_data =
goog_data.assign(LowerBollingerBand20DaySMA2StdevFactor=pd.Series(lower_ban
d, index=goog_data.index))
close_price = goog_data['ClosePrice']
mband = goog_data['MiddleBollingerBand20DaySMA']
uband = goog_data['UpperBollingerBand20DaySMA2StdevFactor']
lband = goog_data['LowerBollingerBand20DaySMA2StdevFactor']

import matplotlib.pyplot as plt

fig = plt.figure()
ax1 = fig.add_subplot(111, ylabel='Google price in $')
close_price.plot(ax=ax1, color='g', lw=2., legend=True)
mband.plot(ax=ax1, color='b', lw=2., legend=True)
uband.plot(ax=ax1, color='g', lw=2., legend=True)
lband.plot(ax=ax1, color='r', lw=2., legend=True)
plt.show()
```

The preceding code will return the following output. Let's have a look at the plot:

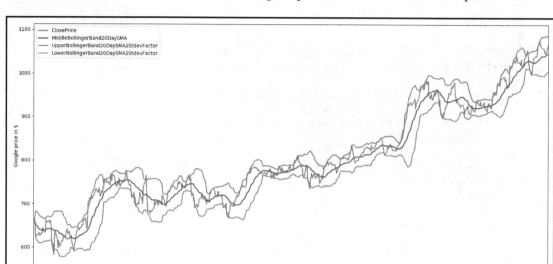

For Bollinger bands, when prices stay within the upper and lower bounds, then not much can be said, but, when prices traverse the upper band, then one interpretation can be that prices are breaking out to the upside and will continue to do so. Another interpretation of the same event can be that the trading instrument is overbought and we should expect a bounce back down.

The other case is when prices traverse the lower band, then one interpretation can be that prices are breaking out to the downside and will continue to do so. Another interpretation of the same event can be that the trading instrument is oversold and we should expect a bounce back up. In either case, Bollinger bands helps us to quantify and capture the exact time when this happens.

Relative strength indicator

The relative strength indicator, which we will refer to as RSI, is quite different from the previous indicators we saw that were based on moving averages of prices. This is based on price changes over periods to capture the strength/magnitude of price moves.

The relative strength indicator was developed by J Welles Wilder. It comprises a lookback period, which it uses to compute the magnitude of the average of gains/price increases over that period, as well as the magnitude of the averages of losses/price decreases over that period. Then, it computes the RSI value that normalizes the signal value to stay between 0 and 100, and attempts to capture if there have been many more gains relative to the losses, or if there have been many more losses relative to the gains. RSI values over 50% indicate an uptrend, while RSI values below 50% indicate a downtrend.

For the last n periods, the following applies:

$$Price > PreviousPrice => AbsoluteLossOverPeriod = 0$$

Otherwise, the following applies:

$$AbsoluteLossOverPeriod = PreviousPrice - Price$$

$$Price < PreviousPrice => AbsoluteGainOverPeriod = 0$$

Otherwise, the following applies:

$$AbsoluteGainOverPeriod = Price - PreviousPrice$$

$$RelativeStrength(RS) = \frac{\frac{\sum|GainsOverLastNPeriods|}{n}}{\frac{\sum|LossesOverLastNPeriods|}{n}}$$

$$RelativeStrength(RS) = \frac{\sum|GainsOverLastNPeriods|}{\sum|LossesOverLastNPeriods|}$$

$$RelativeStrengthIndicator(RSI) = 100 - \frac{100}{(1 + RS)}$$

Implementation of the relative strength indicator

Now, let's implement and plot a relative strength indicator on our dataset:

```
import statistics as stats

time_period = 20 # look back period to compute gains & losses

gain_history = [] # history of gains over look back period (0 if no gain,
magnitude of gain if gain)
loss_history = [] # history of losses over look back period (0 if no loss,
magnitude of loss if loss)
```

```
avg_gain_values = [] # track avg gains for visualization purposes
avg_loss_values = [] # track avg losses for visualization purposes

rsi_values = [] # track computed RSI values

last_price = 0 # current_price - last_price > 0 => gain. current_price -
last_price < 0 => loss.

for close_price in close:
 if last_price == 0:
   last_price = close_price

 gain_history.append(max(0, close_price - last_price))
 loss_history.append(max(0, last_price - close_price))
 last_price = close_price

 if len(gain_history) > time_period: # maximum observations is equal to
lookback period
   del (gain_history[0])
   del (loss_history[0])

 avg_gain = stats.mean(gain_history) # average gain over lookback period
 avg_loss = stats.mean(loss_history) # average loss over lookback period
 avg_gain_values.append(avg_gain)
 avg_loss_values.append(avg_loss)

 rs = 0
 if avg_loss > 0: # to avoid division by 0, which is undefined
   rs = avg_gain / avg_loss
 rsi = 100 - (100 / (1 + rs))
 rsi_values.append(rsi)
```

In the preceding code, the following applies:

- We have used 20 days as our time period over which we computed the average gains and losses and then normalized it to be between 0 and 100 based on our formula for *RSI* values.
- For our dataset where prices have been steadily rising, it is obvious that the *RSI* values are consistently over 50% or more.

Now, let's look at the code to visualize the final signal as well as the components involved:

```
goog_data = goog_data.assign(ClosePrice=pd.Series(close,
index=goog_data.index))
goog_data =
goog_data.assign(RelativeStrengthAvgGainOver20Days=pd.Series(avg_gain_value
s, index=goog_data.index))
```

```
goog_data =
goog_data.assign(RelativeStrengthAvgLossOver20Days=pd.Series(avg_loss_value
s, index=goog_data.index))
goog_data =
goog_data.assign(RelativeStrengthIndicatorOver20Days=pd.Series(rsi_values,
index=goog_data.index))
close_price = goog_data['ClosePrice']
rs_gain = goog_data['RelativeStrengthAvgGainOver20Days']
rs_loss = goog_data['RelativeStrengthAvgLossOver20Days']
rsi = goog_data['RelativeStrengthIndicatorOver20Days']

import matplotlib.pyplot as plt

fig = plt.figure()
ax1 = fig.add_subplot(311, ylabel='Google price in $')
close_price.plot(ax=ax1, color='black', lw=2., legend=True)
ax2 = fig.add_subplot(312, ylabel='RS')
rs_gain.plot(ax=ax2, color='g', lw=2., legend=True)
rs_loss.plot(ax=ax2, color='r', lw=2., legend=True)
ax3 = fig.add_subplot(313, ylabel='RSI')
rsi.plot(ax=ax3, color='b', lw=2., legend=True)
plt.show()
```

The preceding code will return the following output. Let's have a look at the plot:

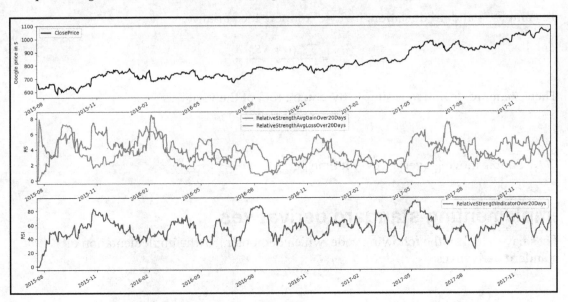

The first observation we can make from our analysis of the RSI signal applied to our GOOGLE dataset is that the `AverageGain` over our time frame of 20 days more often than not exceeds the `AverageLoss` over the same time frame, which intuitively makes sense because Google has been a very successful stock, increasing in value more or less consistently. Based on that, the RSI indicator also stays above 50% for the majority of the lifetime of the stock, again reflecting the continued gains in the Google stock over the course of its lifetime.

Standard deviation

Standard deviation, which will be referred to as **STDEV**, is a basic measure of price volatility that is used in combination with a lot of other technical analysis indicators to improve them. We'll explore that in greater detail in this section.

Standard deviation is a standard measure that is computed by measuring the squared deviation of individual prices from the mean price, and then finding the average of all those squared deviation values. This value is known as **variance**, and the standard deviation is obtained by taking the square root of the variance. Larger STDEVs are a mark of more volatile markets or larger expected price moves, so trading strategies need to factor that increased volatility into risk estimates and other trading behavior.

To compute standard deviation, first we compute the variance:

$$\sigma^2 = \frac{\sum_{i=1}^{n}(Pi - SMA)^2}{n}$$

Then, standard deviation is simply the square root of the variance:

$$\sigma = \sqrt{\sigma^2}$$

SMA: Simple moving average over n time periods.

Implementing standard derivatives

Let's have a look at the following code, which demonstrates the implementation of standard derivatives.

We are going to import the statistics and the math library we need to perform basic mathematical operations. We are defining the loopback period with the variable `time_period`, and we will store the past prices in the list history, while we will store the SMA and the standard deviation in `sma_values` and `stddev_values`. In the code, we calculate the variance, and then we calculate the standard deviation. To finish, we append to the `goog_data` data frame that we will use to display the chart:

```
import statistics as stats
import math as math

time_period = 20 # look back period

history = [] # history of prices
sma_values = [] # to track moving average values for visualization purposes
stddev_values = [] # history of computed stdev values
for close_price in close:
 history.append(close_price)
 if len(history) > time_period: # we track at most 'time_period' number of
prices
    del (history[0])

 sma = stats.mean(history)
 sma_values.append(sma)

 variance = 0 # variance is square of standard deviation
 for hist_price in history:
    variance = variance + ((hist_price - sma) ** 2)

 stdev = math.sqrt(variance / len(history))
 stddev_values.append(stdev)

goog_data = goog_data.assign(ClosePrice=pd.Series(close,
index=goog_data.index))
goog_data =
goog_data.assign(StandardDeviationOver20Days=pd.Series(stddev_values,
index=goog_data.index))
close_price = goog_data['ClosePrice']
stddev = goog_data['StandardDeviationOver20Days']
```

The preceding code will build the final visualizations:

```
import matplotlib.pyplot as plt

fig = plt.figure()
ax1 = fig.add_subplot(211, ylabel='Google price in $')
close_price.plot(ax=ax1, color='g', lw=2., legend=True)
ax2 = fig.add_subplot(212, ylabel='Stddev in $')
stddev.plot(ax=ax2, color='b', lw=2., legend=True)
plt.show()
```

The preceding code will return the following output. Let's have a look at the plot:

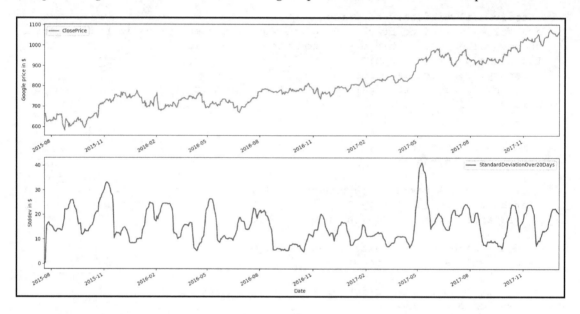

Here, the standard deviation quantifies the volatility in the price moves during the last 20 days. Volatility spikes when the Google stock prices spike up or spike down or go through large changes over the last 20 days. We will revisit the standard deviation as an important volatility measure in later chapters.

Momentum

Momentum, also referred to as **MOM**, is an important measure of speed and magnitude of price moves. This is often a key indicator of trend/breakout-based trading algorithms.

In its simplest form, momentum is simply the difference between the current price and price of some fixed time periods in the past. Consecutive periods of positive momentum values indicate an uptrend; conversely, if momentum is consecutively negative, that indicates a downtrend. Often, we use simple/exponential moving averages of the MOM indicator, as shown here, to detect sustained trends:

$$MOM = Price_t - Price_{t-n}$$

Here, the following applies:

- $Price_t$: Price at time t
- $Price_{t-n}$: Price n time periods before time t

Implementation of momentum

Now, let's have a look at the code that demonstrates the implementation of momentum:

```
time_period = 20 # how far to look back to find reference price to compute
momentum

history = [] # history of observed prices to use in momentum calculation
mom_values = [] # track momentum values for visualization purposes

for close_price in close:
 history.append(close_price)
 if len(history) > time_period: # history is at most 'time_period' number
of observations
    del (history[0])

 mom = close_price - history[0]
 mom_values.append(mom)
```

This maintains a list history of past prices and, at each new observation, computes the momentum to be the difference between the current price and the price time_period days ago, which, in this case, is 20 days:

```
goog_data = goog_data.assign(ClosePrice=pd.Series(close,
index=goog_data.index))
goog_data =
goog_data.assign(MomentumFromPrice20DaysAgo=pd.Series(mom_values,
index=goog_data.index))
close_price = goog_data['ClosePrice']
mom = goog_data['MomentumFromPrice20DaysAgo']

import matplotlib.pyplot as plt
```

```
fig = plt.figure()
ax1 = fig.add_subplot(211, ylabel='Google price in $')
close_price.plot(ax=ax1, color='g', lw=2., legend=True)
ax2 = fig.add_subplot(212, ylabel='Momentum in $')
mom.plot(ax=ax2, color='b', lw=2., legend=True)
plt.show()
```

The preceding code will return the following output. Let's have a look at the plot:

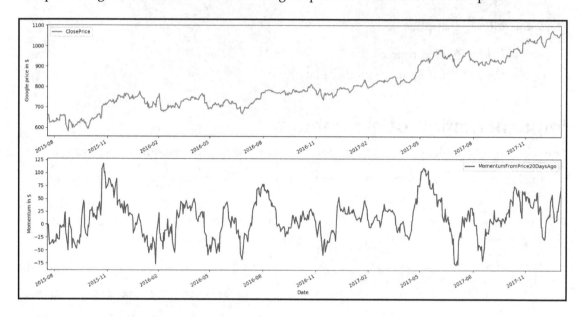

The plot for momentum shows us the following:

- Momentum values peak when the stock price changes by a large amount as compared to the price 20 days ago.
- Here, most momentum values are positive, mainly because, as we discussed in the previous section, Google stock has been increasing in value over the course of its lifetime and has large upward momentum values from time to time.
- During the brief periods where the stock prices drop in value, we can observe negative momentum values.

In this section, we learned how to create trading signals based on technical analysis. In the next section, we will learn how to implement advanced concepts, such as seasonality, in trading instruments.

Implementing advanced concepts, such as seasonality, in trading instruments

In trading, the price we receive is a collection of data points at constant time intervals called time series. They are time dependent and can have increasing or decreasing trends and seasonality trends, in other words, variations specific to a particular time frame. Like any other retail products, financial products follow trends and seasonality during different seasons. There are multiple seasonality effects: weekend, monthly, and holidays.

In this section, we will use the GOOG data from 2001 to 2018 to study price variations based on the months.

1. We will write the code to regroup the data by months, calculate and return the monthly returns, and then compare these returns in a histogram. We will observe that GOOG has a higher return in October:

```python
import pandas as pd
import matplotlib.pyplot as plt
from pandas_datareader import data

start_date = '2001-01-01'
end_date = '2018-01-01'
SRC_DATA_FILENAME='goog_data_large.pkl'

try:
  goog_data = pd.read_pickle(SRC_DATA_FILENAME)
  print('File data found...reading GOOG data')
except FileNotFoundError:
  print('File not found...downloading the GOOG data')
  goog_data = data.DataReader('GOOG', 'yahoo', start_date,
end_date)
  goog_data.to_pickle(SRC_DATA_FILENAME)

goog_monthly_return = goog_data['Adj Close'].pct_change().groupby(
  [goog_data['Adj Close'].index.year,
   goog_data['Adj Close'].index.month]).mean()
goog_montly_return_list=[]

for i in range(len(goog_monthly_return)):
  goog_montly_return_list.append\
      ({'month':goog_monthly_return.index[i][1],
        'monthly_return': goog_monthly_return[i]})

goog_montly_return_list=pd.DataFrame(goog_montly_return_list,
columns=('month','monthly_return'))
```

```
goog_montly_return_list.boxplot(column='monthly_return',
by='month')

ax = plt.gca()
labels = [item.get_text() for item in ax.get_xticklabels()]
labels=['Jan','Feb','Mar','Apr','May','Jun',\
        'Jul','Aug','Sep','Oct','Nov','Dec']
ax.set_xticklabels(labels)
ax.set_ylabel('GOOG return')
plt.tick_params(axis='both', which='major', labelsize=7)
plt.title("GOOG Monthly return 2001-2018")
plt.suptitle("")
plt.show()
```

The preceding code will return the following output. The following screenshot represents the GOOG monthly return:

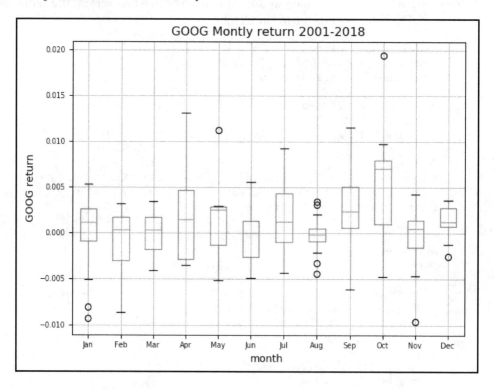

In this screenshot, we observe that there are repetitive patterns. The month of October is the month when the return seems to be the highest, unlike November, where we observe a drop in the return.

2. Since it is a time series, we will study the stationary (mean, variance remain constant over time). In the following code, we will check this property because the following time series models work on the assumption that time series are stationary:

- Constant mean
- Constant variance
- Time-independent autocovariance

```
# Displaying rolling statistics
def plot_rolling_statistics_ts(ts, titletext,ytext,
window_size=12):
    ts.plot(color='red', label='Original', lw=0.5)
    ts.rolling(window_size).mean().plot(
            color='blue',label='Rolling Mean')
    ts.rolling(window_size).std().plot(
            color='black', label='Rolling Std')

    plt.legend(loc='best')
    plt.ylabel(ytext)
    plt.title(titletext)
    plt.show(block=False)

plot_rolling_statistics_ts(goog_monthly_return[1:],'GOOG prices
rolling mean and standard deviation','Monthly return')

plot_rolling_statistics_ts(goog_data['Adj Close'],'GOOG prices
rolling mean and standard deviation','Daily prices',365)
```

The preceding code will return the following two charts, where we will compare the difference using two different time series.

- One shows the GOOG daily prices, and the other one shows the GOOG monthly return.
- We observe that the rolling average and rolling variance are not constant when using the daily prices instead of using the daily return.
- This means that the first time series representing the daily prices is not stationary. Therefore, we will need to make this time series stationary.
- The non-stationary for a time series can generally be attributed to two factors: trend and seasonality.

The following plot shows GOOG daily prices:

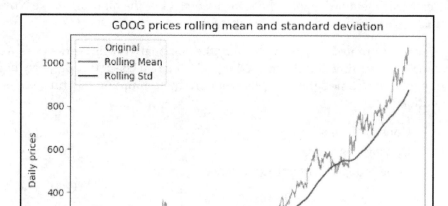

When observing the plot of the GOOG daily prices, the following can be stated:

- We can see that the price is growing over time; this is a trend.
- The wave effect we are observing on the GOOG daily prices comes from seasonality.
- When we make a time series stationary, we remove the trend and seasonality by modeling and removing them from the initial data.
- Once we find a model predicting future values for the data without seasonality and trend, we can apply back the seasonality and trend values to get the actual forecasted data.

The following plot shows the GOOG monthly return:

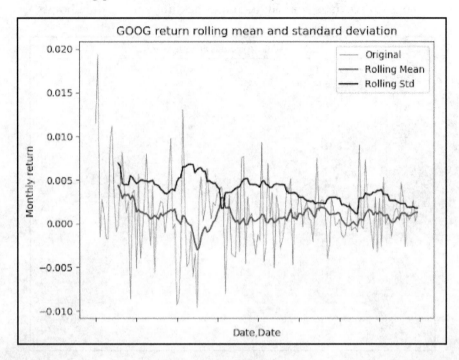

For the data using the GOOG daily prices, we can just remove the trend by subtracting the moving average from the daily prices in order to obtain the following screenshot:

- We can now observe the trend disappeared.
- Additionally, we also want to remove seasonality; for that, we can apply differentiation.

- For the differentiation, we will calculate the difference between two consecutive days; we will then use the difference as data points.

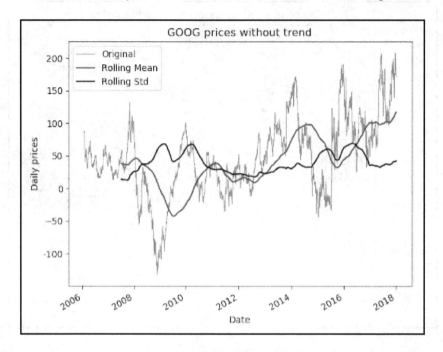

We recommend that you read a book on time series to go deeper in an analysis of the same: *Practical Time Series Analysis: Master Time Series Data Processing, Visualization, and Modeling Using Python*, Packt edition.

3. To confirm our observation, in the code, we use the popular statistical test: the augmented Dickey-Fuller test:

- This determines the presence of a unit root in time series.
- If a unit root is present, the time series is not stationary.
- The null hypothesis of this test is that the series has a unit root.
- If we reject the null hypothesis, this means that we don't find a unit root.

- If we fail to reject the null hypothesis, we can say that the time series is non-stationary:

```
def test_stationarity(timeseries):
  print('Results of Dickey-Fuller Test:')
  dftest = adfuller(timeseries[1:], autolag='AIC')
  dfoutput = pd.Series(dftest[0:4], index=['Test Statistic', 'p-
value', '#Lags Used', 'Number of Observations Used'])
  print (dfoutput)

test_stationarity(goog_data['Adj Close'])
```

4. This test returns a p-value of 0.99. Therefore, the time series is not stationary. Let's have a look at the test:

```
test_stationarity(goog_monthly_return[1:])
```

This test returns a p-value of less than 0.05. Therefore, we cannot say that the time series is not stationary. We recommend using daily returns when studying financial products. In the example of stationary, we could observe that no transformation is needed.

5. The last step of the time series analysis is to forecast the time series. We have two possible scenarios:

- A strictly stationary series without dependencies among values. We can use a regular linear regression to forecast values.
- A series with dependencies among values. We will be forced to use other statistical models. In this chapter, we chose to focus on using the **Auto-Regression Integrated Moving Averages (ARIMA)** model. This model has three parameters:
    - Autoregressive *(AR)* term *(p)*—lags of dependent variables. Example for 3, the predictors for *x(t)* is *x(t-1) + x(t-2) + x(t-3)*.
    - Moving average *(MA)* term *(q)*—lags for errors in prediction. Example for 3, the predictor for *x(t)* is *e(t-1) + e(t-2) + e(t-3)*, where *e(i)* is the difference between the moving average value and the actual value.
    - Differentiation *(d)*— This is the *d* number of occasions where we apply differentiation between values, as was explained when we studied the GOOG daily price. If *d=1*, we proceed with the difference between two consecutive values.

The parameter values for AR(p) and MA(q) can be respectively found by using the **autocorrelation function (ACF)** and the **partial autocorrelation function (PACF)**:

```
from statsmodels.graphics.tsaplots import plot_acf
from statsmodels.graphics.tsaplots import plot_pacf
from matplotlib import pyplot

pyplot.figure()
pyplot.subplot(211)
plot_acf(goog_monthly_return[1:], ax=pyplot.gca(),lags=10)

pyplot.subplot(212)
plot_pacf(goog_monthly_return[1:], ax=pyplot.gca(),lags=10)

pyplot.show()
```

Now, let's have a look at the output of the code:

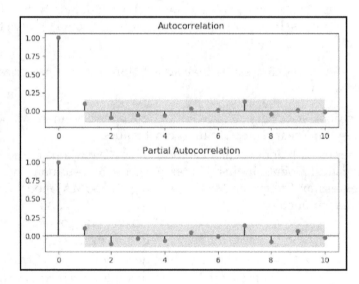

When we observe the two preceding diagrams, we can draw the confidence interval on either side of 0. We will use this confidence interval to determine the parameter values for the AR(p) and MA(q).

- **q**: The lag value is q=1 when the ACF plot crosses the upper confidence interval for the first time.
- **p**: The lag value is p=1 when the PACF chart crosses the upper confidence interval for the first time.

6. These two graphs suggest using *q=1* and *p=1*. We will apply the ARIMA model in the following code:

```
from statsmodels.tsa.arima_model import ARIMA

model = ARIMA(goog_monthly_return[1:], order=(2, 0, 2))

fitted_results = model.fit()

goog_monthly_return[1:].plot()

fitted_results.fittedvalues.plot(color='red')

plt.show()
```

As shown in the code, we applied the ARIMA model to the time series and it is representing the monthly return.

Summary

In this chapter, we explored concepts of generating trading signals, such as support and resistance, based on the intuitive ideas of supply and demand that are fundamental forces that drive market prices. We also briefly explored how you might use support and resistance to implement a simple trading strategy. Then, we looked into a variety of technical analysis indicators, explained the intuition behind them, and implemented and visualized their behavior during different price movements. We also introduced and implemented the ideas behind advanced mathematical approaches, such as **Autoregressive (AR)**, **Moving Average (MA)**, **Differentiation (D)**, **AutoCorrelation Function (ACF)**, and **Partial Autocorrelation Function (PACF)** for dealing with non-stationary time series datasets. Finally, we briefly introduced an advanced concept such as seasonality, which explains how there are repeating patterns in financial datasets, basic time series analysis and concepts of stationary or non-stationary time series, and how you may model financial data that displays that behavior.

In the next chapter, we will review and implement some simple regression and classification methods and understand the advantages of applying supervised statistical learning methods to trading.

3
Predicting the Markets with Basic Machine Learning

In the last chapter, we learned how to design trading strategies, create trading signals, and implement advanced concepts, such as seasonality in trading instruments. Understanding those concepts in greater detail is a vast field comprising stochastic processes, random walks, martingales, and time series analysis, which we leave to you to explore at your own pace.

So what's next? Let's look at an even more advanced method of prediction and forecasting: statistical inference and prediction. This is known as machine learning, the fundamentals of which were developed in the 1800s and early 1900s and have been worked on ever since. Recently, there has been a resurgence in interest in machine learning algorithms and applications owing to the availability of extremely cost-effective processing power and the easy availability of large datasets. Understanding machine learning techniques in great detail is a massive field at the intersection of linear algebra, multivariate calculus, probability theory, frequentist and Bayesian statistics, and an in-depth analysis of machine learning is beyond the scope of a single book. Machine learning methods, however, are surprisingly easily accessible in Python and quite intuitive to understand, so we will explain the intuition behind the methods and see how they find applications in algorithmic trading. But first, let's introduce some basic concepts and notation that we will need for the rest of this chapter.

This chapter will cover the following topics:

- Understanding the terminology and notations
- Creating predictive models that predict price movement using linear regression methods
- Creating predictive models that predict buy and sell signals using linear classification methods

Understanding the terminology and notations

To develop ideas quickly and build an intuition regarding supply and demand, we have a simple and completely hypothetical dataset of height, weight, and race of a few random samples obtained from a survey. Let's have a look at the dataset:

Height (inches)	Weight (lbs)	Race (Asian/African/Caucasian)
72	180	Asian
66	150	Asian
70	190	African
75	210	Caucasian
64	150	Asian
77	220	African
70	200	Caucasian
65	150	African

Let's examine the individual fields:

- Height in inches and weight in lbs are continuous data types because they can take on any values, such as 65, 65.123, and 65.3456667.
- Race, on the other hand, would be an example of a categorical data type, because there are a finite number of possible values that can go in the field. In this example, we assume that possible race values are Asian, African, and Caucasian.

Now, given this dataset, say our task is to build a mathematical model that can *learn* from the data we provide it with. The task or objective we are trying to learn in this example is to find the relationship between the weight of a person as it relates to their height and race. Intuitively, it should be obvious that height will have a major role to play (taller people are much more likely to be heavier), and race should have very little impact. Race may have some impact on the height of an individual, but once the height is known, knowing their race also provides very little additional information in guessing/predicting a person's weight. In this particular problem, note that in the dataset, we are also provided the weight of the samples in addition to their height and race.

Since the variable we are trying to learn how to predict is known, this is known as a **supervised learning problem**. If, on the other hand, we were not provided with the weight variable and were asked to predict whether, based on height and race, someone is more likely to be heavier than someone else, that would be an unsupervised learning problem. For the scope of this chapter, we will focus on supervised learning problems only, since that is the most typical use case of machine learning in algorithmic trading.

Another thing to address in this example is the fact that, in this case, we are trying to predict weight as a function of height and race. So we are trying to predict a continuous variable. This is known as a regression problem, since the output of such a model is a continuous value. If, on the other hand, say our task was to predict the race of a person as a function of their height and weight, in that case, we would be trying to predict a categorical variable type. This is known as a classification problem, since the output of such a model will be one value from a set of finite discrete values.

When we start addressing this problem, we will begin with a dataset that is already available to us and will *train* our model of choice on this dataset. This process (as you've already guessed) is known as training your model. We will use the data provided to us to guess the parameters of the learning model of our choice (we will elaborate more on what this means later). This is known as statistical inference of these parametric learning models. There are also non-parametric learning models, where we try to remember the data we've seen so far to make a guess as regards new data.

Once we are done training our model, we will use it to predict weight for datasets we haven't seen yet. Obviously, this is the part we are interested in. Based on data in the future that we haven't seen yet, can we predict the weight? This is known as testing your model and the datasets used for that are known as test data. The task of using a model where the parameters were learned by statistical inference to actually make predictions on previously unseen data is known as statistical prediction or forecasting.

We need to be able to understand the metrics of how to differentiate between a good model and a bad model. There are several well known and well understood performance metrics for different models. For regression prediction problems, we should try to minimize the differences between predicted value and the actual value of the target variable. This error term is known as residual errors; larger errors mean worse models and, in regression, we try to minimize the sum of these residual errors, or the sum of the square of these residual errors (squaring has the effect of penalizing large outliers more strongly, but more on that later). The most common metric for regression problems is R^2, which tracks the ratio of explained variance vis-à-vis unexplained variance, but we save that for more advanced texts.

In the simple hypothetical prediction problem of guessing weight based on height and race, let's say the model predicts the weight to be 170 and the actual weight is 160. In this case, the error is *160-170 = -10*, the absolute error is *|-10| = 10*, and the squared error is *(-10)^2 = 100*. In classification problems, we want to make sure our predictions are the same discrete value as the actual value. When we predict a label that is different from the actual label, that is a misclassification or error. Obviously, the higher the number of accurate predictions, the better the model, but it gets more complicated than that. There are metrics such as a confusion matrix, a receiver operating characteristic, and the area under the curve, but we save those for more advanced texts. Let's say, in the modified hypothetical problem of guessing race based on height and weight, that we guess the race to be Caucasian while the correct race is African. That is then considered an error, and we can aggregate all such errors to find the aggregate errors across all predictions, but we will talk more on this in the later parts of the book.

So far, we have been speaking in terms of a hypothetical example, but let's tie the terms we've encountered so far into how it applies to financial datasets. As we mentioned, supervised learning methods are most common here because, in historical financial data, we are able to measure the price movements from the data. If we are simply trying to predict that, if a price moves up or down from the current price, then that is a classification problem with two prediction labels – *Price goes up* and *Price goes down*. There can also be three prediction labels since *Price goes up*, *Price goes down*, and *Price remains the same*. If, however, we want to predict the magnitude and direction of price moves, then this is a regression problem where an example of the output could be *Price moves +10.2 dollars*, meaning the prediction is that the price will move up by $10.2. The training dataset is generated from historical data, and this can be historical data that was not used in training the model and the live market data during live trading. We measure the accuracy of such models with the metrics we listed above in addition to the PnL generated from the trading strategies. With this introduction complete, let's now look into these methods in greater detail, starting with regression methods.

Exploring our financial dataset

Before we start applying machine learning techniques to build predictive models, we need to perform some exploratory data wrangling on our dataset with the help of the steps listed here. This is often a large and an underestimated prerequisite when it comes to applying advanced methods to financial datasets.

1. **Getting the data**: We'll continue to use Google stock data that we've used in our previous chapter:

```python
import pandas as pd
from pandas_datareader import data

def load_financial_data(start_date, end_date, output_file):
    try:
        df = pd.read_pickle(output_file)
        print('File data found...reading GOOG data')
    except FileNotFoundError:
        print('File not found...downloading the GOOG data')
        df = data.DataReader('GOOG', 'yahoo', start_date, end_date)
        df.to_pickle(output_file)

    return df
```

   In the code, we revisited how to download the data and implement a method, `load_financial_data`, which we can use moving forward. It can also be invoked, as shown in the following code, to download 17 years' of daily Google data:

```python
goog_data = load_financial_data( start_date='2001-01-01',
    end_date='2018-01-01', output_file='goog_data_large.pkl')
```

   The code will download financial data over a period of 17 years from GOOG stock data. Now, let's move on to the next step.

2. **Creating objectives/trading conditions that we want to predict**: Now that we know how to download our data, we need to operate on it to extract our target for the predictive models, also known as a response or dependent variable; effectively, what we are trying predict.

In our hypothetical example of predicting weight, weight was our response variable. For algorithmic trading, the common target is to be able to predict what the future price will be so that we can take positions in the market right now that will yield a profit in the future. If we model the response variable as future price-current price, then we are trying to predict the direction of the future price with regard to the current price (does it go up, does it go down, or does it remain the same), as well as the magnitude of the price change. So, these variables look like +10, +3.4, -4, and so on. This is the response variable methodology that we will use for regression models, but we will look at it in greater detail later. Another variant of the response variable would be to simply predict the direction but ignore the magnitude, in other words, +1 to signify the future price moving up, -1 to signify the future price moving down, and 0 to signify that the future price remains the same as the current price. That is the response variable methodology that we will use for classification models, but we will explore that later. Let's implement the following code to generate these response variables:

```
def create_classification_trading_condition(df):
    df['Open-Close'] = df.Open - df.Close
    df['High-Low'] = df.High - df.Low
    df = df.dropna()
    X = df[['Open-Close', 'High-Low']]
    Y = np.where(df['Close'].shift(-1) > df['Close'], 1, -1)

    return (X, Y)
```

In this code, the following applies:

- The classification response variable is +1 if the close price tomorrow is higher than the close price today, and -1 if the close price tomorrow is lower than the close price today.
- For this example, we assume that the close price tomorrow is not the same as the close price today, which we can choose to handle by creating a third categorical value, 0.

The regression response variable is *Close price tomorrow-Close price today for each day*. Let's have a look at the code:

```
def create_regression_trading_condition(df):
    df['Open-Close'] = df.Open - df.Close
    df['High-Low'] = df.High - df.Low
    df = df.dropna()
    X = df[['Open-Close', 'High-Low']]
    Y = df['Close'].shift(-1) - df['Close']

    return (X, Y)
```

In this code, the following applies:

- It is a positive value if the price goes up tomorrow, a negative value if the price goes down tomorrow, and zero if the price does not change.
- The sign of the value indicates the direction, and the magnitude of the response variable captures the magnitude of the price move.

3. **Partitioning datasets into training and testing datasets**: One of the key questions regarding a trading strategy is how it will perform on market conditions or datasets that the trading strategy has not seen. Trading performance on datasets that have not been used in training the predictive model is often referred to as out-sample performance for that trading strategy. These results are considered representative of what to expect when the trading strategy is run in live markets. Generally, we divide all of our available datasets into multiple partitions, and then we evaluate models trained on one dataset over a dataset that wasn't used in training it (and optionally validated on yet another dataset after that). For the purpose of our models, we will be partitioning our dataset into two datasets: training and testing. Let's have a look at the code:

```
from sklearn.model_selection import train_test_split

def create_train_split_group(X, Y, split_ratio=0.8):
    return train_test_split(X, Y, shuffle=False,
train_size=split_ratio)
```

In this code, the following applies:

- We used a default split ratio of 80%, so 80% of the entire dataset is used for training, and the remaining 20% is used for testing.
- There are more advanced splitting methods to account for distributions of underlying data (such as we want to avoid ending up with a training/testing dataset that is not truly representative of actual market conditions).

Creating predictive models using linear regression methods

Now that we know how to get the datasets that we need, how to quantify what we are trying to predict (objectives), and how to split data into training and testing datasets to evaluate our trained models on, let's dive into applying some basic machine learning techniques to our datasets:

- First, we will start with regression methods, which can be linear as well as non-linear.
- **Ordinary Least Squares** (OLS) is the most basic linear regression model, which is where we will start from.
- Then, we will look into Lasso and Ridge regression, which are extensions of OLS, but which include regularization and shrinkage features (we will discuss these aspects in more detail later).
- Elastic Net is a combination of both Lasso and Ridge regression methods.
- Finally, our last regression method will be decision tree regression, which is capable of fitting non-linear models.

Ordinary Least Squares

Given $m \times 1$ observations of the target variables, $m \times 1$ rows of features values, and each row of dimension $1 \times n$, OLS seeks to find the weights of dimension $n \times 1$ that minimize the residual sum of squares of differences between the target variable and the predicted variable predicted by linear approximation:

- $min\|X \bullet W - y\|_2^2$, which is the best fit for the equation $X \bullet W = y$, where X is the $m \times n$ matrix of feature values, W is the $n \times 1$ matrix/vector of weights/coefficients assigned to each of the n feature values, and y is the $m \times 1$ matrix/vector of the target variable observation on our training dataset.

Here is an example of the matrix operations involved for $m = 4$ and $n = 2$:

$$
min \left\| \begin{bmatrix} x00 & x01 \\ x10 & x11 \\ x20 & x21 \\ x30 & x31 \end{bmatrix} \bullet \begin{bmatrix} w_0 \\ w_1 \end{bmatrix} - \begin{bmatrix} x_0 \\ x_1 \\ x_2 \\ x_3 \end{bmatrix} \right\|_2^2
$$

- Intuitively, it is very easy to understand OLS with a single feature variable and a single target variable by visualizing it as trying to draw a line that has the *best fit*.
- OLS is just a generalization of this simple idea in much higher dimensions, where m is tens of thousands of observations, and n is thousands of features values.
- The typical setup in m is much larger than n (many more observations in comparison to the number of feature values), otherwise the solution is not guaranteed to be unique.
- There are closed form solutions to this problem where $w = \dfrac{A^T \bullet y}{A^T \bullet A}$ but, in practice, these are better implemented by iterative solutions, but we'll skip the details of all of that for now.
- The reason why we prefer to minimize the sum of the squares of the error terms is so that massive outliers are penalized more harshly and don't end up throwing off the entire fit.

There are many underlying assumptions for OLS in addition to the assumption that the target variable is a linear combination of the feature values, such as the independence of feature values themselves, and normally distributed error terms. The following diagram is a very simple example showing a relatively close linear relationship between two arbitrary variables. Note that it is not a perfect linear relationship, in other words, not all data points lie perfectly on the line and we have left out the X and Y labels because these can be any arbitrary variables. The point here is to demonstrate an example of what a linear relationship visualization looks like. Let's have a look at the following diagram:

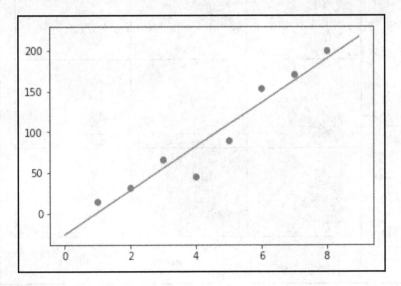

1. Let's start by loading up Google data in the code, using the same method that we introduced in the previous section:

```
goog_data = load_financial_data(
    start_date='2001-01-01',
    end_date='2018-01-01',
    output_file='goog_data_large.pkl')
```

2. Now, we create and populate the target variable vector, Y, for regression in the following code. Remember that what we are trying to predict in regression is magnitude and the direction of the price change from one day to the next:

```
goog_data, X, Y = create_regression_trading_condition(goog_data)
```

3. With the help of the code, let's quickly create a scatter plot for the two features we have: High-Low price of the day and Open-Close price of the day against the target variable, which is Price-Of-Next-Day - Price-Of-Today (future price):

```
pd.plotting.scatter_matrix(goog_data[['Open-Close', 'High-Low',
    'Target']], grid=True, diagonal='kde')
```

This code will return the following output. Let's have a look at the plot:

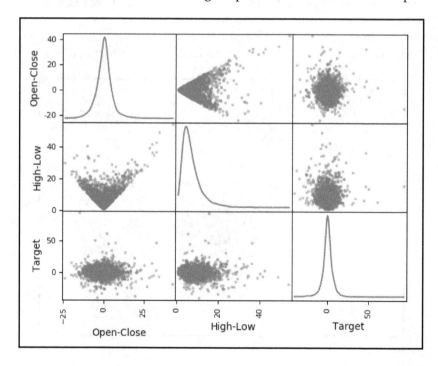

4. Finally, as shown in the code, let's split 80% of the available data into the training feature value and target variable set (X_train, Y_train), and the remaining 20% of the dataset into the out-sample testing feature value and target variable set (X_test, Y_test):

```
X_train,X_test,Y_train,Y_test=create_train_split_group(X,Y,split_ra
tio=0.8)
```

5. Now, let's fit the OLS model as shown here and observe the model we obtain:

```
from sklearn import linear_model
ols = linear_model.LinearRegression()
ols.fit(X_train, Y_train)
```

6. The coefficients are the optimal weights assigned to the two features by the fit method. We will print the coefficients as shown in the code:

```
print('Coefficients: \n', ols.coef_)
```

This code will return the following output. Let's have a look at the coefficients:

```
Coefficients:
[[ 0.02406874 -0.05747032]]
```

7. The next block of code quantifies two very common metrics that test goodness of fit for the linear model we just built. Goodness of fit means how well a given model fits the data points observed in training and testing data. A good model is able to closely fit most of the data points and errors/deviations between observed and predicted values are very low. Two of the most popular metrics for linear regression models are mean_squared_error $\|X \bullet W - y\|_2^2$, which is what we explored as our objective to minimize when we introduced OLS, and R-squared (R^2), which is another very popular metric that measures how well the fitted model predicts the target variable when compared to a baseline model whose prediction output is always the mean of the target variable based on training data, that is, $\bar{y} = \dfrac{\sum_{i=1}^{n} y_i}{n}$. We will skip the exact formulas for computing R^2 but, intuitively, the closer the R^2 value to 1, the better the fit, and the closer the value to 0, the worse the fit. Negative R^2 values mean that the model fits worse than the baseline model. Models with negative R^2 values usually indicate issues in the training data or process and cannot be used:

```
from sklearn.metrics import mean_squared_error, r2_score

# The mean squared error
print("Mean squared error: %.2f"
```

```
        % mean_squared_error(Y_train, ols.predict(X_train)))

# Explained variance score: 1 is perfect prediction
print('Variance score: %.2f' % r2_score(Y_train,
ols.predict(X_train)))

# The mean squared error
print("Mean squared error: %.2f"
      % mean_squared_error(Y_test, ols.predict(X_test)))

# Explained variance score: 1 is perfect prediction
print('Variance score: %.2f' % r2_score(Y_test,
ols.predict(X_test)))
```

This code will return the following output:

```
Mean squared error: 27.36
Variance score: 0.00
Mean squared error: 103.50
Variance score: -0.01
```

8. Finally, as shown in the code, let's use it to predict prices and calculate strategy returns:

```
goog_data['Predicted_Signal'] = ols.predict(X)
goog_data['GOOG_Returns'] = np.log(goog_data['Close'] /
goog_data['Close'].shift(1))

def calculate_return(df, split_value, symbol):
    cum_goog_return = df[split_value:]['%s_Returns' %
symbol].cumsum() * 100
    df['Strategy_Returns'] = df['%s_Returns' % symbol] *
df['Predicted_Signal'].shift(1)
    return cum_goog_return

def calculate_strategy_return(df, split_value, symbol):
    cum_strategy_return =
df[split_value:]['Strategy_Returns'].cumsum() * 100
    return cum_strategy_return

cum_goog_return = calculate_return(goog_data,
split_value=len(X_train), symbol='GOOG')
cum_strategy_return = calculate_strategy_return(goog_data,
split_value=len(X_train), symbol='GOOG')

def plot_chart(cum_symbol_return, cum_strategy_return, symbol):
    plt.figure(figsize=(10, 5))
    plt.plot(cum_symbol_return, label='%s Returns' % symbol)
```

```
        plt.plot(cum_strategy_return, label='Strategy Returns')
        plt.legend()

    plot_chart(cum_goog_return, cum_strategy_return, symbol='GOOG')

    def sharpe_ratio(symbol_returns, strategy_returns):
        strategy_std = strategy_returns.std()
        sharpe = (strategy_returns - symbol_returns) / strategy_std
        return sharpe.mean()

    print(sharpe_ratio(cum_strategy_return, cum_goog_return))
```

This code will return the following output:

```
    2.083840359081768
```

Let's now have a look at the graphical representation that is derived from the code:

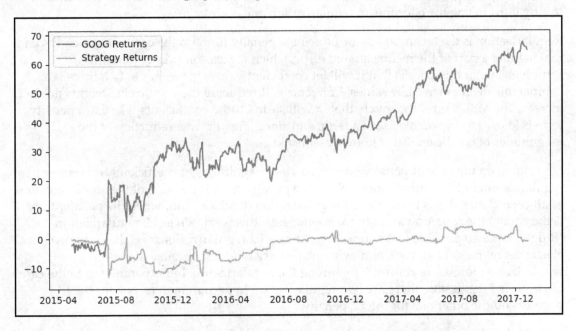

Here, we can observe that the simple linear regression model using only the two features, Open-Close and High-Low, returns positive returns. However, it does not outperform the Google stock's return because it has been increasing in value since inception. But since that cannot be known ahead of time, the linear regression model, which does not assume/expect increasing stock prices, is a good investment strategy.

Regularization and shrinkage – LASSO and Ridge regression

Now that we have covered OLS, we will try to improve on that by using regularization and coefficient shrinkage using LASSO and Ridge regression. One of the problems with OLS is that occasionally, for some datasets, the coefficients assigned to the predictor variables can grow to be very large. Also, OLS can end up assigning non-zero weights to all predictors and the total number of predictors in the final predictive model can be a very large number. Regularization tries to address both problems, that is, the problem of too many predictors and the problem of predictors with very large coefficients. Too many predictors in the final model is disadvantageous because it leads to overfitting, in addition to requiring more computations to predict. Predictors with large coefficients are disadvantageous because a few predictors with large coefficients can overpower the entire model's prediction, and small changes in predictor values can cause large swings in predicted output. We address this by introducing the concepts of regularization and shrinkage.

Regularization is the technique of introducing a penalty term on the coefficient weights and making that a part of the mean squared error, which regression tries to minimize. Intuitively, what this does is that it will let coefficient values grow, but only if there is a comparable decrease in MSE values. Conversely, if reducing the coefficient weights doesn't increase the MSE values too much, then it will shrink those coefficients. The extra penalty term is known as the regularization term, and since it results in a reduction of the magnitudes of coefficients, it is known as shrinkage.

Depending on the type of penalty term involving magnitudes of coefficients, it is either L1 regularization or L2 regularization. When the penalty term is the sum of the absolute values of all coefficients, this is known as L1 regularization (LASSO), and, when the penalty term is the sum of the squared values of the coefficients, this is known as L2 regularization (Ridge). It is also possible to combine both L1 and L2 regularization, and that is known as elastic net regression. To control how much penalty is added because of these regularization terms, we control it by tuning the regularization hyperparameter. In the case of elastic net regression, there are two regularization hyperparameters, one for the L1 penalty and the other one for the L2 penalty.

Let's apply Lasso regression to our dataset and inspect the coefficients in the following code. With a regularization parameter of 0.1, we see that the first predictor gets assigned a coefficient that is roughly half of what was assigned by OLS:

```
from sklearn import linear_model

# Fit the model
lasso = linear_model.Lasso(alpha=0.1)
```

```
lasso.fit(X_train, Y_train)

# The coefficients
print('Coefficients: \n', lasso.coef_)
```

This code will return the following output:

```
Coefficients:
[ 0.01673918 -0.04803374]
```

If the regularization parameter is increased to 0.6, the coefficients shrink much further to [0. -0.00540562], and the first predictor gets assigned a weight of 0, meaning that predictor can be removed from the model. L1 regularization has this additional property of being able to shrink coefficients to 0, thus having the extra advantage of being useful for feature selection, in other words, it can shrink the model size by removing some predictors.

Now, let's apply Ridge regression to our dataset and observe the coefficients:

```
from sklearn import linear_model

# Fit the model
ridge = linear_model.Ridge(alpha=10000)
ridge.fit(X_train, Y_train)

# The coefficients
print('Coefficients: \n', ridge.coef_)
```

This code will return the following output:

```
Coefficients:
[[ 0.01789719 -0.04351513]]
```

Decision tree regression

The disadvantage of the regression methods we've seen so far is that they are all linear models, meaning they can only capture relationships between predictors and target variables if the underlying relationship between them is linear.

Decision tree regression can capture non-linear relationships, thus allowing for more complex models. Decision trees get their name because they are structured like an upside-down tree, with decision nodes or branches and result nodes or leaf nodes. We start at the root of the tree and then, at each step, we inspect the value of our predictors and pick a branch to follow to the next node. We continue following branches until we get to a leaf node and our final prediction is then the value of that leaf node. Decision trees can be used for classification or regression, but here, we will look at using it for regression only.

Creating predictive models using linear classification methods

In the first part of this chapter, we reviewed trading strategies based on regression machine learning algorithms. In this second part, we will focus on the classification of machine learning algorithms and another supervised machine learning method utilizing known datasets to make predictions. Instead of the output variable of the regression being a numerical (or continuous) value, the classification output is a categorical (or discrete value). We will use the same method as the regression analysis by finding the mapping function (f) such that whenever there is new input data (x), the output variable (y) for the dataset can be predicted.

In the following subsections, we will review three classification machine learning methods:

- K-nearest neighbors
- Support vector machine
- Logistic regression

K-nearest neighbors

K-nearest neighbors (or **KNN**) is a supervised method. Like the prior methods we saw in this chapter, the goal is to find a function predicting an output, y, from an unseen observation, x. Unlike a lot of other methods (such as linear regression), this method doesn't use any specific assumption about the distribution of the data (it is referred to as a non-parametric classifier).

The KNN algorithm is based on comparing a new observation to the K most similar instances. It can be defined as a distance metric between two data points. One of the most used frequently methods is the Euclidean distance. The following is the derivative:

$$d(x,y)=(x1-y1)^2+(x2-y2)^2+...+(xn-yn)^2$$

When we review the documentation of the Python function, `KNeighborsClassifier`, we can observe different types of parameters:

One of them is the parameter, *p*, which can pick the type of distance.

- When *p=1*, the Manhattan distance is used. The Manhattan distance is the sum of the horizontal and vertical distances between two points.
- When *p=2*, which is the default value, the Euclidean distance is used.
- When *p>2*, this is the Minkowski distance, which is a generalization of the Manhattan and Euclidean methods.
  $d(x,y)=(|x1-y1|^p+|x2-y2|^p+...+|xn-yn|^p)^1/p.$

The algorithm will calculate the distance between a new observation and all the training data. This new observation will belong to the group of *K* points that are the closest to this new observation. Then, condition probabilities will be calculated for each class. The new observation will be assigned to the class with the highest probability. The weakness of this method is the time to associate the new observation to a given group.

In the code, in order to implement this algorithm, we will use the functions we declared in the first part of this chapter:

1. Let's get the Google data from January 1, 2001 to January 1, 2018:

```
goog_data=load_financial_data(start_date='2001-01-01',
                  end_date = '2018-01-01',
                  output_file='goog_data_large.pkl')
```

2. We create the rule when the strategy will take a long position (+1) and a short position (-1), as shown in the following code:

```
X,Y=create_trading_condition(goog_data)
```

3. We prepare the training and testing dataset as shown in the following code:

```
X_train,X_test,Y_train,Y_test=\
    create_train_split_group(X,Y,split_ratio=0.8)
```

4. In this example, we choose a KNN with *K=15*. We will train this model using the training dataset as shown in the following code:

```
knn=KNeighborsClassifier(n_neighbors=15)
knn.fit(X_train, Y_train)

accuracy_train = accuracy_score(Y_train, knn.predict(X_train))
accuracy_test = accuracy_score(Y_test, knn.predict(X_test))
```

5. Once the model is created, we are going to predict whether the price goes up or down and store the values in the original data frame, as shown in the following code:

```
goog_data['Predicted_Signal']=knn.predict(X)
```

6. In order to compare the strategy using the KNN algorithm, we will use the return of the GOOG symbol without d, as shown in the following code:

```
goog_data['GOOG_Returns']=np.log(goog_data['Close']/
                              goog_data['Close'].shift(1))

cum_goog_return=calculate_return(goog_data,split_value=len(X_train)
,symbol='GOOG')
cum_strategy_return=
calculate_strategy_return(goog_data,split_value=len(X_train))

plot_chart(cum_goog_return, cum_strategy_return,symbol='GOOG')
```

This code will return the following output. Let's have a look at the plot:

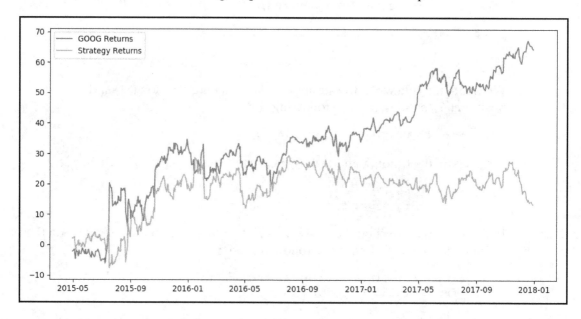

Support vector machine

Support vector machine (**SVM**) is a supervised machine learning method. As previously seen, we can use this method for regression, but also for classification. The principle of this algorithm is to find a hyper plan that separates the data into two classes.

Let's have a look at the following code, that implements the same:

```
# Fit the model
svc=SVC()
svc.fit(X_train, Y_train)

# Forecast value
goog_data['Predicted_Signal']=svc.predict(X)
goog_data['GOOG_Returns']=np.log(goog_data['Close']/
                               goog_data['Close'].shift(1))

cum_goog_return=calculate_return(goog_data,split_value=len(X_train),symbol=
'GOOG')
cum_strategy_return=
calculate_strategy_return(goog_data,split_value=len(X_train))

plot_chart(cum_goog_return, cum_strategy_return,symbol='GOOG')
```

In this example, the following applies:

- Instead of instantiating a class to create a KNN method, we used the SVC class.
- The class constructor has several parameters adjusting the behavior of the method to the data you will work on.
- The most important one is the parameter kernel. This defines the method of building the hyper plan.
- In this example, we just use the default values of the constructor.

Now, let's have a look at the output of the code:

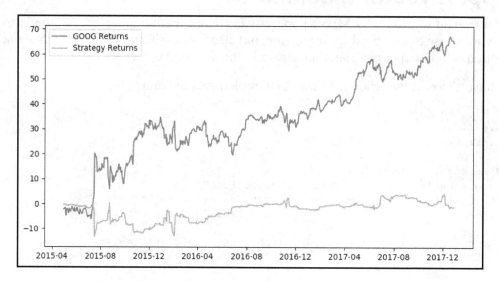

Logistic regression

Logistic regression is a supervised method that works for classification. Based on linear regression, logistic regression transforms its output using the logistic sigmoid, returning a probability value that maps different classes:

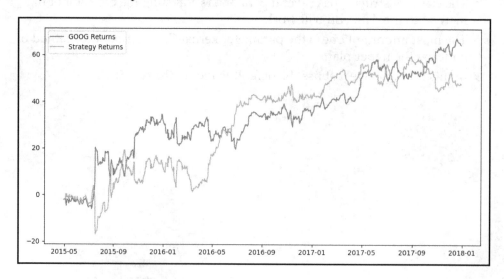

Summary

In this chapter, we got a basic understanding of how to use machine learning in trading. We started with going through the essential terminology and notation. We learned to create predictive models that predict price movement using linear regression methods. We built several codes using Python's scikit-learn library. We saw how to create predictive models that predict buy and sell signals using linear classification methods. We also demonstrated how to apply these machine learning methods to a simple trading strategy. We also went through the tools that we can use to create a trading strategy.

The next chapter will introduce trading rules that can help to improve your trading strategies.

Section 3: Algorithmic Trading Strategies

3

In this section, you will learn about the workings and implementation of some well-known trading strategies as well as learn how to trade on the basis of basic information (trends, seasonality, the correlation between symbols in the market, and correlation between events).

This section comprises the following chapters:

- Chapter 4, *Classical Trading Strategies Driven by Human Intuition*
- Chapter 5, *Sophisticated Algorithmic Strategies*
- Chapter 6, *Managing Risk in Algorithmic Strategies*

4
Classical Trading Strategies Driven by Human Intuition

During the previous chapters, we used statistical methods to predict market price movement from historical data. You may think that you know how to manipulate data, but how can these statistical techniques be applied to real trading? After spending so much time working on data, you may also want to know some key trading strategies that you can apply to make money.

In this chapter, we will talk about basic algorithmic strategies that follow human intuition. We will learn how to create trading strategies based on momentum and trend following, and a strategy that works for markets with mean reversion behavior. We will also talk about their advantages and disadvantages. By the end of this chapter, you will know how to use an idea to create a basic trading strategy.

This chapter will cover the following topics:

- Creating a trading strategy based on momentum and trend following
- Creating a trading strategy that works for markets with mean reversion behavior
- Creating trading strategies that operate on linearly correlated groups of trading instruments

Creating a trading strategy based on momentum and trend following

Momentum strategy uses the trend to predict the future of a price. For instance, if the price of an asset has increased for the last 20 days, it is likely that this price will continue rising. The moving average strategy is one example of momentum strategy.

Momentum strategies assume that the future will follow the past by following an upward or a downward trend (divergence or trend trading). Momentum investment has been used for decades: *buying low, selling high, buying high, and selling higher, selling the losers and letting the winners ride;* all these techniques are the origin of momentum trading. Momentum investing adopts short-term positions in relation to financial products going up and sells them when they go down. When we use a momentum strategy, we try to be ahead of the market; we trade fast, and then we let the market come to the same conclusion. The earlier we realize that there is a change, the more profitable we will be.

When you start working on a momentum strategy, you need to select the assets you are going to focus on while considering the risk for trading these assets. You need to ensure entering at the right time, but also not changing position too late. One of the most important drawback of this kind of strategy is the time and the fees. If your trading system is too slow, you won't manage to capture the opportunity to make money before the competition. Aside from this problem, we have to add the transaction fees, which are not negligible. By the very nature of the momentum strategy, the accuracy of this model is very low if news impacts the market.

Advantages of the momentum strategy:

- This class of strategy is easy to understand.

Disadvantages of the momentum strategy:

- This class of strategy doesn't take into account noises or special events. It has a tendency to smooth out prior events.
- The transaction fees can be potentially high owing to the number of orders.

Examples of momentum strategies

The following are some examples of momentum strategies:

- **Moving average crossover**: This momentum strategy principle revolves around calculating the moving average for a price of an asset and detecting when the price moves from one side of a moving average to the other. This means that when the current price intersects the moving average, there is a change in the momentum. However, this can lead to too many momentum changes. To limit this effect, we can use the dual moving average crossover.

- **Dual moving average crossover**: Because we want to limit the number of switches, we introduce an additional moving average. There will be a short-term moving average and a long-term moving average. With this implementation, the momentum shifts in the direction of the short-term moving average. When the short-term moving average crosses the long-term moving average and its value exceeds that of the long-term moving average, the momentum will be upward and this can lead to the adoption of a long position. If the movement is in the opposite direction, this can lead to take a short position instead.

- **Turtle trading**: Unlike the two other implementations, this momentum strategy doesn't use any moving average but relies on having a number of specific days, which are high and low.

Python implementation

For the Python implementation of this section, we will implement the dual moving average. This strategy is based on the indicator of moving average. It is widely used to smooth out price movements by filtering non-significant noises. Let's have a look at the implementations in the following subsections.

Dual moving average

In this section, we will implement the double moving average strategy. We will use the same code pattern from the prior chapters to get the GOOG data:

1. This code will first check whether the goog_data_large.pkl file exists. If the file does not exist, we will fetch the GOOG data from Yahoo finance:

   ```
   import pandas as pd
   import numpy as np
   ```

```
from pandas_datareader import data

def load_financial_data(start_date, end_date,output_file):
    try:
        df = pd.read_pickle(output_file)
        print('File data found...reading GOOG data')
    except FileNotFoundError:
        print('File not found...downloading the GOOG data')
        df = data.DataReader('GOOG', 'yahoo', start_date,
end_date)
        df.to_pickle(output_file)
    return df

goog_data=load_financial_data(start_date='2001-01-01',
                end_date = '2018-01-01',
                output_file='goog_data_large.pkl')
```

2. Next, as shown in the preceding code, we will create a
   double_moving_average function with parameters fixing the size of the two
   moving averages returning a data frame:

   - short_mavg: Short-term moving average values
   - long_mavg: Long-term moving average values
   - signal: True if the short-term moving average is higher than the long-term
     moving average
   - orders: 1 for the buy order, and −1 for the sell order:

```
def double_moving_average(financial_data, short_window,
long_window):
    signals = pd.DataFrame(index=financial_data.index)
    signals['signal'] = 0.0
    signals['short_mavg'] = financial_data['Close'].\
        rolling(window=short_window,
            min_periods=1, center=False).mean()
    signals['long_mavg'] = financial_data['Close'].\
        rolling(window=long_window,
            min_periods=1, center=False).mean()
    signals['signal'][short_window:] =\
        np.where(signals['short_mavg'][short_window:]
                                        >
signals['long_mavg'][short_window:], 1.0, 0.0)
    signals['orders'] = signals['signal'].diff()
    return signals

ts=double_moving_average(goog_data,20,100)
```

The code will build the data frame, `ts`:

- This data frame will contain the signal column storing the signal of going long (value 1) and going short (value 0)
- The column *orders* will contain the side of the orders (buy or sell)

3. We will now write the code to display the curve representing the orders for the dual moving strategy:

```
fig = plt.figure()
ax1 = fig.add_subplot(111, ylabel='Google price in $')
goog_data["Adj Close"].plot(ax=ax1, color='g', lw=.5)
ts["short_mavg"].plot(ax=ax1, color='r', lw=2.)
ts["long_mavg"].plot(ax=ax1, color='b', lw=2.)

ax1.plot(ts.loc[ts.orders== 1.0].index,
         goog_data["Adj Close"][ts.orders == 1.0],
         '^', markersize=7, color='k')

ax1.plot(ts.loc[ts.orders== -1.0].index,
         goog_data["Adj Close"][ts.orders == -1.0],
         'v', markersize=7, color='k')

plt.legend(["Price","Short mavg","Long mavg","Buy","Sell"])
plt.title("Double Moving Average Trading Strategy")

plt.show()
```

This code will return the following output. Let's have a look at the plot:

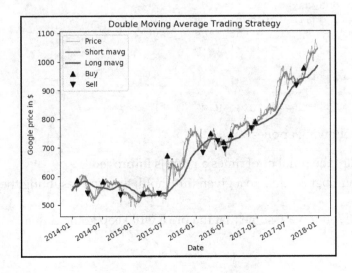

The plot represents the GOOG prices and the two moving averages associated with this price. Each order is represented by an arrow.

Naive trading strategy

In this section, we will implement a naive strategy based on the number of times a price increases or decreases. This strategy is based on the historical price momentum. Let's have a look at the code:

```python
def naive_momentum_trading(financial_data, nb_conseq_days):
    signals = pd.DataFrame(index=financial_data.index)
    signals['orders'] = 0
    cons_day=0
    prior_price=0
    init=True
    for k in range(len(financial_data['Adj Close'])):
        price=financial_data['Adj Close'][k]
        if init:
            prior_price=price
            init=False
        elif price>prior_price:
            if cons_day<0:
                cons_day=0
            cons_day+=1
        elif price<prior_price:
            if cons_day>0:
                cons_day=0
            cons_day-=1
        if cons_day==nb_conseq_days:
            signals['orders'][k]=1
        elif cons_day == -nb_conseq_days:
            signals['orders'][k]=-1

    return signals

ts=naive_momentum_trading(goog_data, 5)
```

In this code, the following applies:

- We count the number of times a price is improved.
- If the number is equal to a given threshold, we buy, assuming the price will keep rising.
- We will sell if we assume that the price will keep going down.

We will display the evolution of the trading strategy by using the following code:

```
fig = plt.figure()
ax1 = fig.add_subplot(111, ylabel='Google price in $')
goog_data["Adj Close"].plot(ax=ax1, color='g', lw=.5)

ax1.plot(ts.loc[ts.orders== 1.0].index,
         goog_data["Adj Close"][ts.orders == 1],
         '^', markersize=7, color='k')

ax1.plot(ts.loc[ts.orders== -1.0].index,
         goog_data["Adj Close"][ts.orders == -1],
         'v', markersize=7, color='k')

plt.legend(["Price","Buy","Sell"])
plt.title("Turtle Trading Strategy")

plt.show()
```

This code will return the following output. This curve represents the orders for the naive momentum trading strategy:

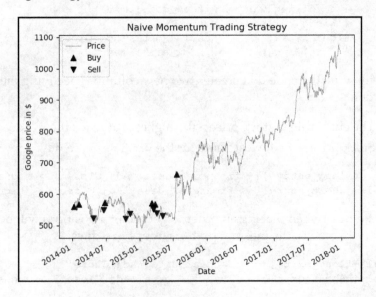

From this plot, the following can be observed:

- The naive trading strategy does not produce many orders.
- We can have a higher return if we have more orders. For that, we will use the following strategy to increase the number of orders.

Turtle strategy

In this more advanced trading strategy, we are going to create a long signal when the price reaches the highest price for the last `window_size` days (in this example, we will choose 50):

1. We will create a short signal when the price reaches its lowest point. We will get out of a position by having the price crossing the moving average of the last `window_size` days. This code starts the `turtle_trading` function by creating a column to store the highs, the lows, and the average with a rolling window `window_size`:

```python
def turtle_trading(financial_data, window_size):
    signals = pd.DataFrame(index=financial_data.index)
    signals['orders'] = 0
    # window_size-days high
    signals['high'] = financial_data['Adj Close'].shift(1).\
        rolling(window=window_size).max()
    # window_size-days low
    signals['low'] = financial_data['Adj Close'].shift(1).\
        rolling(window=window_size).min()
    # window_size-days mean
    signals['avg'] = financial_data['Adj Close'].shift(1).\
        rolling(window=window_size).mean()
```

2. We will write the code that creates two new columns specifying the rules to place an order:

   - The entry rule is stock price > the highest value for the `window_size` day.
   - Stock price < the lowest value for the `window_size` day:

```python
signals['long_entry'] = financial_data['Adj Close'] > signals.high
signals['short_entry'] = financial_data['Adj Close'] < signals.low
```

3. The exit rule (when placing an order to get out of a position) will be when the stock price crosses the mean of past `window_size` days:

```python
signals['long_exit'] = financial_data['Adj Close'] < signals.avg
signals['short_exit'] = financial_data['Adj Close'] > signals.avg
```

4. To draw the chart representing the orders, as shown in the code, we will give the values 1 when we enter a long position, -1 when we enter a short position, and 0 for not changing anything:

```
init=True
position=0
for k in range(len(signals)):
    if signals['long_entry'][k] and position==0:
        signals.orders.values[k] = 1
        position=1
    elif signals['short_entry'][k] and position==0:
        signals.orders.values[k] = -1
        position=-1
    elif signals['short_exit'][k] and position>0:
        signals.orders.values[k] = -1
        position = 0
    elif signals['long_exit'][k] and position < 0:
        signals.orders.values[k] = 1
        position = 0
    else:
        signals.orders.values[k] = 0
return signals
ts=turtle_trading(goog_data, 50)
```

The `turtle_trading` function from the code will display the plot that describes how the strategy behaves:

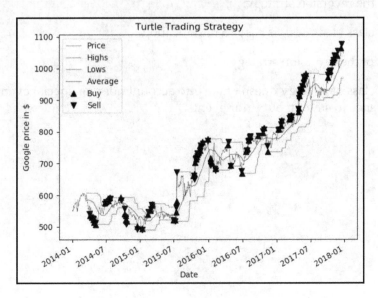

From the plot, the following can be observed:

- The number of orders between the naive momentum strategy and the turtle trading strategy.
- On account of a higher number of orders, this strategy offers more potential of returns than the previous one.

Creating a trading strategy that works for markets with reversion behavior

After the momentum strategy, we will now look at another very popular type of strategy, the mean reversion strategy. The underlying precept is that prices revert toward the mean. Extreme events are followed by more normal events. We will find a time where a value such as the price or the return is very different from the past values. Once established, we will place an order by forecasting that this value will come back to the mean.

Reversion strategy uses the belief that the trend of quantity will eventually reverse. This is the opposite of the previous strategy. If a stock return increases too fast, it will eventually return to its average. Reversion strategies assume that any trend will go back to the average value, either an upward or downward trend (divergence or trend trading).

Advantages of the reversion strategy:

- This class of strategy is easy to understand.

Disadvantages of the reversion strategy:

- This class of strategy doesn't take into account noise or special events. It has a tendency to smooth out prior events.

Examples of reversion strategies

Here are the examples of reversion strategies:

- **Mean reversion strategy**: This strategy assumes that the value of a price/return will return to the average value.
- Unlike the mean reversion strategy, pair trading—mean reversion is based on the correlation between two instruments. If a pair of stocks already has a high correlation and, at some point, the correlation is diminished, it will come back to the original level (correlation mean value). If the stock with the lower price drops, we can long this stock and short the other stock of this pair.

Creating trading strategies that operate on linearly correlated groups of trading instruments

We are going through the process of implementing an example of a pair trading strategy. The first step is to determine the pairs that have a high correlation. This can be based on the underlying economic relationship (for example, companies having similar business plans) or also a financial product created out of some others, such as ETF. Once we figure out which symbols are correlated, we will create the trading signals based on the value of these correlations. The correlation value can be the Pearson's coefficient, or a Z-score.

In case of a temporary divergence, the outperforming stock (the stock that moved up) would have been sold and the underperforming stock (the stock that moved down) would have been purchased. If the two stocks converge by either the outperforming stock moving back down or the underperforming stock moving back up, or both, you will make money in such cases. You won't make money in the event that both stocks move up or down together with no change in the spread between them. Pairs trading is a market neutral trading strategy as it allows traders to profit from changing market conditions:

1. Let's begin by creating a function establishing cointegration between pairs, as shown in the following code. This function takes as inputs a list of financial instruments and calculates the cointegration values of these symbols. The values are stored in a matrix. We will use this matrix to display a heatmap:

```
def find_cointegrated_pairs(data):
    n = data.shape[1]
    pvalue_matrix = np.ones((n, n))
```

```
        keys = data.keys()
        pairs = []
        for i in range(n):
            for j in range(i+1, n):
                result = coint(data[keys[i]], data[keys[j]])
                pvalue_matrix[i, j] = result[1]
                if result[1] < 0.02:
                    pairs.append((keys[i], keys[j]))
        return pvalue_matrix, pairs
```

2. Next, as shown in the code, we will load the financial data by using the `panda` data reader. This time, we load many symbols at the same time. In this example, we use `SPY` (this symbol reflects market movement), `APPL` (technology), `ADBE` (technology), `LUV` (airlines), `MSFT` (technology), `SKYW` (airline industry), `QCOM` (technology), `HPQ` (technology), `JNPR` (technology), `AMD` (technology), and `IBM` (technology).

Since the goal of this trading strategy is to find co-integrated symbols, we narrow down the search space according to industry. This function will load the data of a file from the Yahoo finance website if the data is not in the `multi_data_large.pkl` file:

```
import pandas as pd
pd.set_option('display.max_rows', 500)
pd.set_option('display.max_columns', 500)
pd.set_option('display.width', 1000)
import numpy as np
import matplotlib.pyplot as plt
from statsmodels.tsa.stattools import coint
import seaborn
from pandas_datareader import data

symbolsIds = ['SPY','AAPL','ADBE','LUV','MSFT','SKYW','QCOM',
              'HPQ','JNPR','AMD','IBM']

def load_financial_data(symbols, start_date,
end_date,output_file):
    try:
        df = pd.read_pickle(output_file)
        print('File data found...reading symbols data')
    except FileNotFoundError:
        print('File not found...downloading the symbols data')
        df = data.DataReader(symbols, 'yahoo', start_date,
end_date)
        df.to_pickle(output_file)
    return df
```

```
data=load_financial_data(symbolsIds,start_date='2001-01-01',
                         end_date = '2018-01-01',
                         output_file='multi_data_large.pkl')
```

3. After we call the `load_financial_data` function, we will then call the `find_cointegrated_pairs` function, as shown in the following code:

```
pvalues, pairs = find_cointegrated_pairs(data['Adj Close'])
```

4. We will use the `seaborn` package to draw the heatmap. The code calls the `heatmap` function from the `seaborn` package. Heatmap will use the list of symbols on the *x* and *y* axes. The last argument will mask the p-values higher than 0.98:

```
seaborn.heatmap(pvalues, xticklabels=symbolsIds,
                yticklabels=symbolsIds, cmap='RdYlGn_r',
                mask = (pvalues >= 0.98))
```

This code will return the following map as an output. This map shows the p-values of the return of the coin:

- If a p-value is lower than 0.02, this means the null hypothesis is rejected.
- This means that the two series of prices corresponding to two different symbols can be co-integrated.
- This means that the two symbols will keep the same spread on average. On the heatmap, we observe that the following symbols have p-values lower than 0.02:

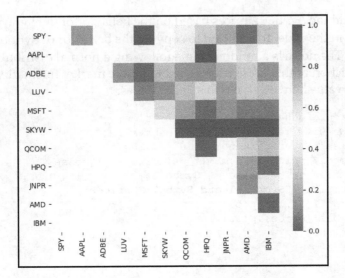

This screenshot represents the heatmap measuring the cointegration between a pair of symbols. If it is red, this means that the p-value is 1, which means that the null hypothesis is not rejected. Therefore, there is no significant evidence that the pair of symbols is co-integrated. After selecting the pairs we will use for trading, let's focus on how to trade these pairs of symbols.

5. First, let's create a pair of symbols artificially to get an idea of how to trade. We will use the following libraries:

```
import numpy as np
import pandas as pd
from statsmodels.tsa.stattools import coint
import matplotlib.pyplot as plt
```

6. As shown in the code, let's create a symbol return that we will call `Symbol1`. The value of the `Symbol1` price starts from a value of 10 and, every day, it will vary based on a random return (following a normal distribution). We will draw the price values by using the function plot of the `matplotlib.pyplot` package:

```
# Set a seed value to make the experience reproducible
np.random.seed(123)
# Generate Symbol1 daily returns
Symbol1_returns = np.random.normal(0, 1, 100)
# Create a series for Symbol1 prices
Symbol1_prices = pd.Series(np.cumsum(Symbol1_returns),
name='Symbol1') + 10
Symbol1_prices.plot(figsize=(15,7))
plt.show()
```

7. We build the `Symbol2` prices based on the behavior of the `Symbol1` prices, as shown in the code. In addition to copying the behavior of `Symbol1`, we will add noises. The noise is a random value following a normal distribution. The introduction of this noise is designed to mimic market fluctuations. It changes the spread value between the two symbol prices:

```
# Create a series for Symbol2 prices
# We will copy the Symbol1 behavior
noise = np.random.normal(0, 1, 100)
Symbol2_prices = Symbol1_prices + 10 + noise
Symbol2_prices.name = 'Symbol2'
plt.title("Symbol 1 and Symbol 2 prices")
Symbol1_prices.plot()
Symbol2_prices.plot()
plt.show()
```

This code will return the following output. The plot shows the evolution of the price of Symbol 1 and Symbol 2:

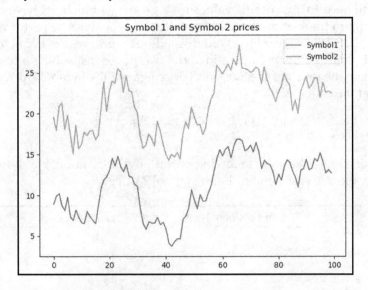

8. In the code, we will check the cointegration between the two symbols by using the `coint` function. This takes two lists/series of values and performs a test to check whether the two series are co-integrated:

```
score, pvalue, _ = coint(Symbol1_prices, Symbol2_prices)
```

In the code, `pvalue` contains the p-score. Its value is 10-13, which means that we can reject the null hypothesis. Therefore, these two symbols are co-integrated.

9. We will define the `zscore` function. This function returns how far a piece of data is from the population mean. This will help us to choose the direction of trading. If the return value of this function is positive, this means that the symbol price is higher than the average price value. Therefore, its price is expected to go down or the paired symbol value will go up. In this case, we will want to short this symbol and long the other one. The code implements the `zscore` function:

```
def zscore(series):
    return (series - series.mean()) / np.std(series)
```

10. We will use the ratio between the two symbol prices. We will need to set the threshold that defines when a given price is far off the mean price value. For that, we will need to use specific values for a given symbol. If we have many symbols we want to trade with, this will imply that this analysis be performed for all the symbols. Since we want to avoid this tedious work, we are going to normalize this study by analyzing the ratio of the two prices instead. As a result, we calculate the ratios of the Symbol 1 price against the Symbol 2 price. Let's have a look at the code:

```
ratios = Symbol1_prices / Symbol2_prices
ratios.plot()
```

This code will return the following output. In the diagram, we show the variation in the ratio between symbol 1 and symbol 2 prices:

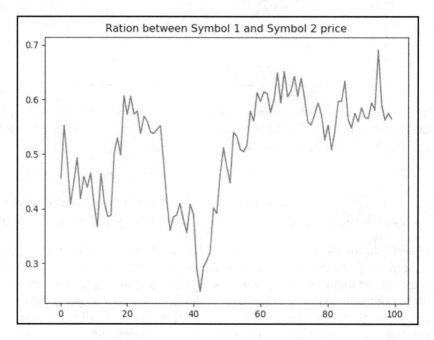

11. Let's draw the chart showing when we will place orders with the following code:

```
train = ratios[:75]
test = ratios[75:]

plt.axhline(ratios.mean())
plt.legend([' Ratio'])
plt.show()
```

```
zscore(ratios).plot()
plt.axhline(zscore(ratios).mean(),color="black")
plt.axhline(1.0, color="red")
plt.axhline(-1.0, color="green")
plt.show()
```

This code will return the following output. The curve demonstrates the following:

- The Z-score evolution with horizontal lines at -1 (green), +1 (red), and the average of Z-score (black).
- The average of Z-score is 0.
- When the Z-score reaches -1 or +1, we will use this event as a trading signal. The values +1 and -1 are arbitrary values.
- It should be set depending on the study we will run in order to create this trading strategy:

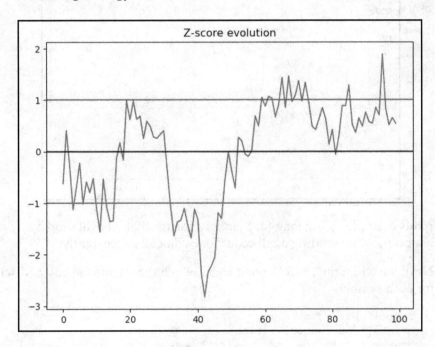

12. Every time the Z-score reaches one of the thresholds, we have a trading signal. As shown in the code, we will present a graph, each time we go long for Symbol 1 with a green marker, and each time we go short with a red marker:

```
ratios.plot()
buy = ratios.copy()
sell = ratios.copy()
```

```
buy[zscore(ratios)>-1] = 0
sell[zscore(ratios)<1] = 0
buy.plot(color="g", linestyle="None", marker="^")
sell.plot(color="r", linestyle="None", marker="v")
x1,x2,y1,y2 = plt.axis()
plt.axis((x1,x2,ratios.min(),ratios.max()))
plt.legend(["Ratio", "Buy Signal", "Sell Signal"])
plt.show()
```

This code will return the following output. Let's have a look at the plot:

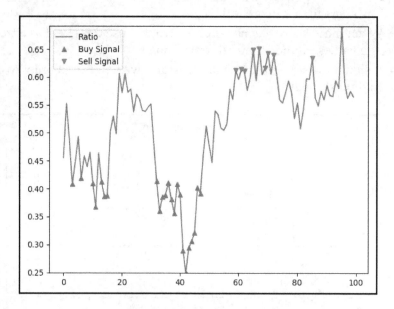

In this example, going long for Symbol 1 means that we will send a buy order for Symbol 1, while sending a sell order for Symbol 2 concurrently.

13. Next, we will write the following code, which represents the buy and sell order for each symbol:

```
Symbol1_prices.plot()
symbol1_buy[zscore(ratios)>-1] = 0
symbol1_sell[zscore(ratios)<1] = 0
symbol1_buy.plot(color="g", linestyle="None", marker="^")
symbol1_sell.plot(color="r", linestyle="None", marker="v")

Symbol2_prices.plot()
symbol2_buy[zscore(ratios)<1] = 0
symbol2_sell[zscore(ratios)>-1] = 0
symbol2_buy.plot(color="g", linestyle="None", marker="^")
```

```
symbol2_sell.plot(color="r", linestyle="None", marker="v")


x1,x2,y1,y2 = plt.axis()
plt.axis((x1,x2,Symbol1_prices.min(),Symbol2_prices.max()))
plt.legend(["Symbol1", "Buy Signal", "Sell Signal","Symbol2"])
plt.show()
```

The following chart shows the buy and sell orders for this strategy. We see that the orders will be placed only when zscore is higher or lower than +/-1:

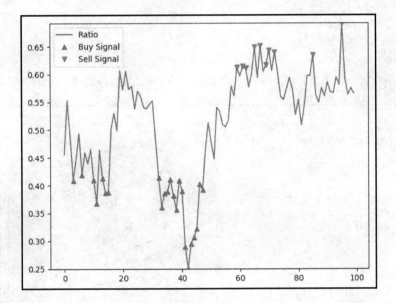

Following the analysis that provided us with an understanding of the pairs that are co-integrated, we observed that the following pairs demonstrated similar behavior:

- ADBE, MSFT
- JNPR, LUV
- JNPR, MSFT
- JNPR, QCOM
- JNPR, SKYW
- JNPR, SPY

14. We will use MSFT and JNPR to implement the strategy based on real symbols. We will replace the code to build Symbol 1 and Symbol 2 with the following code. The following code will get the real prices for MSFT and JNPR:

```
Symbol1_prices = data['Adj Close']['MSFT']
Symbol1_prices.plot(figsize=(15,7))
plt.show()
Symbol2_prices = data['Adj Close']['JNPR']
Symbol2_prices.name = 'JNPR'
plt.title("MSFT and JNPR prices")
Symbol1_prices.plot()
Symbol2_prices.plot()
plt.legend()
plt.show()
```

This code will return the following plots as output. Let's have a look at them:

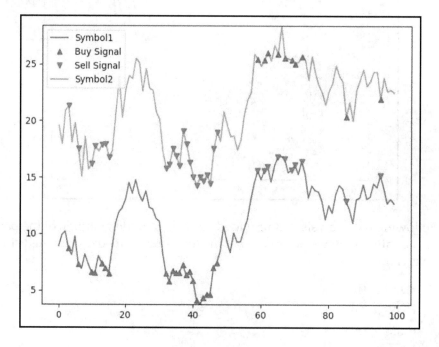

The following screenshot shows the MSFT and JNPR prices. We observe similarities of movement between the two symbols:

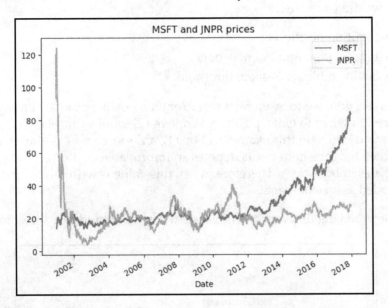

When running the code that we ran previously for Symbol 1 and Symbol 2 by getting the actual prices from JNPR and MSFT, we will obtain the following curves:

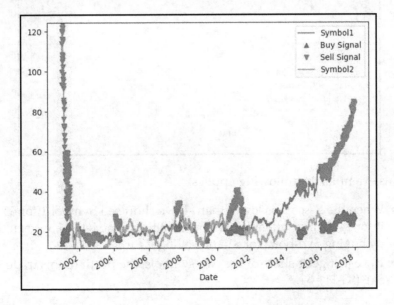

This chart reveals a large quantity of orders. The pair correlation strategy without limitation sends too many orders. We can limit the number of orders in the same way we did previously:

- Limiting positions
- Limiting the number of orders
- Setting a higher Z-score threshold

In this section, we focused on when to enter a position, but we have not addressed when to exit a position. While the Z-score value is above or below the threshold limits (in this example, -1 or +1), a Z-score value within the range between the threshold limits denotes an improbable change of spread between the two symbol prices. Therefore, when this value is within this limit, this can be regarded as an exit signal.

In the following diagram, we illustrate when we should exit a position:

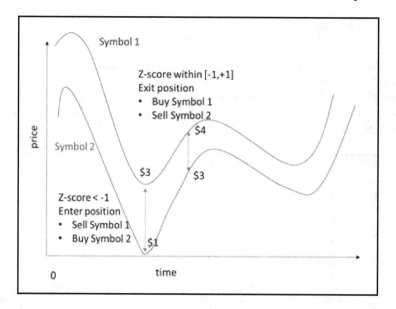

In this example, the following applies:

- When the Z-score is lower than -1, we short sell Symbol 1 for $3 and we buy it for $4, while, when the Z-score is in the range [-1,+1], we exit the position by buying Symbol 2 for $1 and selling it for $3.
- If we just get 1 share of the two symbols, the profit of this trade will be ($3-$4)+($3-$1)=$1.

15. We will create a data frame, `pair_correlation_trading_strategy`, in the code. This contains information relating to orders and position and we will use this data frame to calculate the performance of this pair correlation trading strategy:

```
pair_correlation_trading_strategy =
pd.DataFrame(index=Symbol1_prices.index)
 pair_correlation_trading_strategy['symbol1_price']=Symbol1_prices
pair_correlation_trading_strategy['symbol1_buy']=np.zeros(len(Symbo
l1_prices))
pair_correlation_trading_strategy['symbol1_sell']=np.zeros(len(Symb
ol1_prices))
pair_correlation_trading_strategy['symbol2_buy']=np.zeros(len(Symbo
l1_prices))
pair_correlation_trading_strategy['symbol2_sell']=np.zeros(len(Symb
ol1_prices))
```

16. We will limit the number of orders by reducing the position to one share. This can be a long or short position. For a given symbol, when we have a long position, a sell order is the only one that is allowed. When we have a short position, a buy order is the only one that is allowed. When we have no position, we can either go long (by buying) or go short (by selling). We will store the price we use to send the orders. For the paired symbol, we will do the opposite. When we sell Symbol 1, we will buy Symbol 2, and vice versa:

```
position=0
for i in range(len(Symbol1_prices)):
    s1price=Symbol1_prices[i]
    s2price=Symbol2_prices[i]
    if not position and symbol1_buy[i]!=0:
pair_correlation_trading_strategy['symbol1_buy'][i]=s1price
        pair_correlation_trading_strategy['symbol2_sell'][i] =
s2price
        position=1
    elif not position and symbol1_sell[i]!=0:
        pair_correlation_trading_strategy['symbol1_sell'][i] =
s1price
        pair_correlation_trading_strategy['symbol2_buy'][i] =
s2price
        position = -1
    elif position==-1 and (symbol1_sell[i]==0 or
i==len(Symbol1_prices)-1):
        pair_correlation_trading_strategy['symbol1_buy'][i] =
s1price
        pair_correlation_trading_strategy['symbol2_sell'][i] =
s2price
        position = 0
```

```
        elif position==1 and (symbol1_buy[i] == 0 or
    i==len(Symbol1_prices)-1):
            pair_correlation_trading_strategy['symbol1_sell'][i] =
    s1price
            pair_correlation_trading_strategy['symbol2_buy'][i] =
    s2price
            position = 0
```

This code will return the following output. The plot shows the decrease in the number of orders. We will now calculate the profit and loss generated by this strategy:

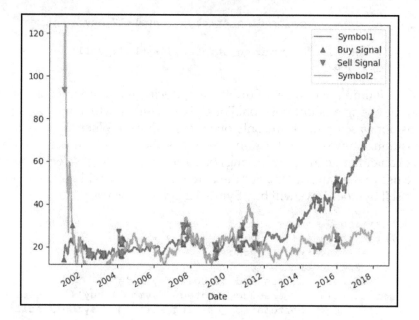

17. We will now write the code that calculates the profit and loss of the pair correlation strategy. We make a subtraction between the vectors containing the Symbol 1 and Symbol 2 prices. We will then add these positions to create a representation of the profit and loss:

```
pair_correlation_trading_strategy['symbol1_position']=\
 pair_correlation_trading_strategy['symbol1_buy']-
pair_correlation_trading_strategy['symbol1_sell']

pair_correlation_trading_strategy['symbol2_position']=\
 pair_correlation_trading_strategy['symbol2_buy']-
pair_correlation_trading_strategy['symbol2_sell']
```

```
pair_correlation_trading_strategy['symbol1_position'].cumsum().plot
() # Calculate Symbol 1 P&L
pair_correlation_trading_strategy['symbol2_position'].cumsum().plot
() # Calculate Symbol 2 P&L

 pair_correlation_trading_strategy['total_position']=\
pair_correlation_trading_strategy['symbol1_position']+pair_correlat
ion_trading_strategy['symbol2_position'] # Calculate total P&L
pair_correlation_trading_strategy['total_position'].cumsum().plot()
```

This code will return the following output. In the plot, the blue line represents the profit and loss for Symbol 1, and the orange line represents the profit and loss for Symbol 2. The green line represents the total profit and loss:

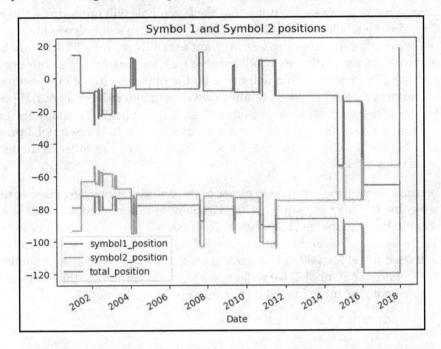

Until this part, we traded only one share. In regular trading, we will trade hundreds/thousands of shares. Let's analyze what can happen when we use a pair-correlation trading strategy.

Suppose we have a pair of two symbols (Symbol 1 and Symbol 2). Let's assume that the Symbol 1 price is $100 and the Symbol 2 price is $10. If we trade a given fixed amount of shares of Symbol 1 and Symbol 2, we can use 100 shares. If we have a long signal for Symbol 1, we will buy Symbol 1 for $100. The notional position will be 100 x $100 = $10,000. Since it is a long signal for Symbol 1, it is a short signal for Symbol 2. We will have a Symbol 2 notional position of 100 x $10 = $1,000. We will have a delta of $9,000 between these two positions.

By having a large price differential, this places more emphasis on the symbol with the higher price. So it means when that symbol leads the return. Additionally, when we trade and invest money on the market, we should hedge positions against market moves. For example, if we invest in an overall long position by buying many symbols, we think that these symbols will outperform the market. Suppose the whole market is depreciating, but these symbols are indeed outperforming the other ones. If we want to sell them, we will certainly lose money since the market will collapse. For that, we usually hedge our positions by investing in something that will move on the opposite side of our positions. In the example of a pair trading correlation, we should aim to have a neutral position by investing the same notional in Symbol 1 and in Symbol 2. By taking the example of having a Symbol 1 price that is markedly different to the Symbol 2 price, we cannot use the hedge of Symbol 2 if we invest the same number of shares as we invest in Symbol 1.

Because we don't want to be in either of the two situations described earlier, we are going to invest the same notional in Symbol 1 and Symbol 2. Let's say we want to buy 100 shares of Symbol 1. The notional position we will have is 100 x $100 = $10,000. To get the same equivalent of notional position for Symbol 2, we will need to get $10,000 / $10 = 1,000 shares. If we get 100 shares of Symbol 1 and 1,000 shares of Symbol 2, we will have a neutral position for this investment, and we will not give more importance to Symbol 1 over Symbol 2.

Now, let's suppose the price of symbol 2 is $3 instead of being $10. When dividing $10,000 / $3 = 3,333 + 1/3. This means we will send an order for 3,333 shares, which means that we will have a Symbol 1 position of $10,000 and a Symbol 2 position of 3,333 x $3 = $9,999, resulting in a delta of $1. Now suppose that the traded amount, instead of being $10,000, was $10,000,000. This will result in a delta of $1,000. Because we need to remove the decimal part when buying stocks, this delta will appear for any symbols. If we trade around 200 pairs of symbols, we may have $200,000 (200 x $1,000) of position that is not hedged. We will be exposed to market moves. Therefore, if the market goes down, we may lose out on this $200,000. That's why it will be important to hedge with a financial instrument going in the opposite direction from this $200,000 position. If we have positions with many symbols, resulting in having a residual of $200,000 of a long position that is not covered, we will get a short position of the ETF SPY behaving in the same way as the market moves.

18. We replace `s1prices` with `s1positions` from the earlier code by taking into account the number of shares we want to allocate for the trading of this pair:

```
pair_correlation_trading_strategy['symbol1_price']=Symbol1_prices
pair_correlation_trading_strategy['symbol1_buy']=np.zeros(len(Symbo
l1_prices))
pair_correlation_trading_strategy['symbol1_sell']=np.zeros(len(Symb
ol1_prices))
pair_correlation_trading_strategy['symbol2_buy']=np.zeros(len(Symbo
l1_prices))
pair_correlation_trading_strategy['symbol2_sell']=np.zeros(len(Symb
ol1_prices))
pair_correlation_trading_strategy['delta']=np.zeros(len(Symbol1_pri
ces))
 position=0
 s1_shares = 1000000
 for i in range(len(Symbol1_prices)):
     s1positions= Symbol1_prices[i] * s1_shares
     s2positions= Symbol2_prices[i] *
int(s1positions/Symbol2_prices[i])
     delta_position=s1positions-s2positions
     if not position and symbol1_buy[i]!=0:
pair_correlation_trading_strategy['symbol1_buy'][i]=s1positions
         pair_correlation_trading_strategy['symbol2_sell'][i] =
s2positions
pair_correlation_trading_strategy['delta'][i]=delta_position
         position=1
     elif not position and symbol1_sell[i]!=0:
         pair_correlation_trading_strategy['symbol1_sell'][i] =
s1positions
         pair_correlation_trading_strategy['symbol2_buy'][i] =
```

```
        s2positions
            pair_correlation_trading_strategy['delta'][i] =
    delta_position
            position = -1
        elif position==-1 and (symbol1_sell[i]==0 or
    i==len(Symbol1_prices)-1):
            pair_correlation_trading_strategy['symbol1_buy'][i] =
    s1positions
            pair_correlation_trading_strategy['symbol2_sell'][i] =
    s2positions
            position = 0
        elif position==1 and (symbol1_buy[i] == 0 or
    i==len(Symbol1_prices)-1):
            pair_correlation_trading_strategy['symbol1_sell'][i] =
    s1positions
            pair_correlation_trading_strategy['symbol2_buy'][i] =
    s2positions
            position = 0
```

This code will return the following output. This graph represent the positions of Symbol 1 and Symbol 2 and the total profit and loss of this pair correlation trading strategy:

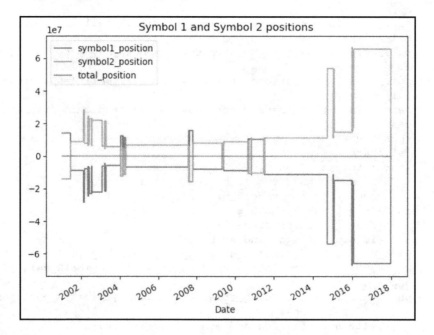

The code displays the delta position. The maximum amount is $25. Because this amount is too low, we don't need to hedge this delta position:

```
pair_correlation_trading_strategy['delta'].plot()
plt.title("Delta Position")
plt.show()
```

This section concludes the implementation of a trading strategy that is based on the correlation/cointegration with another financial product.

Summary

In this chapter, we were introduced to two intuitive trading strategies – the momentum strategy and the mean-reversion strategy. We learned how to create a trading strategy based on momentum and trend following. We also learned to create a trading strategy that works for markets with reversion behavior. These two strategies are very popular in the trading industry and are heavily used. We explained how to implement them. We got to learned how they work, along with their advantages and disadvantages

In the next chapter, we will build on top of the basic algorithmic strategies and learn about more advanced approaches (statistical arbitrage, pair correlation), along with their advantages and disadvantages.

5
Sophisticated Algorithmic Strategies

In this chapter, we will explore more sophisticated trading strategies employed by leading market participants in the algorithmic trading business. We will build on top of the basic algorithmic strategies and learn about more advanced approaches (such as statistical arbitrage and pair correlation) and their advantages and disadvantages. We will learn how to create a trading strategy that adjusts for trading instrument volatility. We will also learn how to create a trading strategy for economic events and understand and implement the basics of statistical arbitrage trading strategies.

This chapter will cover the following topics:

- Creating a trading strategy that adjusts for trading instrument volatility
- Creating a trading strategy for economic events
- Understanding and implementing basic statistical arbitrage trading strategies

Creating a trading strategy that adjusts for trading instrument volatility

An intuitive way to think about price volatility is investor confidence in the specific instrument, that is, how willing the investors are to invest money into the specific instrument and how long they are willing to hold on to a position in that instrument. As price volatility goes up, because prices make bigger swings at faster paces, investor confidence drops. Conversely, as price volatility goes down, investors are more willing to have bigger positions and hold those positions for longer periods of time. Volatility in a few asset classes often spills over into other asset classes, thus slowly spreading volatility over to all economic fields, housing costs, consumer costs, and so on. Obviously, sophisticated strategies need to dynamically adjust to changing volatility in trading instruments by following a similar pattern of being more cautious with respect to the positions they take, how long positions are held, and what the profit/loss expectations are.

In Chapter 2, *Deciphering the Markets with Technical Analysis*, we saw a lot of trading signals; in Chapter 3, *Predicting the Markets with Basic Machine Learning*, we applied machine learning algorithms to those trading signals; and in Chapter 4, *Classical Trading Strategies Driven by Human Intuition*, we explored basic trading strategies. Most of those approaches did not directly consider volatility changes in the underlying trading instrument, or adjust or account for them. In this section, we will discuss the impact of volatility changes in trading instruments and how to deal with that to improve profitability and reduce risk exposure.

Adjusting for trading instrument volatility in technical indicators

In Chapter 2, *Deciphering the Markets with Technical Analysis*, we looked at generating trading signals with predetermined parameters. What we mean by that is we decided beforehand to use, say, 20 days moving average, or the number of time periods to use, or the smoothing constants to use, and these remained constant throughout the entire period of our analysis. These signals have the benefit of being simple, but suffer from the disadvantage of performing differently as the volatility of the trading instrument changed over the course of time.

Then we also looked at signals such as Bollinger Bands and standard deviation, which adjusted for trading instrument volatility, that is, during non-volatile periods, the lower standard deviation in price movements would make the signals more aggressive to entering positions and less aggressive when closing positions. Conversely, during volatile periods, the higher standard deviation in price movements makes the signals less aggressive to entering positions. This is because the bands that depend on standard deviation widen out from the moving average, which in itself has become more volatile. Thus, these signals implicitly had some aspects of adjusting for trading instrument volatility baked right into them.

In general, it is possible to take any of the technical indicators we have seen so far and combine a standard deviation signal with it to have a more sophisticated form of the basic technical indicator that has dynamic values for number of days, or number of time periods or smoothing factors. The parameters become dynamic by depending on the standard deviation as a volatility measure. Thus, moving averages can have a smaller history or number of time periods when volatility is high to capture more observations, and a larger history or number of time periods when volatility is low to capture fewer observations. Similarly, smoothing factors can be made higher or lower in magnitude depending on volatility. In essence, that controls how much weight is assigned to newer observations as compared to older ones. We won't go into any more detail here, but it is easy to apply these concepts to technical indicators once the basic idea of applying volatility measures to simple indicators to form complex indicators is clear.

Adjusting for trading instrument volatility in trading strategies

We can apply the same concepts of adjusting for volatility measures to trading strategies. Momentum or trend-following strategies can use changing volatility to dynamically change the time period parameters used in the moving averages, or change the thresholds for how many up/down days to count as an entry signal. Another area of improvement would be using changing volatility to dynamically adjust thresholds on when to enter a position when a trend is detected, and dynamically adjust thresholds on when to exit a position when trend reversal is detected.

For mean reversion based strategies, applying volatility measures is pretty similar. In this case, we can use dynamically changing time periods for moving averages, and dynamically changing thresholds for entering positions when overbuying and overselling is detected, or dynamically changing thresholds for exiting positions when reversal to equilibrium prices are detected. Let's explore, in the rest of this chapter, different ideas of adjusting for volatility measures in trading strategies in greater detail and see the impact on the trading strategy behavior.

Volatility adjusted mean reversion trading strategies

We explored mean reversion trading strategies in great detail in Chapter 4, *Classical Trading Strategies Driven by Human Intuition*. For the purposes of this chapter, we will first create a very simple variant of a mean reversion strategy and then show how one would apply volatility adjustment to the strategy to optimize and stabilize its risk-adjusted returns.

Mean reversion strategy using the absolute price oscillator trading signal

Let's explain and implement a mean reversion strategy that relies on the **Absolute Price Oscillator** (**APO**) trading signal indicator we explored in Chapter 2, *Deciphering the Markets with Technical Analysis*. It will use a static constant of 10 days for the Fast EMA and a static constant of 40 days for the Slow EMA. It will perform buy trades when the APO signal value drops below -10 and perform sell trades when the APO signal value goes above +10. In addition, it will check that new trades are made at prices that are different from the last trade price to prevent overtrading. Positions are closed when the APO signal value changes sign, that is, close short positions when APO goes negative and close long positions when APO goes positive.

In addition, positions are also closed if currently open positions are profitable above a certain amount, regardless of APO values. This is used to algorithmically lock profits and initiate more positions instead of relying only on the trading signal value. Now, let's look at the implementation in the next few sections:

1. We will fetch data the same way we have done in the past. Let's fetch 4 years of GOOG data. This code will use the DataReader function from the pandas_datareader package. This function will fetch the GOOG prices from Yahoo Finance between 2014-01-2014 and 2018-01-01. If the .pkl file used to store the data on the disk is not present, the GOOG_data.pkl file will be created. By doing that, we ensure that we will use the file to fetch the GOOG data for future use:

```
import pandas as pd
from pandas_datareader import data

# Fetch daily data for 4 years
SYMBOL='GOOG'
start_date = '2014-01-01'
end_date = '2018-01-01'
SRC_DATA_FILENAME=SYMBOL + '_data.pkl'

try:
    data = pd.read_pickle(SRC_DATA_FILENAME)
except FileNotFoundError:
    data = data.DataReader(SYMBOL, 'yahoo', start_date, end_date)
    data.to_pickle(SRC_DATA_FILENAME)
```

2. Now we will define some constants and variables we will need to perform Fast and Slow EMA calculations and APO trading signal:

```
# Variables/constants for EMA Calculation:
NUM_PERIODS_FAST = 10 # Static time period parameter for the fast
EMA
K_FAST = 2 / (NUM_PERIODS_FAST + 1) # Static smoothing factor
parameter for fast EMA
ema_fast = 0
ema_fast_values = [] # we will hold fast EMA values for
visualization purposes

NUM_PERIODS_SLOW = 40 # Static time period parameter for slow EMA
K_SLOW = 2 / (NUM_PERIODS_SLOW + 1) # Static smoothing factor
parameter for slow EMA
ema_slow = 0
ema_slow_values = [] # we will hold slow EMA values for
visualization purposes
```

```
apo_values = [] # track computed absolute price oscillator value
signals
```

3. We will also need variables that define/control strategy trading behavior and position and PnL management:

```
# Variables for Trading Strategy trade, position & pnl management:
orders = [] # Container for tracking buy/sell order, +1 for buy
order, -1 for sell order, 0 for no-action
positions = [] # Container for tracking positions, positive for
long positions, negative for short positions, 0 for flat/no
position
pnls = [] # Container for tracking total_pnls, this is the sum of
closed_pnl i.e. pnls already locked in and open_pnl i.e. pnls for
open-position marked to market price

last_buy_price = 0 # Price at which last buy trade was made, used
to prevent over-trading at/around the same price
last_sell_price = 0 # Price at which last sell trade was made, used
to prevent over-trading at/around the same price
position = 0 # Current position of the trading strategy
buy_sum_price_qty = 0 # Summation of products of buy_trade_price
and buy_trade_qty for every buy Trade made since last time being
flat
buy_sum_qty = 0 # Summation of buy_trade_qty for every buy Trade
made since last time being flat
sell_sum_price_qty = 0 # Summation of products of sell_trade_price
and sell_trade_qty for every sell Trade made since last time being
flat
sell_sum_qty = 0 # Summation of sell_trade_qty for every sell Trade
made since last time being flat
open_pnl = 0 # Open/Unrealized PnL marked to market
closed_pnl = 0 # Closed/Realized PnL so far
```

4. Finally, we clearly define the entry thresholds, the minimum price change since last trade, the minimum profit to expect per trade, and the number of shares to trade per trade:

```
# Constants that define strategy behavior/thresholds
APO_VALUE_FOR_BUY_ENTRY = -10 # APO trading signal value below
which to enter buy-orders/long-position
APO_VALUE_FOR_SELL_ENTRY = 10 # APO trading signal value above
which to enter sell-orders/short-position
MIN_PRICE_MOVE_FROM_LAST_TRADE = 10 # Minimum price change since
last trade before considering trading again, this is to prevent
over-trading at/around same prices
MIN_PROFIT_TO_CLOSE = 10 # Minimum Open/Unrealized profit at which
to close positions and lock profits
```

```
NUM_SHARES_PER_TRADE = 10 # Number of shares to buy/sell on every
trade
```

5. Now, let's look at the main section of the trading strategy, which has logic for the following:

- Computation/updates to Fast and Slow EMA and the APO trading signal
- Reacting to trading signals to enter long or short positions
- Reacting to trading signals, open positions, open PnLs, and market prices to close long or short positions:

```
close=data['Close']
for close_price in close:
   # This section updates fast and slow EMA and computes APO trading
signal
   if (ema_fast == 0): # first observation
     ema_fast = close_price
     ema_slow = close_price
   else:
     ema_fast = (close_price - ema_fast) * K_FAST + ema_fast
     ema_slow = (close_price - ema_slow) * K_SLOW + ema_slow

   ema_fast_values.append(ema_fast)
   ema_slow_values.append(ema_slow)

   apo = ema_fast - ema_slow
   apo_values.append(apo)
```

6. The code will check for trading signals against trading parameters/thresholds and positions, to trade. We will perform a sell trade at close_price if the following conditions are met:

- The APO trading signal value is above the Sell-Entry threshold and the difference between the last trade price and current price is different enough.
- We are long (positive position) and either the APO trading signal value is at or above 0 or current position is profitable enough to lock profit:

```
   if ((apo > APO_VALUE_FOR_SELL_ENTRY and abs(close_price -
last_sell_price) > MIN_PRICE_MOVE_FROM_LAST_TRADE) # APO above sell
entry threshold, we should sell
     or
     (position > 0 and (apo >= 0 or open_pnl >
MIN_PROFIT_TO_CLOSE))): # long from negative APO and APO has gone
positive or position is profitable, sell to close position
       orders.append(-1) # mark the sell trade
       last_sell_price = close_price
```

```
      position -= NUM_SHARES_PER_TRADE # reduce position by the size
of this trade
      sell_sum_price_qty += (close_price*NUM_SHARES_PER_TRADE) #
update vwap sell-price
      sell_sum_qty += NUM_SHARES_PER_TRADE
      print( "Sell ", NUM_SHARES_PER_TRADE, " @ ", close_price,
"Position: ", position )
```

7. We will perform a buy trade at `close_price` if the following conditions are met: the APO trading signal value is below the Buy-Entry threshold and the difference between the last trade price and current price is different enough. We are short (negative position) and either the APO trading signal value is at or below 0 or current position is profitable enough to lock profit:

```
      elif ((apo < APO_VALUE_FOR_BUY_ENTRY and abs(close_price -
last_buy_price) > MIN_PRICE_MOVE_FROM_LAST_TRADE) # APO below buy
entry threshold, we should buy
          or
          (position < 0 and (apo <= 0 or open_pnl >
MIN_PROFIT_TO_CLOSE))): # short from positive APO and APO has gone
negative or position is profitable, buy to close position
          orders.append(+1) # mark the buy trade
          last_buy_price = close_price
          position += NUM_SHARES_PER_TRADE # increase position by the
size of this trade
          buy_sum_price_qty += (close_price*NUM_SHARES_PER_TRADE) #
update the vwap buy-price
          buy_sum_qty += NUM_SHARES_PER_TRADE
          print( "Buy ", NUM_SHARES_PER_TRADE, " @ ", close_price,
"Position: ", position )
      else:
          # No trade since none of the conditions were met to buy or sell
          orders.append(0)
      positions.append(position)
```

8. The code of the trading strategy contains logic for position/PnL management. It needs to update positions and compute open and closed PnLs when market prices change and/or trades are made causing a change in positions:

```
  # This section updates Open/Unrealized & Closed/Realized positions
      open_pnl = 0
      if position > 0:
          if sell_sum_qty > 0: # long position and some sell trades have
been made against it, close that amount based on how much was sold
against this long position
              open_pnl = abs(sell_sum_qty) *
(sell_sum_price_qty/sell_sum_qty - buy_sum_price_qty/buy_sum_qty)
```

```
        # mark the remaining position to market i.e. pnl would be what
it would be if we closed at current price
        open_pnl += abs(sell_sum_qty - position) * (close_price -
buy_sum_price_qty / buy_sum_qty)
    elif position < 0:
        if buy_sum_qty > 0: # short position and some buy trades have
been made against it, close that amount based on how much was
bought against this short position
            open_pnl = abs(buy_sum_qty) *
(sell_sum_price_qty/sell_sum_qty - buy_sum_price_qty/buy_sum_qty)
        # mark the remaining position to market i.e. pnl would be what
it would be if we closed at current price
        open_pnl += abs(buy_sum_qty - position) *
(sell_sum_price_qty/sell_sum_qty - close_price)
    else:
        # flat, so update closed_pnl and reset tracking variables for
positions & pnls
        closed_pnl += (sell_sum_price_qty - buy_sum_price_qty)
        buy_sum_price_qty = 0
        buy_sum_qty = 0
        sell_sum_price_qty = 0
        sell_sum_qty = 0
        last_buy_price = 0
        last_sell_price = 0

    print( "OpenPnL: ", open_pnl, " ClosedPnL: ", closed_pnl )
    pnls.append(closed_pnl + open_pnl)
```

9. Now we look at some Python/Matplotlib code to see how to gather the relevant results of the trading strategy such as market prices, Fast and Slow EMA values, APO values, Buy and Sell trades, Positions and PnLs achieved by the strategy over its lifetime and then plot them in a manner that gives us insight into the strategy's behavior:

```
# This section prepares the dataframe from the trading strategy
results and visualizes the results
data = data.assign(ClosePrice=pd.Series(close, index=data.index))
data = data.assign(Fast10DayEMA=pd.Series(ema_fast_values,
index=data.index))
data = data.assign(Slow40DayEMA=pd.Series(ema_slow_values,
index=data.index))
data = data.assign(APO=pd.Series(apo_values, index=data.index))
data = data.assign(Trades=pd.Series(orders, index=data.index))
data = data.assign(Position=pd.Series(positions, index=data.index))
data = data.assign(Pnl=pd.Series(pnls, index=data.index))
```

10. Now we will add columns to the data frame with different series that we computed in the previous sections, first the Market Price and then the fast and slow EMA values. We will also have another plot for the APO trading signal value. In both plots, we will overlay buy and sell trades so we can understand when the strategy enters and exits positions:

```python
import matplotlib.pyplot as plt

data['ClosePrice'].plot(color='blue', lw=3., legend=True)
data['Fast10DayEMA'].plot(color='y', lw=1., legend=True)
data['Slow40DayEMA'].plot(color='m', lw=1., legend=True)
plt.plot(data.loc[ data.Trades == 1 ].index,
data.ClosePrice[data.Trades == 1 ], color='r', lw=0, marker='^',
markersize=7, label='buy')
plt.plot(data.loc[ data.Trades == -1 ].index,
data.ClosePrice[data.Trades == -1 ], color='g', lw=0, marker='v',
markersize=7, label='sell')
plt.legend()
plt.show()

data['APO'].plot(color='k', lw=3., legend=True)
plt.plot(data.loc[ data.Trades == 1 ].index, data.APO[data.Trades
== 1 ], color='r', lw=0, marker='^', markersize=7, label='buy')
plt.plot(data.loc[ data.Trades == -1 ].index, data.APO[data.Trades
== -1 ], color='g', lw=0, marker='v', markersize=7, label='sell')
plt.axhline(y=0, lw=0.5, color='k')
for i in range( APO_VALUE_FOR_BUY_ENTRY, APO_VALUE_FOR_BUY_ENTRY*5,
APO_VALUE_FOR_BUY_ENTRY ):
  plt.axhline(y=i, lw=0.5, color='r')
for i in range( APO_VALUE_FOR_SELL_ENTRY,
APO_VALUE_FOR_SELL_ENTRY*5, APO_VALUE_FOR_SELL_ENTRY ):
  plt.axhline(y=i, lw=0.5, color='g')
plt.legend()
plt.show()
```

Let's take a look at what our trading behavior looks like, paying attention to the EMA and APO values when the trades are made. When we look at the positions and PnL plots, this will become completely clear:

In the plot, we can see where the buy and sell trades were made as the price of the Google stock change over the last 4 years, but now, let's look at what the APO trading signal values where the buy trades were made and sell trades were made. According to the design of these trading strategies, we expect sell trades when APO values are positive and expect buy trades when APO values are negative:

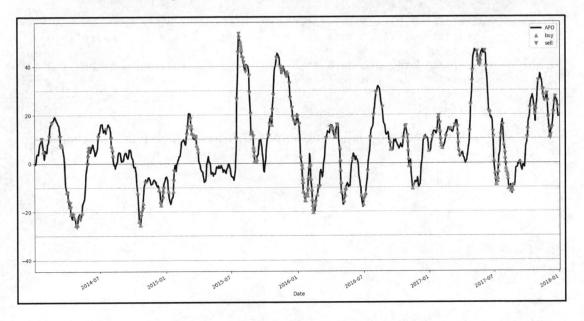

In the plot, we can see that a lot of sell trades are executed when APO trading signal values are positive and a lot of buy trades are executed when APO trading signal values are negative. We also observe that some buy trades are executed when APO trading signal values are positive and some sell trades are executed when APO trading signal values are negative. How do we explain that?

11. As we will see in the following code, those trades are the ones executed to close profits. Let's observe the position and PnL evolution over the lifetime of this strategy:

```
data['Position'].plot(color='k', lw=1., legend=True)
plt.plot(data.loc[ data.Position == 0 ].index, data.Position[
data.Position == 0 ], color='k', lw=0, marker='.', label='flat')
plt.plot(data.loc[ data.Position > 0 ].index, data.Position[
data.Position > 0 ], color='r', lw=0, marker='+', label='long')
plt.plot(data.loc[ data.Position < 0 ].index, data.Position[
data.Position < 0 ], color='g', lw=0, marker='_', label='short')
plt.axhline(y=0, lw=0.5, color='k')
for i in range( NUM_SHARES_PER_TRADE, NUM_SHARES_PER_TRADE*25,
NUM_SHARES_PER_TRADE*5 ):
   plt.axhline(y=i, lw=0.5, color='r')
for i in range( -NUM_SHARES_PER_TRADE, -NUM_SHARES_PER_TRADE*25, -
NUM_SHARES_PER_TRADE*5 ):
   plt.axhline(y=i, lw=0.5, color='g')
plt.legend()
plt.show()

data['Pnl'].plot(color='k', lw=1., legend=True)
plt.plot(data.loc[ data.Pnl > 0 ].index, data.Pnl[ data.Pnl > 0 ],
color='g', lw=0, marker='.')
plt.plot(data.loc[ data.Pnl < 0 ].index, data.Pnl[ data.Pnl < 0 ],
color='r', lw=0, marker='.')
plt.legend()
plt.show()
```

The code will return the following output. Let's have a look at the two charts:

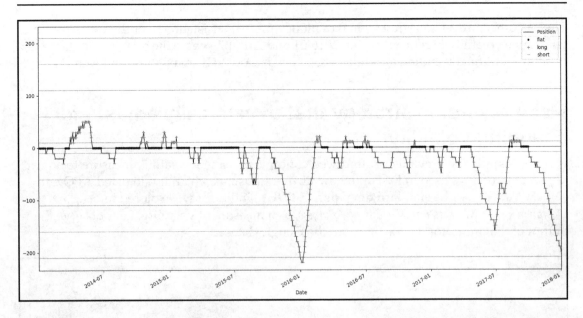

From the position plot, we can see some large short positions around 2016-01, then again in 2017-07, and finally again in 2018-01. If we go back to the APO trading signal values, that is when APO values went through large patches of positive values. Finally, let's look at how the PnL evolves for this trading strategy over the course of the stock's life cycle:

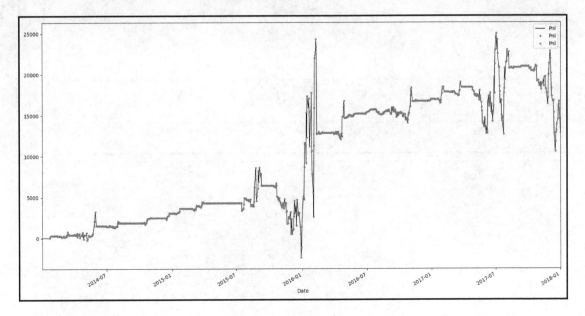

The basic mean reversion strategy makes money pretty consistently over the course of time, with some volatility in returns during 2016-01 and 2017-07, where the strategy has large positions, but finally ending around $15K, which is close to its maximum achieved PnL.

Mean reversion strategy that dynamically adjusts for changing volatility

Now, let's apply the previously introduced concepts of using a volatility measure to adjust the number of days used in Fast and Slow EMA and using a volatility-adjusted APO entry signal. We will use the **standard deviation (STDEV)** indicator we explored in Chapter 2, *Deciphering the Markets with Technical Analysis*, as a measure of volatility. Let's observe the output of that indicator quickly to recap the Google dataset:

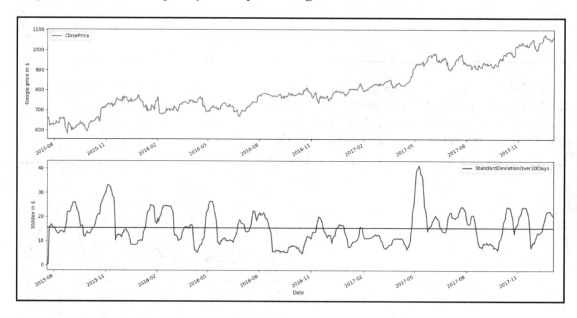

From the output, it seems like volatility measure ranges from somewhere between $8 over 20 days to $40 over 20 days, with $15 over 20 days being the average. So we will use a volatility factor that ranges from 0 to 1, by designing it to be $stdev_factor = stdev/15$, where values closer to 0 indicate very low volatility, values around 1 indicate normal volatility, and values above 1 indicate above-normal volatility. The way in which we incorporate STDEV into our strategy is through the following changes:

- Instead of having static `K_FAST` and `K_SLOW` smoothing factors for the fast and slow EMA, we will instead make them additionally a function of volatility and use `K_FAST * stdev_factor` and `K_SLOW * stdev_factor`, to make them more reactive to newest observations during periods of higher than normal volatility, which makes intuitive sense.

- Instead of using static `APO_VALUE_FOR_BUY_ENTRY` and `APO_VALUE_FOR_SELL_ENTRY` thresholds for entering positions based on the primary trading signal APO, we will also incorporate volatility to have dynamic thresholds `APO_VALUE_FOR_BUY_ENTRY * stdev_factor` and `APO_VALUE_FOR_SELL_ENTRY * stdev_factor`. This makes us less aggressive in entering positions during periods of higher volatility, by increasing the threshold for entry by a factor of volatility, which also makes intuitive sense based on what we discussed in the previous section.

- Finally, we will incorporate volatility in one last threshold and that is by having a dynamic expected profit threshold to lock in profit in a position. In this case, instead of using the static `MIN_PROFIT_TO_CLOSE` threshold, we will use a dynamic `MIN_PROFIT_TO_CLOSE / stdev_factor`. Here, the idea is to be more aggressive in exciting positions during periods of increased volatility, because as we discussed before, during periods of higher than normal volatility, it is riskier to hold on to positions for longer periods of time.

Let's look at the modifications needed to the basic mean reversion strategy to achieve this. First, we need some code to track and update the volatility measure (STDEV):

```
import statistics as stats
import math as math

# Constants/variables that are used to compute standard deviation as a
volatility measure
SMA_NUM_PERIODS = 20 # look back period
price_history = [] # history of prices
```

Then the main strategy loop simply becomes this, while the position and PnL management section of the strategy remains the same:

```
close=data['Close']
for close_price in close:
  price_history.append(close_price)
  if len(price_history) > SMA_NUM_PERIODS: # we track at most 'time_period'
number of prices
    del (price_history[0])

  sma = stats.mean(price_history)
  variance = 0 # variance is square of standard deviation
  for hist_price in price_history:
    variance = variance + ((hist_price - sma) ** 2)

  stdev = math.sqrt(variance / len(price_history))
  stdev_factor = stdev/15
  if stdev_factor == 0:
    stdev_factor = 1

  # This section updates fast and slow EMA and computes APO trading signal
  if (ema_fast == 0): # first observation
    ema_fast = close_price
    ema_slow = close_price
  else:
    ema_fast = (close_price - ema_fast) * K_FAST*stdev_factor + ema_fast
    ema_slow = (close_price - ema_slow) * K_SLOW*stdev_factor + ema_slow

  ema_fast_values.append(ema_fast)
  ema_slow_values.append(ema_slow)

  apo = ema_fast - ema_slow
  apo_values.append(apo)
```

And as we said, the use of the trading signal to manage positions has the same trading logic as before. First, let's look at the sell trade logic:

```
  # We will perform a sell trade at close_price if the following conditions
are met:
  # 1. The APO trading signal value is above Sell-Entry threshold and the
difference between last trade-price and current-price is different enough.
  # 2. We are long( positive position ) and either APO trading signal value
is at or above 0 or current position is profitable enough to lock profit.
    if ((apo > APO_VALUE_FOR_SELL_ENTRY*stdev_factor and abs(close_price -
last_sell_price) > MIN_PRICE_MOVE_FROM_LAST_TRADE*stdev_factor) # APO above
sell entry threshold, we should sell
      or
      (position > 0 and (apo >= 0 or open_pnl >
```

```
MIN_PROFIT_TO_CLOSE/stdev_factor))): # long from negative APO and APO has
gone positive or position is profitable, sell to close position
    orders.append(-1) # mark the sell trade
    last_sell_price = close_price
    position -= NUM_SHARES_PER_TRADE # reduce position by the size of this
trade
    sell_sum_price_qty += (close_price*NUM_SHARES_PER_TRADE) # update vwap
sell-price
    sell_sum_qty += NUM_SHARES_PER_TRADE
    print( "Sell ", NUM_SHARES_PER_TRADE, " @ ", close_price, "Position: ",
position )
```

Now, let's look at similar logic for buy trades:

```
    # We will perform a buy trade at close_price if the following conditions
are met:
    # 1. The APO trading signal value is below Buy-Entry threshold and the
difference between last trade-price and current-price is different enough.
    # 2. We are short( negative position ) and either APO trading signal
value is at or below 0 or current position is profitable enough to lock
profit.
    elif ((apo < APO_VALUE_FOR_BUY_ENTRY*stdev_factor and abs(close_price -
last_buy_price) > MIN_PRICE_MOVE_FROM_LAST_TRADE*stdev_factor) # APO below
buy entry threshold, we should buy
        or
        (position < 0 and (apo <= 0 or open_pnl >
MIN_PROFIT_TO_CLOSE/stdev_factor))): # short from positive APO and APO has
gone negative or position is profitable, buy to close position
    orders.append(+1) # mark the buy trade
    last_buy_price = close_price
    position += NUM_SHARES_PER_TRADE # increase position by the size of
this trade
    buy_sum_price_qty += (close_price*NUM_SHARES_PER_TRADE) # update the
vwap buy-price
    buy_sum_qty += NUM_SHARES_PER_TRADE
    print( "Buy ", NUM_SHARES_PER_TRADE, " @ ", close_price, "Position: ",
position )
  else:
    # No trade since none of the conditions were met to buy or sell
    orders.append(0)
```

Let's compare PnLs from a static constant thresholds mean reversion strategy and a volatility-adjusted mean reversion strategy to see whether we improved performance or not:

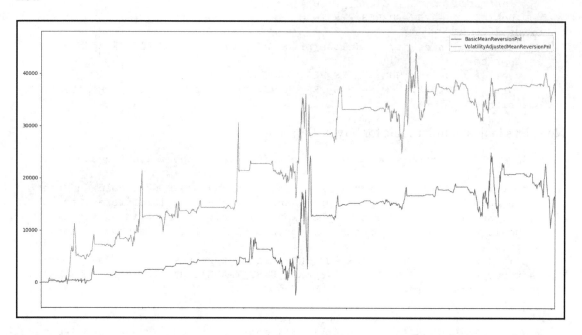

In this case, adjusting the trading strategy for volatility increases the strategy performance by 200%!

Trend-following strategy using absolute price oscillator trading signal

Similar to the mean reversion strategy we explored, we can build a trend-following strategy that uses the APO trading signal. The only difference here is that we enter long positions when the APO is above a certain value, expecting price moves to continue in that direction, and we enter short positions when the APO is below a certain value, expecting price moves to continue going down.

In effect, this is the exact opposite trading strategy with some differences in position management. One might expect this trading strategy to be exactly opposite in performance but, as we will see, that is not the case, that is, both trend-following and mean reversion strategies can be profitable in the same market conditions:

1. First, we define the APO values we will use to enter long/short positions. In this case, the buy entry APO threshold is positive and the sell entry APO threshold is negative:

```
# Constants that define strategy behavior/thresholds
APO_VALUE_FOR_BUY_ENTRY = 10 # APO trading signal value above which
to enter buy-orders/long-position
APO_VALUE_FOR_SELL_ENTRY = -10 # APO trading signal value below
which to enter sell-orders/short-position
```

2. Next, let's look at the core trading logic that enters and exits positions.

First, look at the signal and position management code that leads to sell trades:

```
    # This section checks trading signal against trading
parameters/thresholds and positions, to trade.
# We will perform a sell trade at close_price if the following
conditions are met:
    # 1. The APO trading signal value is below Sell-Entry threshold
and the difference between last trade-price and current-price is
different enough.
    # 2. We are long( positive position ) and either APO trading
signal value is at or below 0 or current position is profitable
enough to lock profit.
    if ((apo < APO_VALUE_FOR_SELL_ENTRY and abs(close_price -
last_sell_price) > MIN_PRICE_MOVE_FROM_LAST_TRADE) # APO above sell
entry threshold, we should sell
        or
        (position > 0 and (apo <= 0 or open_pnl >
MIN_PROFIT_TO_CLOSE))): # long from positive APO and APO has gone
negative or position is profitable, sell to close position
        orders.append(-1) # mark the sell trade
        last_sell_price = close_price
        position -= NUM_SHARES_PER_TRADE # reduce position by the size
of this trade
        sell_sum_price_qty += (close_price*NUM_SHARES_PER_TRADE) #
update vwap sell-price
        sell_sum_qty += NUM_SHARES_PER_TRADE
        print( "Sell ", NUM_SHARES_PER_TRADE, " @ ", close_price,
"Position: ", position )
```

Now, let's look at the signal and position management code that leads to buy trades:

```
    # We will perform a buy trade at close_price if the following conditions
are met:
    # 1. The APO trading signal value is above Buy-Entry threshold and the
difference between last trade-price and current-price is different enough.
    # 2. We are short( negative position ) and either APO trading signal
value is at or above 0 or current position is profitable enough to lock
profit.
    elif ((apo > APO_VALUE_FOR_BUY_ENTRY and abs(close_price -
last_buy_price) > MIN_PRICE_MOVE_FROM_LAST_TRADE) # APO above buy entry
threshold, we should buy
        or
        (position < 0 and (apo >= 0 or open_pnl > MIN_PROFIT_TO_CLOSE))): #
short from negative APO and APO has gone positive or position is
profitable, buy to close position
        orders.append(+1) # mark the buy trade
        last_buy_price = close_price
        position += NUM_SHARES_PER_TRADE # increase position by the size of
this trade
        buy_sum_price_qty += (close_price*NUM_SHARES_PER_TRADE) # update the
vwap buy-price
        buy_sum_qty += NUM_SHARES_PER_TRADE
        print( "Buy ", NUM_SHARES_PER_TRADE, " @ ", close_price, "Position: ",
position )
    else:
        # No trade since none of the conditions were met to buy or sell
        orders.append(0)
```

The code to generate the visualization plots remains the same, so we've skipped it here. Let's look at trend-following trading strategy performance:

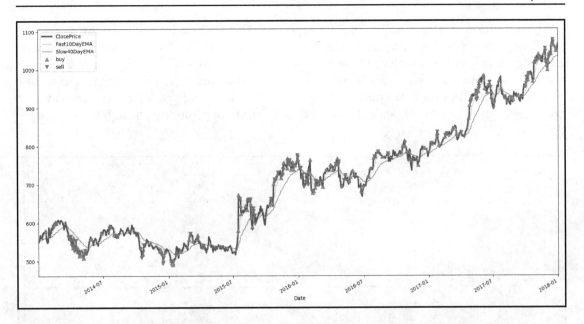

The plot shows at what prices the buy and sell trades are made throughout the lifetime of the trading strategy applied to Google stock data. The trading strategy behavior will make more sense when we inspect the APO signal values to go along with the actual trade prices. Let's look at that in the next plot:

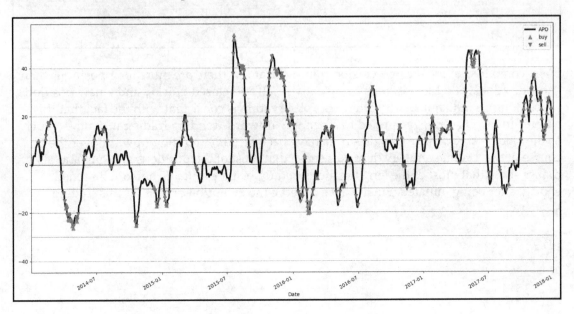

By the definition of a trend-following strategy using the APO trading signal values, intuitively we expect buy trades when APO signal values are positive and sell trades when APO signal values are negative. There are also some buy trades when APO signal values are negative and some sell trades when APO signal values are positive, which might seem counterintuitive, but these are trades made to close out profitable positions, similar to the mean reversion strategy. Now, let's look at the evolution of positions through the course of this trading strategy:

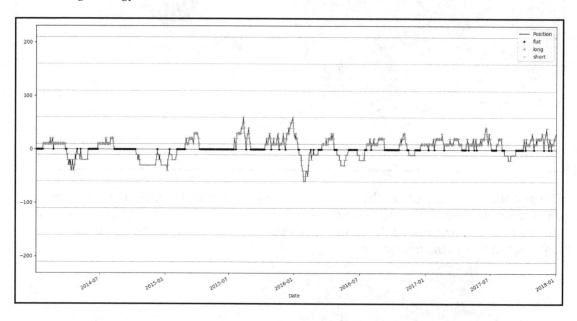

Here, compared to the mean reversion trading strategy, there are more long positions than short positions, and the positions are usually small and closed quickly and a new position (likely long) is initiated shortly after. This observation is consistent with the fact that this is a trend-following strategy applied to a strongly upward-trending trading instrument such as the Google stock. Since Google stocks have been steadily trending upward over the course of this trading strategy, it makes sense that most of the positions are long and also makes sense that most of the long positions end up being profitable and are flattened shortly after being initiated. Finally, let's observe the evolution of PnL for this trading strategy:

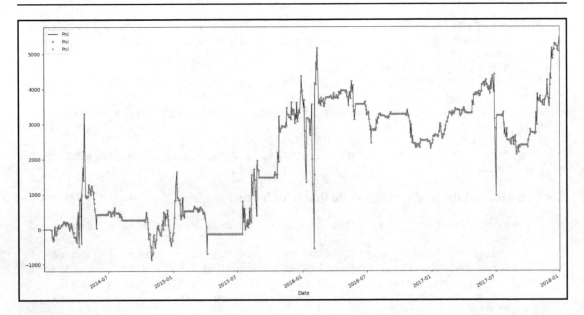

So, for this case, the trend-following strategy makes a third of the money that the mean reversion strategy makes; however, the trend-following strategy also makes money for the same market conditions by entering and exiting positions at different price points.

Trend-following strategy that dynamically adjusts for changing volatility

Let's use STDEV as a measure of volatility and adjust the trend-following strategy to adapt to changing market volatility. We will use an identical approach to the one we used when adjusting the mean reversion trading strategy for market volatility.

The main trading logic for the trend-following strategy adjusted for market volatility looks like the following. Let's start with the trading logic that controls sell trades first:

```
    # This section checks trading signal against trading
parameters/thresholds and positions, to trade.
    # We will perform a sell trade at close_price if the following conditions
are met:
    # 1. The APO trading signal value is below Sell-Entry threshold and the
difference between last trade-price and current-price is different enough.
    # 2. We are long( positive position ) and either APO trading signal value
is at or below 0 or current position is profitable enough to lock profit.
    if ((apo < APO_VALUE_FOR_SELL_ENTRY/stdev_factor and abs(close_price -
last_sell_price) > MIN_PRICE_MOVE_FROM_LAST_TRADE*stdev_factor) # APO below
sell entry threshold, we should sell
        or
        (position > 0 and (apo <= 0 or open_pnl >
```

```
MIN_PROFIT_TO_CLOSE/stdev_factor))): # long from positive APO and APO has
gone negative or position is profitable, sell to close position
    orders.append(-1) # mark the sell trade
    last_sell_price = close_price
    position -= NUM_SHARES_PER_TRADE # reduce position by the size of this
trade
    sell_sum_price_qty += (close_price*NUM_SHARES_PER_TRADE) # update vwap
sell-price
    sell_sum_qty += NUM_SHARES_PER_TRADE
    print( "Sell ", NUM_SHARES_PER_TRADE, " @ ", close_price, "Position: ",
position )
```

Now, let's look at the trading logic code that handles buy trades:

```
# We will perform a buy trade at close_price if the following conditions
are met:
# 1. The APO trading signal value is above Buy-Entry threshold and the
difference between last trade-price and current-price is different enough.
# 2. We are short( negative position ) and either APO trading signal
value is at or above 0 or current position is profitable enough to lock
profit.
    elif ((apo > APO_VALUE_FOR_BUY_ENTRY/stdev_factor and abs(close_price -
last_buy_price) > MIN_PRICE_MOVE_FROM_LAST_TRADE*stdev_factor) # APO above
buy entry threshold, we should buy
    or
    (position < 0 and (apo >= 0 or open_pnl >
MIN_PROFIT_TO_CLOSE/stdev_factor))): # short from negative APO and APO has
gone positive or position is profitable, buy to close position
    orders.append(+1) # mark the buy trade
    last_buy_price = close_price
    position += NUM_SHARES_PER_TRADE # increase position by the size of
this trade
    buy_sum_price_qty += (close_price*NUM_SHARES_PER_TRADE) # update the
vwap buy-price
    buy_sum_qty += NUM_SHARES_PER_TRADE
    print( "Buy ", NUM_SHARES_PER_TRADE, " @ ", close_price, "Position: ",
position )
  else:
    # No trade since none of the conditions were met to buy or sell
    orders.append(0)
```

Finally, let's compare trend-following strategy performance with and without accounting for volatility changes:

So, for trend-following strategies, having dynamic trading thresholds degrades strategy performance. We can explore tweaking the application of the volatility measure to see whether there are variants that actually improve performance compared to static trend-following.

Creating a trading strategy for economic events

In this section, we will explore a new class of trading strategies that is different from what we've seen before. Instead of using technical indicators, we can research economic releases and use various economic releases to estimate/predict the impact on the trading instruments and trade them accordingly. Let's first take a look at what economic releases are and how instrument pricing is influenced by releases.

Economic releases

Economic indicators are a measure of economic activity for a certain country or region or asset classes. These indicators are measured, researched, and released by different entities. Some of these entities are government agencies and some are private research firms. Most of these are released on a schedule, known as an economic calendar. In addition, there is plenty of data available for past releases, expected releases, and actual releases. Each economic indicator captures different economic activity measures: some might affect housing prices, some show employment information, some affect grain, corn, and wheat instruments, others affect precious metals and energy commodities. For example, possibly the most well-known economic indicator, Nonfarm Payrolls in America, is a monthly indicator released by the US Department of Labor (`https://www.bls.gov/ces/`) that represents the number of new jobs created in all non-agricultural industries. This economic release has a huge impact on almost all asset classes. Another example is the EIA Crude Oil Stockpiles report, which is a weekly indicator released by the Energy Information Administration that measures change in the number of barrels of crude oil available. This is a high-impact release for energy products, oil, gas, and so on, but does not usually directly affect things such as stocks, and interest rates.

Now that we have an intuitive idea of what economic indicators are and what economic releases capture and signify, let's look at a short list of important US economic releases. We will not be covering the details of these releases here, but we encourage the reader to explore the economic indicators mentioned here as well as others in greater detail:

ADP Employment, API Crude, Balance of Trade, Baker Hughes Oil Rig Count, Business Optimism, Business Inventories, Case-Shiller, CB Consumer Confidence, CB Leading Index, Challenger Job Cuts, Chicago PMI, Construction Spending, Consumer Credit, Consumer Inflation Expectations, Durable Goods, EIA Crude, EIA Natural Gas, Empire State Manufacturing Index, Employment Cost Index, Factory Orders, Fed Beige Book, Fed Interest Rate Decision, Fed Press Conference, Fed Manufacturing Index, Fed National Activity, FOMC Economic Projections, FOMC Minutes, GDP, Home Sales, Housing Starts, House Price Index, Import Prices, Industrial Production, Inflation Rate, ISM Manufacturing, ISM Non-Manufacturing, ISM New York Index, Jobless Claims, JOLTs, Markit Composite PMI, Markit Manufacturing PMI, Michigan Consumer Sentiment, Mortgage Applications, NAHB Housing Market Index, Nonfarm Payrolls, Nonfarm Productivity, PCE, PPI, Personal Spending, Redbook, Retail Sales, Total Vehicle Sales, WASDE & Wholesale Inventories

More information about these releases is available at `https://tradingeconomics.com/`.

Economic release format

There are plenty of free and paid economic release calendars available, which can be scraped for historical release data or accessed through a proprietary API. Since the focus of this section is utilizing economic release data in trading, we will skip the details of accessing historical data, but it is quite straightforward. Most common economic release calendars look like this:

Calendar	CST	Economic indicator	Actual	Previous	Consensus	Forecast
2019-05-03	07:30 AM	Non Farm Payrolls Apr	263K	189K	185K	178K
2019-06-07	07:30 AM	Non Farm Payrolls May	75K	224K	185K	190K
2019-07-05	07:30 AM	Non Farm Payrolls Jun	224K	72K	160K	171K
2019-08-02	07:30 AM	Non Farm Payrolls Jul	164K	193K	164K	160K

As we discussed earlier, the date and time of releases are set well in advance. Most calendars also provide the previous year's release, or sometimes the previous month's release. The Consensus estimate is what multiple economists or firms expect the release to be; this is generally treated as the expected value of the release, and any large misses from this expectation will cause large price volatility. A lot of calendars, in addition, provide a Forecast field, which is the calendar provider's expected value for that economic release. At the time of writing, `https://tradingeconomics.com/`, `https://www.forexfactory.com/`, and `https://www.fxstreet.com/` are some of the many free and paid economic calendar providers.

Electronic economic release services

One last concept we need to understand before we can look into the analysis of economic releases and price movement is how to deliver these economic releases electronic to trading strategies right to the trading servers. There are a lot of service providers that provide economic releases directly to trading servers electronically via low-latency direct lines. Most providers cover most of the major economic indicators and usually deliver releases to the trading strategies in machine-parsable feeds. These releases can reach the trading servers anywhere from a few microseconds up to a few milliseconds after the official release. Nowadays, it's quite common for a lot of algorithmic trading market participants to make use of such electronic economic release providers as alternative data providers to improve trading performance.

Economic releases in trading

Now that we have a good grasp of what economic indicators are, how the economic releases are scheduled, and how they can be delivered electronically directly to trading servers, let's dive in and look at some possible edge trading strategies gain from economic indicator releases. There are a couple of different ways to use economic indicator releases in algorithmic trading, but we will explore the most common and most intuitive approach. Given the history of expected economic indicator values and actual releases similar to the format we saw before, it is possible to correlate the difference between expected and actual values with price movement that follows. Generally, there are two approaches. One capitalizes on price moves that are less than expected for a big miss in expected and actual economic indicator release, that is, the price should have moved a certain amount based on historical research, but moved much less. This strategy takes a position with the view that prices will move further and tries to capture a profit if it does, similar to trend-following trading strategies in some sense.

The other approach is the opposite one, which tries to detect overreactions in price movements and make the opposite bet, that is, prices will go back to previous price levels, similar to a mean reversion strategy in some sense. In practice, this approach is often improved by using classification methods we explored in `Chapter 3`, *Predicting the Markets with Basic Machine Learning*. Classification methods allow us to improve the process of combining multiple economic releases that occur at the same time in addition to having multiple possible value-boundaries for each release, to provide greater granularity and thresholds. For the purposes of this example, we will not dive into the complexity of applying classification methods to this economic release trading strategy.

Let's look at a couple of Non Farm Payroll releases and observe the impact on the S&P futures. Because this requires tick data, which is not freely available, we will skip the actual analysis code, but it should be easy to conceptualize this analysis and understand how to apply it to different datasets:

	A	B	C	D	E	F	G
1	date	time CST	actual	consensus	miss	bid price change	ask price change
2	2019-03-08	7:30:00	25000	170000	-145000	-17	-16
3	2019-06-07	7:30:00	90000	175000	-85000	-11	-11
4	2018-10-05	7:30:00	121000	180000	-59000	18	18
5	2018-12-07	7:30:00	161000	200000	-39000	15	16
6	2018-08-03	7:30:00	170000	189000	-19000	-1	-1
7	2019-08-02	7:30:00	148000	160000	-12000	-8	-8
8	2019-04-05	7:30:00	182000	170000	12000	22	23
9	2018-07-06	7:30:00	202000	190000	12000	12	12
10	2018-09-07	7:30:00	204000	190000	14000	1	1
11	2019-07-05	7:30:00	191000	153000	38000	-3	-2
12	2019-05-03	7:30:00	236000	180000	56000	10	10
13	2018-11-02	7:30:00	246000	183000	63000	11	11
14	2019-01-04	7:30:00	301000	175000	126000	-6	-6
15	2019-02-01	7:30:00	296000	170000	126000	23	23

Let's quickly put together a scatter plot to easily visualize how price moves correspond to misses in economic indicator releases:

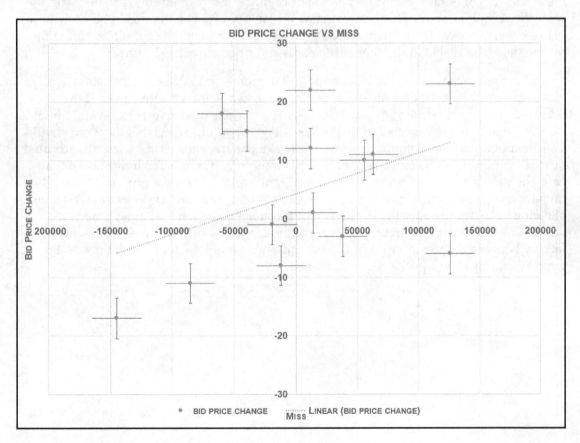

As you can observe, positive misses (actual indicator value higher than consensus indicator values) cause prices to move higher. Conversely, negative misses (actual indicator value lower than consensus indicator values) cause prices to move lower. In general, higher NonFarm Payroll job additions are considered to indicate a healthy economy and thus cause the S&P, which tracks major stocks, to increase in value. Another interesting thing to observe is that the larger the miss, in general, the bigger the price move. So with this simple analysis, we have expected reaction for two unknowns: the direction of a price move due to a miss and the magnitude of the price move as a function of the magnitude of the miss. Now, let's look at how to use this information.

As we discussed before, one of the approaches is to use the miss value and the research to use a trend-following approach and buy on a large positive miss and sell on a large negative miss, with the expectation that prices will move up or down a certain amount. The strategy then closes the long or short position when the expected price move has materialized. This strategy works when the price move and magnitude are in line with the research. Another important consideration is the latency between the release and when the prices begin to move. The strategy needs to be fast enough to initiate a position before the information is available to all other participants and price move has finished.

The other approach is to use the miss value and the research to detect overreaction in price moves and then take the opposite position. In this instance, for a positive miss, if the price decreases, we can have the view that this move is a mistake or an overreaction and initiate a long position with the expectation that prices will go up as our research indicates it should. The other overreaction is if prices move up due to a positive miss as our research indicated but the magnitude of the move is significantly larger than our research indicates. In that case, the strategy waits till prices have moved significantly outside of expectation and then initiates a short position, expecting the overreaction to die down and prices to revert a bit, allowing us to capture a profit. The benefit of the mean reversion trading approach to economic releases over the trend-following approach is that the latter is less sensitive to latency between economic indicator release and time window within which the trading strategy must initiate a position.

Understanding and implementing basic statistical arbitrage trading strategies

Statistical arbitrage trading strategies (StatArb) first became popular in the 1980s, delivering many firms double-digit returns. It is a class of strategies that tries to capture relationships between short-term price movements in many correlated products. Then it uses relationships that have been found to be statistically significant in the past research to make predictions in the instrument being traded based on price movements in a large group of correlated products.

Basics of StatArb

Statistical arbitrage or StatArb is in some way similar to pairs trading that takes offsetting positions in co-linearly related products that we explored in `Chapter 4`, *Classical Trading Strategies Driven by Human Intuition*. However, the difference here is that StatArb trading strategies often have *baskets* or portfolios of hundreds of trading instrument, whether they are futures instruments, equities, options, or even currencies. Also, StatArb strategies have a mixture of mean reversion and trend-following strategies. One possibility is that price deviation in the instrument being traded is less than the expected price deviation based on the expected relationship with the price deviations for the portfolio of instruments. In that case, StatArb strategies resemble a trend-following strategy by positioning themselves on the expectation that the trading instrument's price will catch up to the portfolio.

The other case is that price deviation in the instrument being traded is more than the expected price deviation based on the expected relationship with the price deviations for the portfolio of instruments. Here, StatArb strategies resemble a mean reversion strategy by positioning themselves on the expectation that the trading instrument's price will revert back to the portfolio. Most widespread applications of StatArb trading strategies lean more toward mean reversion strategies. StatArb strategies can be considered HFT but can also be medium frequency if the strategy positions last longer than a few milliseconds or a few seconds.

Lead-lag in StatArb

Another important consideration is that this strategy implicitly expects the portfolio to lead and the trading instrument is lagging in terms of reaction by market participants. When this is not true, for example, when the trading instrument we are trying to trade is actually the one leading price moves across the portfolio, then this strategy doesn't perform well, because instead of the trading instrument price catching up to the portfolio, now the portfolio prices catch up to the trading instrument. This is the concept of lead-lag in StatArb; to be profitable, we need to find trading instruments that are mostly lagging and build a portfolio of instruments that are mostly leading.

A lot of the time, the way this manifests itself is that during some market hours, some instruments lead others and during other market hours, that relationship is reversed. For example, intuitively one can understand that during Asia market hours, trading instruments traded in Asian electronic exchanges such as Singapore, India, Hong Kong, and Japan lead price moves in global assets. During European market hours, trading instruments traded in Germany, London, and other European countries lead most price moves across global assets. Finally, during American market hours, trading instruments in America lead price moves. So the ideal approach is to construct portfolios and establish relationships between lead and lag instruments differently in different trading sessions.

Adjusting portfolio composition and relationships

Another important factor to build StatArb strategies that perform well consistently is understanding and building systems to adapt to changing portfolio compositions and relationships between different trading instruments. The drawback of having the StatArb trading strategy depend primarily on the short-term relationships between large number of trading instruments is that it is hard to understand and adapt to changing relationships between price moves in all the different instruments that constitute a portfolio. The portfolio weights themselves change over time. Principal component analysis, a statistical tool from dimensionality reduction techniques, can be used to construct, adapt, and monitor portfolio weights and significance that change over time.

The other important issue is dealing with relationships between the trading instrument and the leading instruments and also between the trading instrument and the portfolio of leading instruments. Sometimes, localized volatility and country-specific economic events cause the fundamental relationship needed to make StatArb profitable break down. For example, political or economic conditions in Brazil can start affecting the Brazilian real currency price moves to no longer be driven by major currencies around the world. Similarly, during periods of localized economic distress in Britain, say for Brexit, or in America, say due to trade wars against China, these portfolio relationships as well as the lead-lag relationships break down from historical expectations and kill the profitability of StatArb trading strategies. Trying to deal with such conditions can require a lot more statistical edges and sophistication beyond just StatArb techniques.

Infrastructure expenses in StatArb

The last big consideration in StatArb trading is the fact that to be successful in StatArb trading strategies as a business, it is very important to be connected to a lot of electronic trading exchanges to get market data across different exchanges across different countries/continents/markets. Being co-located in so many trading exchanges is extremely expensive from an infrastructure cost perspective. The other problem is that one needs to not only be connected to as many exchanges as possible, but a lot of software development investment needs to make to receive, decode, and store market data and also to send orders, since a lot of these exchanges likely use different market data feed and order gateway communication formats.

The final big consideration is that since StatArb strategies need to receive market data from all exchanges, now every venue needs a physical data link from every other venue, which gets exponentially expensive for every exchange added. Then, if one considers using the much more expensive microwave services to deliver data faster to the trading boxes, that makes it even worse. So to summarize, StatArb trading strategies can be significantly more expensive than some of the other trading strategies from an infrastructure perspective when it comes to running an algorithmic trading business.

StatArb trading strategy in Python

Now that we have a good understanding of the principles involved in StatArb trading strategies and some practical considerations in building and operating an algorithmic trading business utilizing StatArb trading strategies, let's look at a realistic trading strategy implementation and understand its behavior and performance. In practice, modern algorithmic trading businesses that operate with high frequency usually use a low-level programming language such as C++.

StatArb data set

Let's first get the data set we will need to implement a StatArb trading strategy. For this section, we will use the following major currencies across the world:

- **Austrian Dollar versus American Dollar (AUD/USD)**
- **British Pound versus American Dollar (GBP/USD)**
- **Canadian Dollar versus American Dollar (CAD/USD)**
- **Swiss Franc versus American Dollar (CHF/USD)**
- **Euro versus American Dollar (EUR/USD)**
- **Japanese Yen versus American Dollar (JPY/USD)**
- **New Zealand Kiwi versus American Dollar (NZD/USD)**

And for this implementation of the StatArb trading strategy, we will try to trade CAD/USD using its relationship with the other currency pairs:

1. Let's fetch 4 years' worth of data for these currency pairs and set up our data frames:

```
import pandas as pd
from pandas_datareader import data

# Fetch daily data for 4 years, for 7 major currency pairs
TRADING_INSTRUMENT = 'CADUSD=X'
SYMBOLS = ['AUDUSD=X', 'GBPUSD=X', 'CADUSD=X', 'CHFUSD=X',
'EURUSD=X', 'JPYUSD=X', 'NZDUSD=X']
START_DATE = '2014-01-01'
END_DATE = '2018-01-01'

# DataSeries for each currency
symbols_data = {}
for symbol in SYMBOLS:
  SRC_DATA_FILENAME = symbol + '_data.pkl'
```

```
try:
  data = pd.read_pickle(SRC_DATA_FILENAME)
except FileNotFoundError:
  data = data.DataReader(symbol, 'yahoo', START_DATE, END_DATE)
  data.to_pickle(SRC_DATA_FILENAME)

symbols_data[symbol] = data
```

2. Let's quickly visualize each currency pair's prices over the period of our data set and see what we observe. We scale the JPY/USD pair by `100.0` purely for visualization scaling purposes:

```
# Visualize prices for currency to inspect relationship between
them
import matplotlib.pyplot as plt
import numpy as np
from itertools import cycle

cycol = cycle('bgrcmky')

price_data = pd.DataFrame()
for symbol in SYMBOLS:
  multiplier = 1.0
  if symbol == 'JPYUSD=X':
    multiplier = 100.0

  label = symbol + ' ClosePrice'
  price_data =
price_data.assign(label=pd.Series(symbols_data[symbol]['Close'] *
multiplier, index=symbols_data[symbol].index))
  ax = price_data['label'].plot(color=next(cycol), lw=2.,
label=label)
plt.xlabel('Date', fontsize=18)
plt.ylabel('Scaled Price', fontsize=18)
plt.legend(prop={'size': 18})
plt.show()
```

The code will return the following output. Let's have a look at the plot:

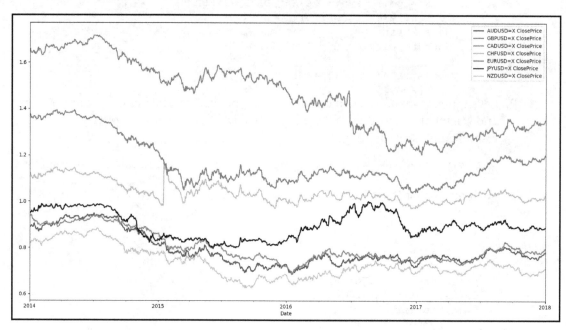

As one would expect and can observe, these currency pairs' price moves are all similar to each other in varying degrees. CAD/USD, AUD/USD, and NZD/USD seem to be most correlated, with CHF/USD and JPY/USD being least correlated to CAD/USD. For the purposes of this strategy, we will use all currencies in the trading model because these relationships are obviously not known ahead of time.

Defining StatArb signal parameters

Now, let's define and quantify some parameters we will need to define moving averages, price deviation from moving averages, history of price deviations, and variables to compute and track correlations:

```
import statistics as stats

# Constants/variables that are used to compute simple moving average and
price deviation from simple moving average
SMA_NUM_PERIODS = 20 # look back period
price_history = {} # history of prices

PRICE_DEV_NUM_PRICES = 200 # look back period of ClosePrice deviations from
SMA
```

```
price_deviation_from_sma = {} # history of ClosePrice deviations from SMA

# We will use this to iterate over all the days of data we have
num_days = len(symbols_data[TRADING_INSTRUMENT].index)
correlation_history = {} # history of correlations per currency pair
delta_projected_actual_history = {} # history of differences between
Projected ClosePrice deviation and actual ClosePrice deviation per currency
pair

final_delta_projected_history = [] # history of differences between final
Projected ClosePrice deviation for TRADING_INSTRUMENT and actual ClosePrice
deviation
```

Defining StatArb trading parameters

Now, before we get into the main strategy loop, let's define some final variables and thresholds we will need to build our StatArb trading strategy:

```
# Variables for Trading Strategy trade, position & pnl management:
orders = [] # Container for tracking buy/sell order, +1 for buy order, -1
for sell order, 0 for no-action
positions = [] # Container for tracking positions, positive for long
positions, negative for short positions, 0 for flat/no position
pnls = [] # Container for tracking total_pnls, this is the sum of
closed_pnl i.e. pnls already locked in and open_pnl i.e. pnls for open-
position marked to market price

last_buy_price = 0 # Price at which last buy trade was made, used to
prevent over-trading at/around the same price
last_sell_price = 0 # Price at which last sell trade was made, used to
prevent over-trading at/around the same price
position = 0 # Current position of the trading strategy
buy_sum_price_qty = 0 # Summation of products of buy_trade_price and
buy_trade_qty for every buy Trade made since last time being flat
buy_sum_qty = 0 # Summation of buy_trade_qty for every buy Trade made since
last time being flat
sell_sum_price_qty = 0 # Summation of products of sell_trade_price and
sell_trade_qty for every sell Trade made since last time being flat
sell_sum_qty = 0 # Summation of sell_trade_qty for every sell Trade made
since last time being flat
open_pnl = 0 # Open/Unrealized PnL marked to market
closed_pnl = 0 # Closed/Realized PnL so far

# Constants that define strategy behavior/thresholds
StatArb_VALUE_FOR_BUY_ENTRY = 0.01 # StatArb trading signal value above
which to enter buy-orders/long-position
StatArb_VALUE_FOR_SELL_ENTRY = -0.01 # StatArb trading signal value below
```

```
which to enter sell-orders/short-position
MIN_PRICE_MOVE_FROM_LAST_TRADE = 0.01 # Minimum price change since last
trade before considering trading again, this is to prevent over-trading
at/around same prices
NUM_SHARES_PER_TRADE = 1000000 # Number of currency to buy/sell on every
trade
MIN_PROFIT_TO_CLOSE = 10 # Minimum Open/Unrealized profit at which to close
positions and lock profits
```

Quantifying and computing StatArb trading signals

1. We will see over available prices a day at a time and see what calculations need
    to be performed, starting with the computation of SimpleMovingAverages and
    price deviation from the rolling SMA first:

```
for i in range(0, num_days):
  close_prices = {}

  # Build ClosePrice series, compute SMA for each symbol and price-
  deviation from SMA for each symbol
  for symbol in SYMBOLS:
    close_prices[symbol] = symbols_data[symbol]['Close'].iloc[i]
    if not symbol in price_history.keys():
      price_history[symbol] = []
      price_deviation_from_sma[symbol] = []

    price_history[symbol].append(close_prices[symbol])
    if len(price_history[symbol]) > SMA_NUM_PERIODS: # we track at
most SMA_NUM_PERIODS number of prices
        del (price_history[symbol][0])

    sma = stats.mean(price_history[symbol]) # Rolling
SimpleMovingAverage
    price_deviation_from_sma[symbol].append(close_prices[symbol] -
sma) # price deviation from mean
    if len(price_deviation_from_sma[symbol]) >
PRICE_DEV_NUM_PRICES:
        del (price_deviation_from_sma[symbol][0])
```

2. Next, we need to compute the relationships between the CAD/USD currency pair price deviations and the other currency pair price deviations. We will use covariance and correlation between the series of price deviations from SMA that we computed in the previous section. In this same loop, we will also compute the CAD/USD price deviation as projected by every other lead currency pair, and see what the difference between the projected price deviation and actual price deviation is. We will need these individual deltas between projected price deviation and actual price deviation to get a final delta value that we will use for trading.

First, let's look at the code block that populates the `correlation_history` and the `delta_projected_actual_history` dictionaries:

```
    # Now compute covariance and correlation between
TRADING_INSTRUMENT and every other lead symbol
    # also compute projected price deviation and find delta between
projected and actual price deviations.
    projected_dev_from_sma_using = {}
    for symbol in SYMBOLS:
        if symbol == TRADING_INSTRUMENT: # no need to find relationship
between trading instrument and itself
            continue

        correlation_label = TRADING_INSTRUMENT + '<-' + symbol
        if correlation_label not in correlation_history.keys(): # first
entry for this pair in the history dictionary
            correlation_history[correlation_label] = []
            delta_projected_actual_history[correlation_label] = []

        if len(price_deviation_from_sma[symbol]) < 2: # need atleast
two observations to compute covariance/correlation
            correlation_history[correlation_label].append(0)
            delta_projected_actual_history[correlation_label].append(0)
            continue
```

Now, let's look at the code block to compute correlation and covariance between the currency pairs:

```
    corr =
np.corrcoef(price_deviation_from_sma[TRADING_INSTRUMENT],
price_deviation_from_sma[symbol])
    cov = np.cov(price_deviation_from_sma[TRADING_INSTRUMENT],
price_deviation_from_sma[symbol])
    corr_trading_instrument_lead_instrument = corr[0, 1] # get the
correlation between the 2 series
    cov_trading_instrument_lead_instrument = cov[0, 0] / cov[0, 1]
# get the covariance between the 2 series

correlation_history[correlation_label].append(corr_trading_instrume
nt_lead_instrument)
```

Finally, let's look at the code block that computes the projected price movement, uses that to find the difference between the projected movement and actual movement, and saves it in our `delta_projected_actual_history` list per currency pair:

```
    # projected-price-deviation-in-TRADING_INSTRUMENT is covariance
* price-deviation-in-lead-symbol
    projected_dev_from_sma_using[symbol] =
price_deviation_from_sma[symbol][-1] *
cov_trading_instrument_lead_instrument

    # delta positive => signal says TRADING_INSTRUMENT price should
have moved up more than what it did
    # delta negative => signal says TRADING_INSTRUMENT price should
have moved down more than what it did.
    delta_projected_actual = (projected_dev_from_sma_using[symbol]
- price_deviation_from_sma[TRADING_INSTRUMENT][-1])
delta_projected_actual_history[correlation_label].append(delta_proj
ected_actual)
```

3. Let's combine these individual deltas between projected and actual price deviation in CAD/USD to get one final StatArb signal value for CAD/USD that is a combination of projections from all the other currency pairs. To combine these different projections, we will use the magnitude of the correlation between CAD/USD and the other currency pairs to weigh the delta between projected and actual price deviations in CAD/USD as predicted by the other pairs. Finally, we will normalize the final delta value by the sum of each individual weight (magnitude of correlation) and that is what we will use as our final signal to build our trading strategy around:

```
# weigh predictions from each pair, weight is the correlation
between those pairs
sum_weights = 0 # sum of weights is sum of correlations for each
symbol with TRADING_INSTRUMENT
for symbol in SYMBOLS:
  if symbol == TRADING_INSTRUMENT: # no need to find relationship
between trading instrument and itself
    continue

  correlation_label = TRADING_INSTRUMENT + '<-' + symbol
  sum_weights += abs(correlation_history[correlation_label][-1])

final_delta_projected = 0 # will hold final prediction of price
deviation in TRADING_INSTRUMENT, weighing projections from all
other symbols.
close_price = close_prices[TRADING_INSTRUMENT]
for symbol in SYMBOLS:
  if symbol == TRADING_INSTRUMENT: # no need to find relationship
between trading instrument and itself
    continue

  correlation_label = TRADING_INSTRUMENT + '<-' + symbol

  # weight projection from a symbol by correlation
  final_delta_projected +=
(abs(correlation_history[correlation_label][-1]) *
delta_projected_actual_history[correlation_label][-1])

# normalize by diving by sum of weights for all pairs
if sum_weights != 0:
  final_delta_projected /= sum_weights
else:
  final_delta_projected = 0

final_delta_projected_history.append(final_delta_projected)
```

StatArb execution logic

Let's execute a strategy for the StatArb signal using the following steps:

1. Now, using the StatArb signal we just computed, we can build a strategy similar to the trend-following strategy we saw before. Let's start by looking at the trading logic that controls the sell trades:

```
    if ((final_delta_projected < StatArb_VALUE_FOR_SELL_ENTRY and
abs(close_price - last_sell_price) >
MIN_PRICE_MOVE_FROM_LAST_TRADE) # StatArb above sell entry
threshold, we should sell
        or
        (position > 0 and (open_pnl > MIN_PROFIT_TO_CLOSE))): # long
from negative StatArb and StatArb has gone positive or position is
profitable, sell to close position
        orders.append(-1) # mark the sell trade
        last_sell_price = close_price
        position -= NUM_SHARES_PER_TRADE # reduce position by the size
of this trade
        sell_sum_price_qty += (close_price * NUM_SHARES_PER_TRADE) #
update vwap sell-price
        sell_sum_qty += NUM_SHARES_PER_TRADE
        print("Sell ", NUM_SHARES_PER_TRADE, " @ ", close_price,
"Position: ", position)
        print("OpenPnL: ", open_pnl, " ClosedPnL: ", closed_pnl, "
TotalPnL: ", (open_pnl + closed_pnl))
```

2. Now, let's look at the buy trade logic, which is quite similar to the sell trade logic:

```
    elif ((final_delta_projected > StatArb_VALUE_FOR_BUY_ENTRY and
abs(close_price - last_buy_price) > MIN_PRICE_MOVE_FROM_LAST_TRADE)
# StatArb below buy entry threshold, we should buy
        or
        (position < 0 and (open_pnl > MIN_PROFIT_TO_CLOSE))): #
short from positive StatArb and StatArb has gone negative or
position is profitable, buy to close position
        orders.append(+1) # mark the buy trade
        last_buy_price = close_price
        position += NUM_SHARES_PER_TRADE # increase position by the
size of this trade
        buy_sum_price_qty += (close_price * NUM_SHARES_PER_TRADE) #
update the vwap buy-price
        buy_sum_qty += NUM_SHARES_PER_TRADE
        print("Buy ", NUM_SHARES_PER_TRADE, " @ ", close_price,
"Position: ", position)
        print("OpenPnL: ", open_pnl, " ClosedPnL: ", closed_pnl, "
TotalPnL: ", (open_pnl + closed_pnl))
```

```
    else:
        # No trade since none of the conditions were met to buy or sell
        orders.append(0)
    positions.append(position)
```

3. Finally, let's also look at the position management and PnL update logic, very similar to previous trading strategies:

```
    # This section updates Open/Unrealized & Closed/Realized
positions
    open_pnl = 0
    if position > 0:
        if sell_sum_qty > 0: # long position and some sell trades have
been made against it, close that amount based on how much was sold
against this long position
            open_pnl = abs(sell_sum_qty) * (sell_sum_price_qty /
sell_sum_qty - buy_sum_price_qty / buy_sum_qty)
        # mark the remaining position to market i.e. pnl would be what
it would be if we closed at current price
        open_pnl += abs(sell_sum_qty - position) * (close_price -
buy_sum_price_qty / buy_sum_qty)
    elif position < 0:
        if buy_sum_qty > 0: # short position and some buy trades have
been made against it, close that amount based on how much was
bought against this short position
            open_pnl = abs(buy_sum_qty) * (sell_sum_price_qty /
sell_sum_qty - buy_sum_price_qty / buy_sum_qty)
        # mark the remaining position to market i.e. pnl would be what
it would be if we closed at current price
        open_pnl += abs(buy_sum_qty - position) * (sell_sum_price_qty /
sell_sum_qty - close_price)
    else:
        # flat, so update closed_pnl and reset tracking variables for
positions & pnls
        closed_pnl += (sell_sum_price_qty - buy_sum_price_qty)
        buy_sum_price_qty = 0
        buy_sum_qty = 0
        sell_sum_price_qty = 0
        sell_sum_qty = 0
        last_buy_price = 0
        last_sell_price = 0

    pnls.append(closed_pnl + open_pnl)
```

StatArb signal and strategy performance analysis

Now, let's analyze the StatArb signal using the following steps:

1. Let's visualize a few more details about the signals in this trading strategy, starting with the correlations between CAD/USD and the other currency pairs as it evolves over time:

```
# Plot correlations between TRADING_INSTRUMENT and other currency
pairs
correlation_data = pd.DataFrame()
for symbol in SYMBOLS:
  if symbol == TRADING_INSTRUMENT:
    continue

  correlation_label = TRADING_INSTRUMENT + '<-' + symbol
  correlation_data =
correlation_data.assign(label=pd.Series(correlation_history[correla
tion_label], index=symbols_data[symbol].index))
  ax = correlation_data['label'].plot(color=next(cycol), lw=2.,
label='Correlation ' + correlation_label)

for i in np.arange(-1, 1, 0.25):
  plt.axhline(y=i, lw=0.5, color='k')
plt.legend()
plt.show()
```

This plot shows the correlation between `CADUSD` and other currency pairs as it evolves over the course of this trading strategy. Correlations close to -1 or +1 signify strongly correlated pairs, and correlations that hold steady are the stable correlated pairs. Currency pairs where correlations swing around between negative and positive values indicate extremely uncorrelated or unstable currency pairs, which are unlikely to yield good predictions in the long run. However, we do not know how the correlation would evolve ahead of time, so we have no choice but to use all currency pairs available to us in our StatArb trading strategy:

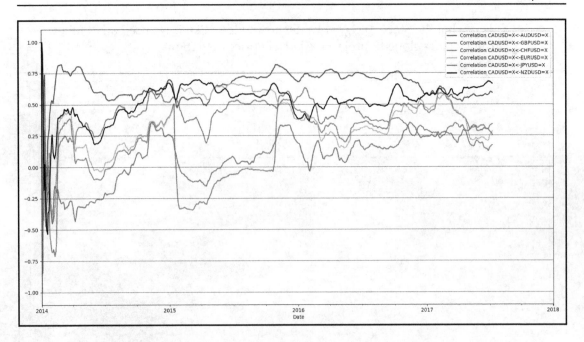

As we suspected, the currency pairs that are most strongly correlated to CAD/USD price deviations are AUD/USD and NZD/USD. JPY/USD is the least correlated to CAD/USD price deviations.

2. Now, let's inspect the delta between projected and actual price deviations in CAD/USD as projected by each individual currency pair individually:

```
# Plot StatArb signal provided by each currency pair
delta_projected_actual_data = pd.DataFrame()
for symbol in SYMBOLS:
  if symbol == TRADING_INSTRUMENT:
    continue

  projection_label = TRADING_INSTRUMENT + '<-' + symbol
  delta_projected_actual_data =
delta_projected_actual_data.assign(StatArbTradingSignal=pd.Series(d
elta_projected_actual_history[projection_label],
index=symbols_data[TRADING_INSTRUMENT].index))
  ax =
delta_projected_actual_data['StatArbTradingSignal'].plot(color=next
(cycol), lw=1., label='StatArbTradingSignal ' + projection_label)
plt.legend()
plt.show()
```

This is what the StatArb signal values would look like if we used any of the currency pairs alone to project CAD/USD price deviations:

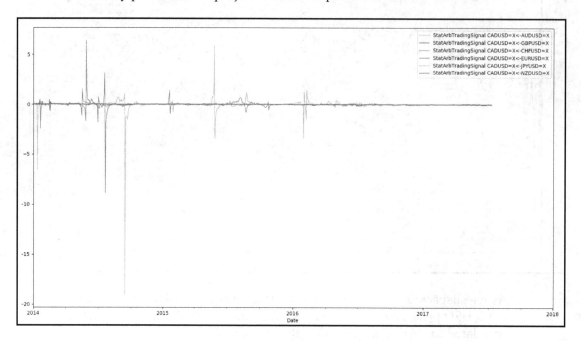

Here, the plot seems to suggest that JPYUSD and CHFUSD have very large predictions, but as we saw before those pairs do not have good correlations with CADUSD, so these are likely to be bad predictions due to poor predictive relationships between CADUSD - JPYUSD and CADUSD - CHFUSD. One lesson to take away from this is that StatArb benefits from having multiple leading trading instruments, because when relationships break down between specific pairs, the other strongly correlated pairs can help offset bad predictions, which we discussed earlier.

3. Now, let's set up our data frames to plot the close price, trades, positions, and PnLs we will observe:

```
delta_projected_actual_data =
delta_projected_actual_data.assign(ClosePrice=pd.Series(symbols_dat
a[TRADING_INSTRUMENT]['Close'],
index=symbols_data[TRADING_INSTRUMENT].index))
delta_projected_actual_data =
delta_projected_actual_data.assign(FinalStatArbTradingSignal=pd.Ser
ies(final_delta_projected_history,
index=symbols_data[TRADING_INSTRUMENT].index))
delta_projected_actual_data =
delta_projected_actual_data.assign(Trades=pd.Series(orders,
index=symbols_data[TRADING_INSTRUMENT].index))
delta_projected_actual_data =
delta_projected_actual_data.assign(Position=pd.Series(positions,
index=symbols_data[TRADING_INSTRUMENT].index))
delta_projected_actual_data =
delta_projected_actual_data.assign(Pnl=pd.Series(pnls,
index=symbols_data[TRADING_INSTRUMENT].index))

plt.plot(delta_projected_actual_data.index,
delta_projected_actual_data.ClosePrice, color='k', lw=1.,
label='ClosePrice')
plt.plot(delta_projected_actual_data.loc[delta_projected_actual_dat
a.Trades == 1].index,
delta_projected_actual_data.ClosePrice[delta_projected_actual_data.
Trades == 1], color='r', lw=0, marker='^', markersize=7,
label='buy')
plt.plot(delta_projected_actual_data.loc[delta_projected_actual_dat
a.Trades == -1].index,
delta_projected_actual_data.ClosePrice[delta_projected_actual_data.
Trades == -1], color='g', lw=0, marker='v', markersize=7,
label='sell')
plt.legend()
plt.show()
```

The following plot tells us at what prices the buy and sell trades are made in CADUSD. We will need to inspect the final trading signal in addition to this plot to fully understand the behavior of this StatArb signal and strategy:

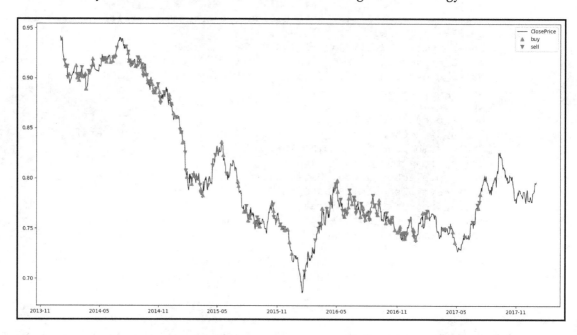

Now, let's look at the actual code to build visualization for the final StatArb trading signal, and overlay buy and sell trades over the lifetime of the signal evolution. This will help us understand for what signal values buy and sell trades are made and if that is in line with our expectations:

```
plt.plot(delta_projected_actual_data.index,
delta_projected_actual_data.FinalStatArbTradingSignal, color='k',
lw=1., label='FinalStatArbTradingSignal')
plt.plot(delta_projected_actual_data.loc[delta_projected_actual_dat
a.Trades == 1].index,
delta_projected_actual_data.FinalStatArbTradingSignal[delta_project
ed_actual_data.Trades == 1], color='r', lw=0, marker='^',
markersize=7, label='buy')
plt.plot(delta_projected_actual_data.loc[delta_projected_actual_dat
a.Trades == -1].index,
delta_projected_actual_data.FinalStatArbTradingSignal[delta_project
ed_actual_data.Trades == -1], color='g', lw=0, marker='v',
markersize=7, label='sell')
plt.axhline(y=0, lw=0.5, color='k')
for i in np.arange(StatArb_VALUE_FOR_BUY_ENTRY,
StatArb_VALUE_FOR_BUY_ENTRY * 10, StatArb_VALUE_FOR_BUY_ENTRY * 2):
```

```
    plt.axhline(y=i, lw=0.5, color='r')
for i in np.arange(StatArb_VALUE_FOR_SELL_ENTRY,
StatArb_VALUE_FOR_SELL_ENTRY * 10, StatArb_VALUE_FOR_SELL_ENTRY *
2):
    plt.axhline(y=i, lw=0.5, color='g')
plt.legend()
plt.show()
```

Since we adopted the trend-following approach in our StatArb trading strategy, we expect to buy when the signal value is positive and sell when the signal value is negative. Let's see whether that's the case in the plot:

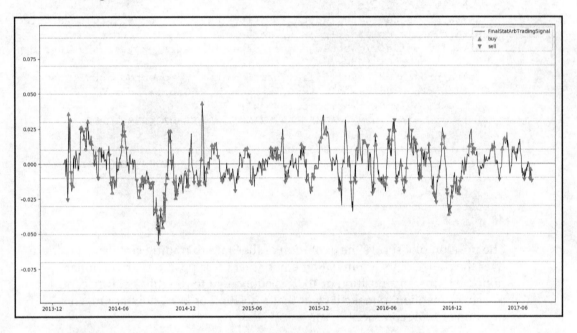

Based on this plot and our understanding of trend-following strategies in addition to the StatArb signal we built, we do indeed see many buy trades when the signal value is positive and sell trades when the signal values are negative. The buy trades made when signal values are negative and sell trades made when signal values are positive can be attributed to the trades that close profitable positions, as we saw in our previous mean reversion and trend-following trading strategies.

4. Let's wrap up our analysis of StatArb trading strategies by visualizing the positions and PnLs:

```
plt.plot(delta_projected_actual_data.index,
delta_projected_actual_data.Position, color='k', lw=1.,
label='Position')
plt.plot(delta_projected_actual_data.loc[delta_projected_actual_dat
a.Position == 0].index,
delta_projected_actual_data.Position[delta_projected_actual_data.Po
sition == 0], color='k', lw=0, marker='.', label='flat')
plt.plot(delta_projected_actual_data.loc[delta_projected_actual_dat
a.Position > 0].index,
delta_projected_actual_data.Position[delta_projected_actual_data.Po
sition > 0], color='r', lw=0, marker='+', label='long')
plt.plot(delta_projected_actual_data.loc[delta_projected_actual_dat
a.Position < 0].index,
delta_projected_actual_data.Position[delta_projected_actual_data.Po
sition < 0], color='g', lw=0, marker='_', label='short')
plt.axhline(y=0, lw=0.5, color='k')
for i in range(NUM_SHARES_PER_TRADE, NUM_SHARES_PER_TRADE * 5,
NUM_SHARES_PER_TRADE):
  plt.axhline(y=i, lw=0.5, color='r')
for i in range(-NUM_SHARES_PER_TRADE, -NUM_SHARES_PER_TRADE * 5, -
NUM_SHARES_PER_TRADE):
  plt.axhline(y=i, lw=0.5, color='g')
plt.legend()
plt.show()
```

The position plot shows the evolution of the StatArb trading strategy's position over the course of its lifetime. Remember that these positions are in dollar notional terms, so a position of 100K is equivalent to roughly 1 future contract, which we mention to make it clear that a position of 100K does not mean a position of 100K contracts!

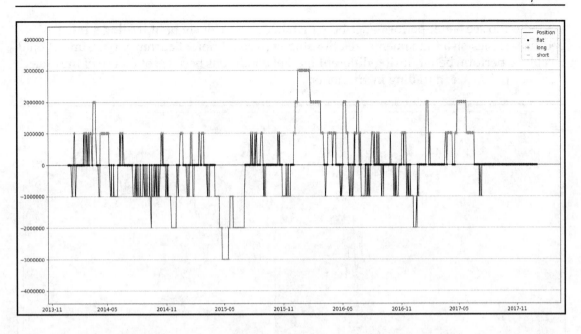

5. Finally, let's have a look at the code for the PnL plot, identical to what we've been using before:

```
plt.plot(delta_projected_actual_data.index,
delta_projected_actual_data.Pnl, color='k', lw=1., label='Pnl')
plt.plot(delta_projected_actual_data.loc[delta_projected_actual_dat
a.Pnl > 0].index,
delta_projected_actual_data.Pnl[delta_projected_actual_data.Pnl >
0], color='g', lw=0, marker='.')
plt.plot(delta_projected_actual_data.loc[delta_projected_actual_dat
a.Pnl < 0].index,
delta_projected_actual_data.Pnl[delta_projected_actual_data.Pnl <
0], color='r', lw=0, marker='.')
plt.legend()
plt.show()
```

We expect to see better performance here than in our previously built trading strategies because it relies on a fundamental relationship between different currency pairs and should be able to perform better during different market conditions because of its use of multiple currency pairs as lead trading instruments:

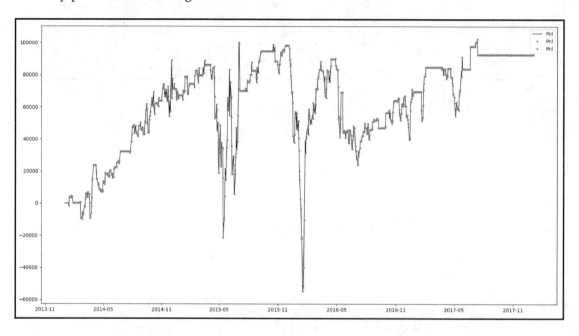

And that's it, now you have a working example of a profitable statistical arbitrage strategy and should be able to improve and extend it to other trading instruments!

Summary

This chapter made use of some of the trading signals we've seen in the previous chapters to build realistic and robust trend-following and mean reversion trading strategies. In addition, we went another step further and made those basic strategies more sophisticated by adding a volatility measure trading signal to make it more dynamic and adaptive to different market conditions. We also looked at a completely new form of trading strategy in the form of trading strategies dealing with economic releases and how to carry out the analysis for that flavor of trading strategies for our sample Non Farm Payroll data. Finally, we looked at our most sophisticated and complex trading strategy so far, which was the statistical arbitrage strategy, and applied it to CAD/USD with the major currency pairs as leading trading signals. We investigated in great detail how to quantify and parameterize the StatArb trading signal and trading strategy and visualized every step of that process and concluded that the trading strategy delivered excellent results for our data set.

In the next chapter, you will learn how to measure and manage the risk (market risk, operational risk, and software implementation bugs) of algorithmic strategies.

Summary

6

Managing the Risk of Algorithmic Strategies

So far, we have built a good understanding of how algorithmic trading works and how we can build trading signals from market data. We also looked into some basic trading strategies, as well as more sophisticated trading strategies, so it may seem like we are in a good place to start trading, right? Not quite. Another very important requirement to be successful at algorithmic trading is understanding risk management and using good risk management practices.

Bad risk management practices can turn any good algorithmic trading strategy into a non-profitable one. On the other hand, good risk management practices can turn a seemingly inferior trading strategy into an actually profitable one. In this chapter, we will examine the different kinds of risk in algorithmic trading, look at how to quantitatively measure and compare these risks, and explore how to build a good risk management system to adhere to these risk management practices.

In this chapter, we will cover the following topics:

- Differentiating between the types of risk and risk factors
- Quantifying the risk
- Differentiating between the measures of risk
- Making a risk management algorithm

Differentiating between the types of risk and risk factors

Risks in algorithmic trading strategies can basically be of two things: risks that cause money loss and risks that cause illegal/forbidden behavior in markets that cause regulatory actions. Let's take a look at the risks involved before we look at what factors lead to increasing/decreasing these risks in the business of algorithmic trading.

Risk of trading losses

This is the most obvious and intuitive one—we want to trade to make money, but we always run through the risk of losing money against other market participants. Trading is a zero-sum game: some participants will make money, while some will lose money. The amount that's lost by the losing participants is the amount that's gained by the winning participants. This simple fact is what also makes trading quite challenging. Generally, less informed participants will lose money to more informed participants. Informed is a loose term here; it can mean participants with access to information that others don't have. This can include access to secretive or expensive or even illegal information sources, the ability to transport and consume such information that other participants don't have, and so on. Information edge can also be gained by participants with a superior ability to glean information from the available information, that is, some participants will have better signals, better analytics abilities, and better predictive abilities to edge out less informed participants. Obviously, more sophisticated participants will also beat less sophisticated participants.

Sophistication can be gained from technology advantages as well, such as faster reacting trading strategies. The use of a low-level language such as C/C++ is harder to develop software in but allows us to build trading software systems that react in single-digit microseconds processing time. An extreme speed advantage is available to participants that use **Field Programmable Gate Arrays** (**FPGAs**) to achieve sub-microsecond response times to market data updates. Another avenue of gaining sophistication is by having more complex trading algorithms with more complex logic that's meant to squeeze out as much edge as possible. It should be clear that algorithmic trading is an extremely complex and competitive business and that all the participants are doing their best to squeeze out every bit of profit possible by being more *informed* and *sophisticated*.

https://news.efinancialcareers.com/us-en/291459/xr-trading-2016 discusses an example of trading losses due to decreased profitability, which occurs due to competition among market participants.

Regulation violation risks

The other risk that isn't everyone's first thought has to do with making sure that algorithmic trading strategies are not violating any regulatory rules. Failing to do so often results in astronomical fines, massive legal fees, and can often get participants banned from trading from certain or all exchanges. Since setting up successful algorithmic trading businesses are multi-year, multi-million dollar ventures, getting shut down due to regulatory reasons can be crushing. The SEC (`https://www.sec.gov/`), FINRA (`https://www.finra.org/`), and CFTC (`https://www.cftc.gov/`) are just some of many regulatory governing bodies watching over algorithmic trading activity in equity, currency, futures, and options markets.

These regulatory firms enforce global and local regulations. In addition, the electronic trading exchanges themselves impose regulations and laws, the violation of which can also incur severe penalties. There are many market participants or algorithmic trading strategy behaviors that are forbidden. Some incur a warning or an audit and some incur penalties. Insider trading reports are quite well known by people inside and outside of the algorithmic trading business. While insider trading doesn't really apply to algorithmic trading or high-frequency trading, we will introduce some of the common issues in algorithmic trading here.

This list is nowhere near complete, but these are the top regulatory issues in algorithmic trading or high-frequency trading.

Spoofing

Spoofing typically refers to the practice of entering orders into the market that are not considered bonafide. A **bonafide** order is one that is entered with the intent of trading. Spoofing orders are entered into the market with the intent of misleading other market participants, and these orders were never entered with the intent of being executed. The purpose of these orders is to make other participants believe that there are more real market participants who are willing to buy or sell than there actually are. By spoofing on the bid side, market participants are misled into thinking there is a lot of interest in buying. This usually leads to other market participants adding more orders to the bid side and moving or removing orders on the ask side with the expectation that prices will go up.

When prices go up, the spoofer then sells at a higher price than would've been possible without the spoofing orders. At this point, the spoofer initiates a short position and cancels all the spoofing bid orders, causing other market participants to do the same. This drive prices back down from these synthetically raised higher prices. When prices have dropped sufficiently, the spoofer then buys at lower prices to cover the short position and lock in a profit.

Spoofing algorithms can repeat this over and over in markets that are mostly algorithmically trading and make a lot of money. This, however, is illegal in most markets because it causes market price instability, provides participants with misleading information about available market liquidity, and adversely affects non-algorithmic trading investors/strategies. In summary, if such behavior was not made illegal, it would cause cascading instability and make most market participants exit providing liquidity. Spoofing is treated as a serious violation in most electronic exchanges, and exchanges have sophisticated algorithms/monitoring systems to detect such behavior and flag market participants who are spoofing.

The first case of spoofing got a lot of publicity, and those of you who are interested can learn more at `https://www.justice.gov/usao-ndil/pr/high-frequency-trader-sentenced-three-years-prison-disrupting-futures-market-first`.

Quote stuffing

Quote stuffing is a manipulation tactic that was employed by high-frequency trading participants. Nowadays, most exchanges have many rules that make quote stuffing infeasible as a profitable trading strategy. Quote stuffing is the practice of using very fast trading algorithms and hardware to enter, modify, and cancel large amounts of orders in one or more trading instruments. Since each order action by a market participant causes the generation of public market data, it is possible for very fast participants to generate a massive amount of market data and massively slow down slower participants who can no longer react in time, thereby causing profits for high-frequency trading algorithms.

This is not as feasible in modern electronic trading markets, mainly because exchanges have put in rules on messaging limits on individual market participants. Exchanges have the ability to analyze and flag short-lived non-bonafide order flow, and modern matching engines are able to better synchronize market data feeds with order flow feeds.

`https://www.businessinsider.com/huge-first-high-frequency-trading-firm-is-charged-with-quote-stuffing-and-manipulation-2010-9` discusses a recent quote stuffing market manipulation incident that caused regulatory actions.

Banging the close

Banging the close is a disruptive and manipulative trading practice that still happens periodically in electronic trading markets, either intentionally or accidentally, by trading algorithms. This practice has to do with illegally manipulating the closing price of a derivative, also known as the settlement price. Since positions in derivatives markets such as futures are marked at the settlement price at the end of the day, this tactic uses large orders during the final few minutes or seconds of closing where many market participants are out of the market already to drive less liquid market prices in an illegal and disruptive way.

This is, in some sense, similar to spoofing, but in this case, often, the participants banging the close may not pick up new executions during the closing period, but may simply try to move market prices to make their already existing positions more profitable. For cash-settled derivatives contracts, the more favorable settlement price leads to more profit. This is why trading closes are also monitored quite closely by electronic trading derivative exchanges to detect and flag this disruptive practice.

`https://www.cftc.gov/PressRoom/PressReleases/pr5815-10` discusses an incident of banging the close for those who are interested.

Sources of risk

Now that we have a good understanding of the different kinds of risk in algorithmic trading, let's look at the factors in algorithmic trading strategy development, optimization, maintenance, and operation that causes them.

Software implementation risk

A modern algorithmic trading business is essentially a technology business, hence giving birth to the new term **FinTech** to mean the intersection of finance and technology. Computer software is designed, developed, and tested by humans who are error-prone and sometimes, these errors creep into trading systems and algorithmic trading strategies. Software implementation bugs are often the most overlooked source of risk in algorithmic trading. While operation risk and market risk are extremely important, software implementation bugs have the potential to cause millions of dollars in losses, and there have been many cases of firms going bankrupt due to software implementation bugs within minutes.

In recent times, there was the infamous Knight Capital incident, where a software implementation bug combined with an operations risk issue caused them to lose $440 million within 45 minutes and they ended up getting shut down. Software implementation bugs are also very tricky because software engineering is a very complex process, and when we add the additional complexity of having sophisticated and complex algorithmic trading strategies and logic, it is hard to guarantee that the implementation of trading strategies and systems are safe from bugs. More information can be found at `https://dealbook.nytimes.com/2012/08/02/knight-capital-says-trading-mishap-cost-it-440-million/`.

Modern algorithmic trading firms have rigorous software development practices to safeguard themselves against software bugs. These include rigorous unit tests, which are small tests on individual software components to verify their behavior doesn't change to an incorrect behavior as software development/maintenance being made to existing components is performed. There are also regression tests, which are tests that test larger components that are composed of smaller components as a whole to ensure the higher-level behavior remains consistent. All electronic trading exchanges also provide a test market environment with test market data feeds and test order entry interfaces where market participants have to build, test, and certify their components with the exchange before they are even allowed to trade in live markets.

Most sophisticated algorithmic trading participants also have backtesting software that simulates a trading strategy over historically recorded data to ensure strategy behavior is in line with expectations. We will explore backtesting further in `Chapter 9`, *Creating a Backtester in Python*. Finally, other software management practices, such as code reviews and change management, are also performed on a daily basis to verify the integrity of algorithmic trading systems and strategies on a daily basis. Despite all of these precautions, software implementation bugs do slip into live trading markets, so we should always be aware and cautious because software is never perfect and the cost of mistakes/bugs is very high in the algorithmic trading business, and even higher in the HFT business.

DevOps risk

DevOps risk is the term that is used to describe the risk potential when algorithmic trading strategies are deployed to live markets. This involves building and deploying correct trading strategies and configuring the configuration, the signal parameters, the trading parameters, and starting, stopping, and monitoring them. Most modern trading firms trade markets electronically almost 23 hours a day, and they have a large number of staff whose only job is to keep an eye on the automated algorithmic trading strategies that are deployed to live markets to ensure they are behaving as expected and no erroneous behavior goes uninvestigated. They are known as the Trading Desk, or TradeOps or DevOps.

These people have a decent understanding of software development, trading rules, and exchange for provided risk monitoring interfaces. Often, when software implementation bugs end up going to live markets, they are the final line of defense, and it is their job to monitor the systems, detect issues, safely pause or stop the algorithms, and contact and resolve the issues that have emerged. This is the most common understanding of where operation risk can show up. Another source of operation risk is in algorithmic trading strategies that are not 100% black box. Black box trading strategies are trading strategies that do not require any human feedback or interaction. These are started at a certain time and then stopped at a certain time, and the algorithms themselves make all the decisions.

Gray box trading strategies are trading strategies that are not 100% autonomous. These strategies still have a lot of automated decision-making built into them, but they also have external controls that allow the traders or TradeOps engineers to monitor the strategies, as well as adjust parameters and trading strategy behavior, and even send manual orders. Now, during these manual human interventions, there is another source of risk, which is basically the risk of humans making mistakes in the commands/adjustments that are sent to these strategies. Sending incorrect parameters can cause the algorithm to behave incorrectly and cause losses.

There are also cases of sending bad commands, which can cause an unexpected and unintentional large impact on the market, causing trading losses and market disruptions that add regulatory fines. One of the common errors is the fat finger error, where prices, sizes, and buy/sell instructions are sent incorrectly due to a *fat finger*. Some examples can be found at https://www.bloomberg.com/news/articles/2019-01-24/oops-a-brief-history-of-some-of-the-market-s-worst-fat-fingers.

Market risk

Finally, we have market risk, which is what is commonly thought of when we think of risk in algorithmic trading. This is the risk of trading against and losing money to more informed participants. Every market participant, at some point or the other, on some trade or the other, will lose money to a more informed participant. We discussed what makes an informed participant superior to a non-informed one in the previous section. Obviously, the only way to avoid market risk is to get access to more information, improve the trading edge, improve sophistication, and improve technology advantages. But since market risk is a truth of all algorithmic trading strategies, a very important aspect is to understand the behavior of the algorithmic trading strategy before deploying it to live markets.

This involves understanding what to expect normal behavior to look like and, more importantly, understanding when a certain strategy makes and loses money and quantifying loss metrics to set up expectations. Then, risk limits are set up at multiple places in an algorithmic trading pipeline in the trading strategy, then in a central risk monitoring system, then in the order gateway, sometimes at the clearing firm, and finally sometimes even at the exchange level. Each extra layer of risk check can slow down a market participant's ability to react to fast-moving markets, but it is essential to have these to prevent runaway trading algorithms from causing a lot of damage.

Once the trading strategy has violated maximum trading risk limits assigned to it, it will be shut down at one or more places where the risk validation is set up. Market risk is very important to understand, implement, and configure correctly because incorrect risk estimates can kill a profitable trading strategy by increasing the frequency and magnitude of losing trades, losing positions, losing days, and even losing weeks or months. This is because the trading strategy could have lost its profitable edge and if you leave it running for too long without adapting it to changing markets, it can erode all the profits the strategy may have generated in the past. Sometimes, market conditions are very different than what is expected and strategies can go through periods of larger than normal losses, in which cases it is important to have risk limits set up to detect outsized losses and adjust trading parameters or stop trading.

We will look at what risk measures are common in algorithmic trading, how to quantify and research them from historical data, and how to configure and calibrate algorithmic strategies before deploying them to live markets. For now, the summary is that market risk is a normal part of algorithmic trading, but failing to understand and prepare for it can destroy a lot of good trading strategies.

Quantifying the risk

Now, let's get started with understanding what realistic risk constraints look like and how to quantify them. We will list, define, and implement some of the most commonly used risk limits in the modern algorithmic trading industry today. We will use the volatility adjusted mean reversion strategy we built in Chapter 5, *Sophisticated Algorithmic Strategies*, as our realistic trading strategy, which we now need to define and quantify risk measures for.

The severity of risk violations

One thing to understand before diving into all the different risk measures is defining what the severity of a risk violation means. So far, we've been discussing risk violations as being maximum risk limit violations. But in practice, there are multiple levels of every risk limit, and each level of risk limit violation is not equally as catastrophic to algorithmic trading strategies. The lowest severity risk violation would be considered a warning risk violation, which means that this risk violation, while not expected to happen regularly, can happen normally during a trading strategy operation. Intuitively, it is easy to think of this as, say, on most days, trading strategies do not send more than 5,000 orders a day, but on certain volatile days, it is possible and acceptable that the trading strategy sends 20,000 orders on that day. This would be considered an example of a warning risk violation – this is unlikely, but not a sign of trouble. The purpose of this risk violation is to warn the trader that something unlikely is happening in the market or trading strategy.

The next level of risk violation is what would be considered as something where the strategy is still functioning correctly but has reached the limits of what it is allowed to do, and must safely liquidate and shut down. Here, the strategy is allowed to send orders and make trades that flatten the position and cancel new entry orders, if there are any. Basically, the strategy is done trading but is allowed to automatically handle the violation and finish trading until a trader checks on what happens and decides to either restart and allocate higher risk limits to the trading strategy.

The final level of risk violation is what would be considered a maximum possible risk violation, which is a violation that should never, ever happen. If a trading strategy ever triggers this risk violation, it is a sign that something went very wrong. This risk violation means that the strategy is no longer allowed to send any more order flow to the live markets. This risk violation would only be triggered during periods of extremely unexpected events, such as a flash crash market condition. This severity of risk violation basically means that the algorithmic trading strategy is not designed to deal with such an event automatically and must freeze trading and then resort to external operators to manage open positions and live orders.

Differentiating the measures of risk

Let's explore different measures of risk. We will use the trading performance from the volatility adjusted mean reversion strategy we saw in Chapter 5, *Sophisticated Algorithmic Strategies*, as an example of a trading strategy in which we wish to understand the risks behind and quantify and calibrate them.

In Chapter 5, *Sophisticated Algorithmic Trading Strategies*, we built the Mean Reversion, Volatility Adjusted Mean Reversion, Trend Following, and Volatility Adjusted Trend Following strategies. During the analysis of their performance, we wrote the results into the corresponding CSV files. These can also be found in this book's GitHub repository, https:/ /github.com/PacktPublishing/Learn-Algorithmic-Trading---Fundamentals-of-Algorithmic-Trading, or by running the volatility adjusted mean reversion strategy (volatility_mean_reversion.py) in Chapter 5, *Sophisticated Algorithmic Strategies*, in the *Mean Reversion Strategy that dynamically adjusts for changing volatility* section. Let's load up the trading performance .csv file, as shown in the following code block, and quickly look at what fields we have available:

```
import pandas as pd
import matplotlib.pyplot as plt

results = pd.read_csv('volatility_adjusted_mean_reversion.csv')
print(results.head(1))
```

The code will return the following output:

```
      Date       Open High       Low Close Adj Close  \
0  2014-01-02  555.647278 556.788025   552.06073 554.481689 554.481689
     Volume  ClosePrice  Fast10DayEMA  Slow40DayEMA APO  Trades Position PnL
0  3656400  554.481689   554.481689 554.481689  0.0 0 0 0.0
```

For the purposes of implementing and quantifying risk measures, the fields we are interested in are Date, High, Low, ClosePrice, Trades, Position, and PnL. We will ignore the other fields since we do not require them for the risk measures we are currently interested in. Now, let's dive into understanding and implementing our risk measures.

Stop-loss

The first risk limit we will look at is quite intuitive and is called **stop-loss**, or **max-loss**. This limit is the maximum amount of money a strategy is allowed to lose, that is, the minimum PnL allowed. This often has a notion of a time frame for that loss, meaning stop-loss can be for a day, for a week, for a month, or for the entire lifetime of the strategy. A stop-loss with a time frame of a day means that if the strategy loses a stop-loss amount of money in a single day, it is not allowed to trade any more on that day, but can resume the next day. Similarly, for a stop-loss amount in a week, it is not allowed to trade anymore for that week, but can resume next week.

Now, let's compute stop-loss levels on a week and month for the volatility adjusted mean reversion strategy, as shown in the following code:

```python
num_days = len(results.index)

pnl = results['PnL']

weekly_losses = []
monthly_losses = []

for i in range(0, num_days):
  if i >= 5 and pnl[i - 5] > pnl[i]:
    weekly_losses.append(pnl[i] - pnl[i - 5])

  if i >= 20 and pnl[i - 20] > pnl[i]:
    monthly_losses.append(pnl[i] - pnl[i - 20])

plt.hist(weekly_losses, 50)
plt.gca().set(title='Weekly Loss Distribution', xlabel='$',
ylabel='Frequency')
plt.show()

plt.hist(monthly_losses, 50)
plt.gca().set(title='Monthly Loss Distribution', xlabel='$',
ylabel='Frequency')
plt.show()
```

The code will return the following plots as output. Let's have a look at the weekly loss distribution plot shown here:

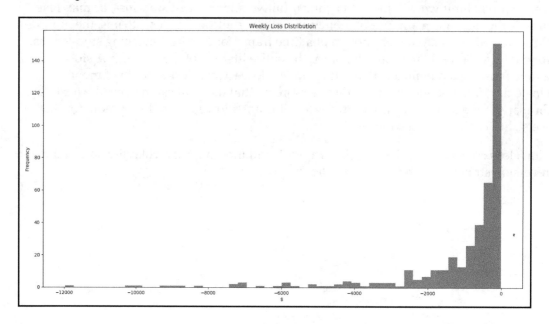

Now, let's take a look at the monthly loss distribution plot shown here:

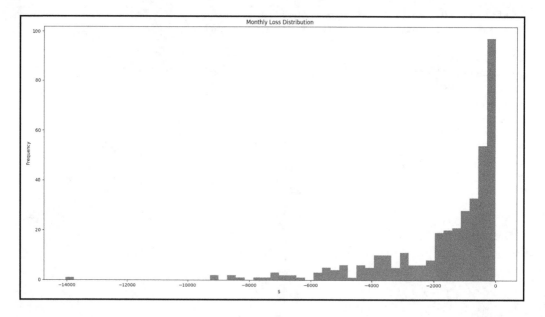

The plots show the distribution of weekly and monthly losses. From these, we can observe the following:

- A weekly loss of anything more than $4K and a monthly loss of anything more than $6K is highly unexpected.
- A weekly loss of more than $12K and a monthly loss of $14K have never happened, so it can be considered an unprecedented event, but we will revisit this later.

Max drawdown

Max drawdown is also a PnL metric, but this measures the maximum loss that a strategy can take over a series of days. This is defined as the peak to trough decline in a trading strategy's account value. This is important as a risk measure so that we can get an idea of what the historical maximum decline in the account value can be. This is important because we can get unlucky during the deployment of a trading strategy and run it in live markets right at the beginning of the drawdown.

Having an expectation of what the maximum drawdown is can help us understand whether the strategy loss streak is still within our expectations or whether something unprecedented is happening. Let's look at how to compute it:

```
max_pnl = 0
max_drawdown = 0
drawdown_max_pnl = 0
drawdown_min_pnl = 0

for i in range(0, num_days):
  max_pnl = max(max_pnl, pnl[i])
  drawdown = max_pnl - pnl[i]

  if drawdown > max_drawdown:
    max_drawdown = drawdown
    drawdown_max_pnl = max_pnl
    drawdown_min_pnl = pnl[i]

print('Max Drawdown:', max_drawdown)

results['PnL'].plot(x='Date', legend=True)
plt.axhline(y=drawdown_max_pnl, color='g')
plt.axhline(y=drawdown_min_pnl, color='r')
plt.show()
```

The code will return the following output:

```
Max Drawdown: 15340.41716347829
```

The plots that follow are a result of the preceding code. Let's have a look:

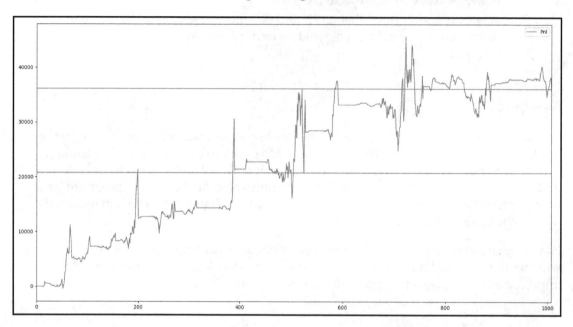

In the plot, the max drawdown occurs roughly during the middle of this PnL series, with the maximum PnL being 37K and the minimum PnL after that high being 22K, causing the maximum drawdown achieved to be roughly 15K:

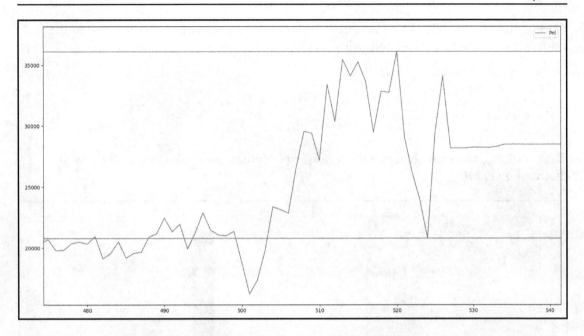

The plot is simply the same plot as before but zoomed in to the exact observations where the drawdown occurs. As we mentioned previously, after achieving a high of roughly 37K, PnLs have a large drawdown of 15K and drop down to roughly 22K, before rebounding.

Position limits

Position limits are also quite straightforward and intuitive to understand. It is simply the maximum position, long or short, that the strategy should have at any point in its trading lifetime. It is possible to have two different position limits, one for the maximum long position and another for the maximum short position, which can be useful, for instance, where shorting stocks have different rules/risks associated with them than being long on stocks does. Every unit of open position has a risk associated with it. Generally, the larger the position a strategy puts on, the larger the risk associated with it. So, the best strategies are the ones that can make money while getting into as small a position as possible. In either case, before a strategy is deployed to production, it is important to quantify and estimate what the maximum positions the strategy can get into, based on historical performance, so that we can find out when a strategy is within its normal behavior parameters and when it is outside of historical norms.

Finding the maximum position is straightforward. Let's find a quick distribution of the positions with the help of the following code:

```
position = results['Position']
plt.hist(position, 20)
plt.gca().set(title='Position Distribution', xlabel='Shares',
ylabel='Frequency')
plt.show()
```

The preceding code will generate the following output. Let's have a look at the position distribution chart:

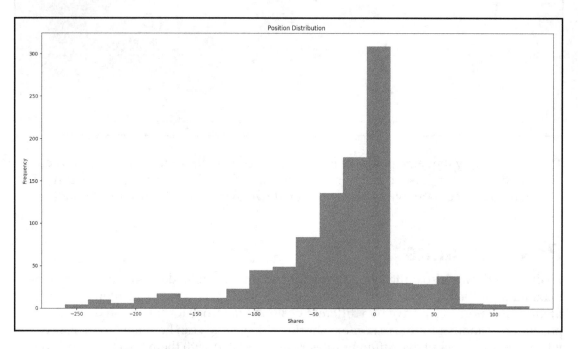

We can see the following from the preceding chart:

- For this trading strategy, which has been applied to Google stock data, the strategy is unlikely to have a position exceeding 200 shares and has never had a position exceeding 250.
- If it gets into position levels exceeding 250, we should be careful that the trading strategy is still performing as expected.

Position holding time

While analyzing positions that a trading strategy gets into, it is also important to measure how long a position stays open until it is closed and returned to its flat position or opposition position. The longer a position stays open, the more risk it is taking on, because the more time there is for markets to make massive moves that can potentially go against the open position. A long position is initiated when the position goes from being short or flat to being long and is closed when the position goes back to flat or short. Similarly, short positions are initiated when the position goes from being long or flat to being short and is closed when the position goes back to flat or long.

Now, let's find the distribution of open position durations with the help of the following code:

```
position_holding_times = []
current_pos = 0
current_pos_start = 0
for i in range(0, num_days):
  pos = results['Position'].iloc[i]

  # flat and starting a new position
  if current_pos == 0:
    if pos != 0:
      current_pos = pos
      current_pos_start = i
    continue

  # going from long position to flat or short position or
  # going from short position to flat or long position
  if current_pos * pos <= 0:
    current_pos = pos
    position_holding_times.append(i - current_pos_start)
    current_pos_start = i

print(position_holding_times)
plt.hist(position_holding_times, 100)
plt.gca().set(title='Position Holding Time Distribution', xlabel='Holding
time days', ylabel='Frequency')
plt.show()
```

The preceding code will return the following output. Let's have a look at the position holding time distribution plot:

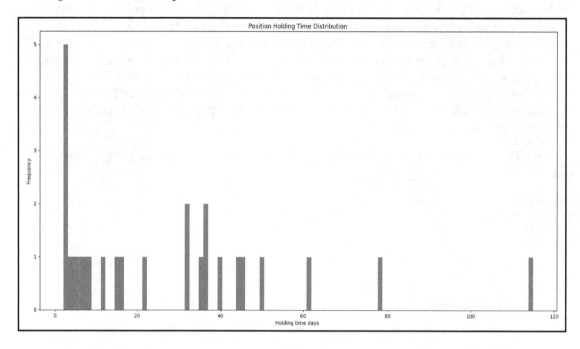

So, for this strategy, we can see that the holding time is pretty distributed, with the longest one lasting around 115 days and the shortest one lasting around 3 days.

Variance of PnLs

We need to measure how much the PnLs can vary from day to day or even week to week. This is an important measure of risk because if a trading strategy has large swings in PnLs, the account value is very volatile and it is hard to run a trading strategy with such a profile. Often, we compute the Standard Deviation of returns over different days or weeks or whatever timeframe we choose to use as our investment time horizon. Most optimization methods try to find optimal trading performance as a balance between PnLs and the Standard Deviation of returns.

Computing the standard deviation of returns is easy. Let's compute the standard deviation of weekly returns, as shown in the following code:

```
last_week = 0
weekly_pnls = []
```

```
for i in range(0, num_days):
  if i - last_week >= 5:
    weekly_pnls.append(pnl[i] - pnl[last_week])
    last_week = i

from statistics import stdev
print('Weekly PnL Standard Deviation:', stdev(weekly_pnls))

plt.hist(weekly_pnls, 50)
plt.gca().set(title='Weekly PnL Distribution', xlabel='$',
ylabel='Frequency')
plt.show()
```

The preceding code will return the following output:

```
Weekly PnL Standard Deviation: 1995.1834727008127
```

The following plot shows the weekly PnL distribution that was created from the preceding code:

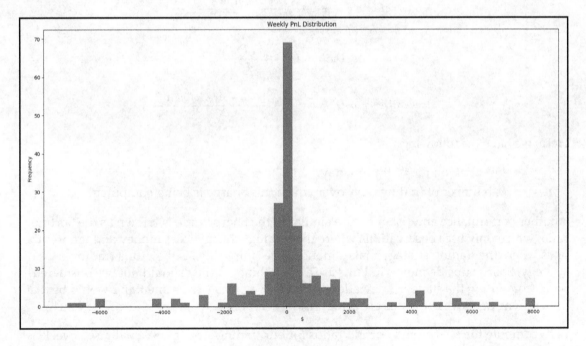

We can see that the weekly PnLs are close to being normally distributed around a mean of $0, which intuitively makes sense. The distribution is right skewed, which yields the positive cumulative PnLs for this trading strategy. There are some very large profits and losses for some weeks, but they are very rare, which is also within the expectations of what the distribution should look like.

Sharpe ratio

Sharpe ratio is a very commonly used performance and risk metric that's used in the industry to measure and compare the performance of algorithmic trading strategies. Sharpe ratio is defined as the ratio of average PnL over a period of time and the PnL standard deviation over the same period. The benefit of the Sharpe ratio is that it captures the profitability of a trading strategy while also accounting for the risk by using the volatility of the returns. Let's have a look at the mathematical representation:

$$SharpeRatio = \frac{AvgDailyPnl}{StandardDeviationOfDailyPnls}$$

$$AvgDailyPnl = \frac{\sum_{i=1}^{N} Pnl_i}{N}$$

$$StandardDeviationOfPnls = \frac{\sum_{i=1}^{N} (Pnl_i - AvgDailyPnl)^2}{N}$$

Here, we have the following:

- Pnl_i: PnL on the ith trading day.
- N: Number of trading days over which this Sharpe is being computed.

Another performance and risk measure similar to the Sharpe ratio is known as the Sortino ratio, which only uses observations where the trading strategy loses money and ignores the ones where the trading strategy makes money. The simple idea is that, for a trading strategy, Sharpe upside moves in PnLs are a good thing, so they should not be considered when computing the standard deviation. Another way to say the same thing would be that only downside moves or losses are actual risk observations.

Let's compute the Sharpe and Sortino ratios for our trading strategy. We will use a week as the time horizon for our trading strategy:

```
last_week = 0
weekly_pnls = []
weekly_losses = []
```

```
for i in range(0, num_days):
  if i - last_week >= 5:
    pnl_change = pnl[i] - pnl[last_week]
    weekly_pnls.append(pnl_change)
    if pnl_change < 0:
      weekly_losses.append(pnl_change)
    last_week = i

from statistics import stdev, mean

sharpe_ratio = mean(weekly_pnls) / stdev(weekly_pnls)
sortino_ratio = mean(weekly_pnls) / stdev(weekly_losses)

print('Sharpe ratio:', sharpe_ratio)
print('Sortino ratio:', sortino_ratio)
```

The preceding code will return the following output:

```
Sharpe ratio: 0.09494748065583607
Sortino ratio: 0.11925614548156238
```

Here, we can see that the Sharpe ratio and the Sortino ratio are close to each other, which is what we expect since both are risk-adjusted return metrics. The Sortino ratio is slightly higher than the Sharpe ratio, which also makes sense since, by definition, the Sortino ratio does not consider large increases in PnLs as being contributions to the drawdown/risk for the trading strategy, indicating that the Sharpe ratio was, in fact, penalizing some large +ve jumps in PnLs.

Maximum executions per period

This risk measure is an interval-based risk check. An interval-based risk is a counter that resets after a fixed amount of time and the risk check is imposed within such a time slice. So, while there is no final limit, it's important that the limit isn't exceeded within the time interval that is meant to detect and avoid over-trading. The interval-based risk measure we will inspect is maximum executions per period. This measures the maximum number of trades allowed in a given timeframe. Then, at the end of the timeframe, the counter is reset and starts over. This would detect and prevent a runaway strategy that buys and sells at a very fast pace.

Let's look at the distribution of executions per period for our strategy using a week as our timeframe, as shown here:

```
executions_this_week = 0
executions_per_week = []
```

```
last_week = 0
for i in range(0, num_days):
  if results['Trades'].iloc[i] != 0:
    executions_this_week += 1

  if i - last_week >= 5:
    executions_per_week.append(executions_this_week)
    executions_this_week = 0
    last_week = i

plt.hist(executions_per_week, 10)
plt.gca().set(title='Weekly number of executions Distribution',
xlabel='Number of executions', ylabel='Frequency')
plt.show()
```

The code will return the following output. Let's have a look at the plot:

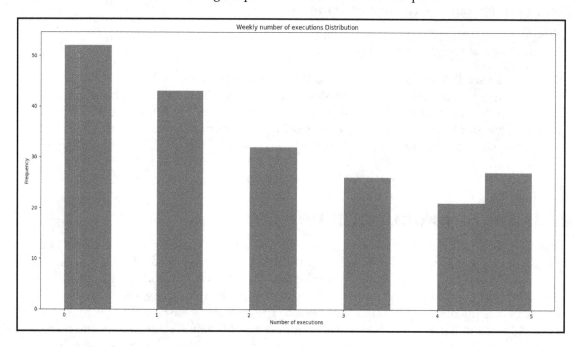

As we can see, for this trading strategy, it's never traded more than five times a week in the past, which is when it trades every day of the week, which doesn't help us much. Now, let's look at the maximum executions per month:

```
executions_this_month = 0
executions_per_month = []
last_month = 0
for i in range(0, num_days):
```

```
    if results['Trades'].iloc[i] != 0:
      executions_this_month += 1

    if i - last_month >= 20:
      executions_per_month.append(executions_this_month)
      executions_this_month = 0
      last_month = i

  plt.hist(executions_per_month, 20)
  plt.gca().set(title='Monthly number of executions Distribution',
  xlabel='Number of executions', ylabel='Frequency')
  plt.show()
```

The preceding code will return the following output. Let's have a look at the plot:

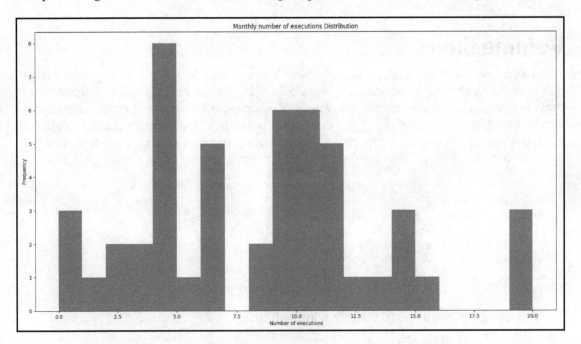

We can observe the following from the preceding plot:

- It is possible for the strategy to trade every day in a month, so this risk measure can't really be used for this strategy.
- However, this is still an important risk measure to understand and calibrate, especially for algorithmic trading strategies that trade frequently, and especially for HFT strategies.

Maximum trade size

This risk metric measures what the maximum possible trade size for a single trade for the trading strategy is. In our previous examples, we use static trade sizes, but it is not very difficult to build a trading strategy that sends a larger order when the trading signal is stronger and a smaller order when the trading signal is weaker. Alternatively, a strategy can choose to liquidate a larger than normal position in one trade if it's profitable, in which case it will send out a pretty large order. This risk measure is also very helpful when the trading strategy is a gray box trading strategy as it prevents fat-finger errors, among other things. We will skip implementing this risk measure here, but all we do is find a distribution of per trade size, which should be straightforward to implement based on our implementation of previous risk measures.

Volume limits

This risk metric measures the traded volume, which can also have an interval-based variant that measures volume per period. This is another risk measure that is meant to detect and prevent overtrading. For example, some of the catastrophic software implementation bugs we discussed in this chapter could've been prevented if they had a tight volume limit in place that warned operators about risk violations and possibly a volume limit that shut down trading strategies. Let's observe the traded volume for our strategy, which is shown in the following code:

```
traded_volume = 0
for i in range(0, num_days):
  if results['Trades'].iloc[i] != 0:
    traded_volume += abs(results['Position'].iloc[i] -
results['Position'].iloc[i-1])

print('Total traded volume:', traded_volume)
```

The preceding code will return the following output:

```
Total traded volume: 4050
```

In this case, the strategy behavior is as expected, that is, no overtrading is detected. We can use this to calibrate what total traded volume to expect from this strategy when it is deployed to live markets. If it ever trades significantly more than what is expected, we can detect that to be an over-trading condition.

Making a risk management algorithm

By now, we're aware of the different types of risks and factors, including the risks in a trading strategy and the most common risk metrics for algorithmic trading strategies. Now, let's have a look at incorporating these risk measures into our volatility adjusted mean reversion trading strategy to make it safer before deploying it into live markets. We will set the risk limits to 150% of the maximum achieved historically. We are doing this because it is possible that there is a day in the future that is very different from what we've seen historically. Let's get started:

1. Let's define our risk limits, which we are not allowed to breach. As we discussed previously, it will be set to 150% of the historically observed maximums:

```
# Risk limits
RISK_LIMIT_WEEKLY_STOP_LOSS = -12000 * 1.5
RISK_LIMIT_MONTHLY_STOP_LOSS = -14000 * 1.5
RISK_LIMIT_MAX_POSITION = 250 * 1.5
RISK_LIMIT_MAX_POSITION_HOLDING_TIME_DAYS = 120 * 1.5
RISK_LIMIT_MAX_TRADE_SIZE = 10 * 1.5
RISK_LIMIT_MAX_TRADED_VOLUME = 4000 * 1.5
```

2. We will maintain some variables to track and check for risk violations with the help of the following code:

```
risk_violated = False

traded_volume = 0
current_pos = 0
current_pos_start = 0
```

3. As we can see, we have some code for computing the Simple Moving Average and Standard Deviation for volatility adjustments. We will compute the fast and slow EMAs and the APO value, which we can use as our mean reversion trading signal:

```
close = data['Close']
for close_price in close:
  price_history.append(close_price)
  if len(price_history) > SMA_NUM_PERIODS: # we track at most
'time_period' number of prices
    del (price_history[0])

  sma = stats.mean(price_history)
  variance = 0 # variance is square of standard deviation
  for hist_price in price_history:
    variance = variance + ((hist_price - sma) ** 2)
```

```
    stdev = math.sqrt(variance / len(price_history))
    stdev_factor = stdev / 15
    if stdev_factor == 0:
      stdev_factor = 1

    # This section updates fast and slow EMA and computes APO trading
  signal
    if (ema_fast == 0): # first observation
      ema_fast = close_price
      ema_slow = close_price
    else:
      ema_fast = (close_price - ema_fast) * K_FAST * stdev_factor +
  ema_fast
      ema_slow = (close_price - ema_slow) * K_SLOW * stdev_factor +
  ema_slow

    ema_fast_values.append(ema_fast)
    ema_slow_values.append(ema_slow)

    apo = ema_fast - ema_slow
    apo_values.append(apo)
```

4. Now, before we can evaluate our signal and check whether we can send an order
   out, we need to perform a risk check to ensure that the trade size we may attempt
   is within `MAX_TRADE_SIZE` limits:

```
    if NUM_SHARES_PER_TRADE > RISK_LIMIT_MAX_TRADE_SIZE:
      print('RiskViolation NUM_SHARES_PER_TRADE',
  NUM_SHARES_PER_TRADE, ' > RISK_LIMIT_MAX_TRADE_SIZE',
  RISK_LIMIT_MAX_TRADE_SIZE )
      risk_violated = True
```

5. Now, the next section checks the trading signal to see if we should send orders as
   usual. However, with an additional check, that would prevent the orders from
   going out if risk limits have been violated. Let's look at the changes that we need
   to make to the sell trades:

```
    # We will perform a sell trade at close_price if the following
  conditions are met:
    # 1. The APO trading signal value is above Sell-Entry threshold
  and the difference between last trade-price and current-price is
  different enough.
    # 2. We are long( +ve position ) and either APO trading signal
  value is at or above 0 or current position is profitable enough to
  lock profit.
    if (not risk_violated and
        ((apo > APO_VALUE_FOR_SELL_ENTRY * stdev_factor and
```

```
abs(close_price - last_sell_price) > MIN_PRICE_MOVE_FROM_LAST_TRADE
* stdev_factor) # APO above sell entry threshold, we should sell
      or
      (position > 0 and (apo >= 0 or open_pnl >
MIN_PROFIT_TO_CLOSE / stdev_factor)))): # long from -ve APO and APO
has gone positive or position is profitable, sell to close position
    orders.append(-1) # mark the sell trade
    last_sell_price = close_price
    position -= NUM_SHARES_PER_TRADE # reduce position by the size
of this trade
    sell_sum_price_qty += (close_price * NUM_SHARES_PER_TRADE) #
update vwap sell-price
    sell_sum_qty += NUM_SHARES_PER_TRADE
    traded_volume += NUM_SHARES_PER_TRADE
    print("Sell ", NUM_SHARES_PER_TRADE, " @ ", close_price,
"Position: ", position)
```

Similarly, let's look at the buy trade logic:

```
# We will perform a buy trade at close_price if the following
conditions are met:
# 1. The APO trading signal value is below Buy-Entry threshold
and the difference between last trade-price and current-price is
different enough.
# 2. We are short( -ve position ) and either APO trading signal
value is at or below 0 or current position is profitable enough to
lock profit.
  elif (not risk_violated and
        ((apo < APO_VALUE_FOR_BUY_ENTRY * stdev_factor and
abs(close_price - last_buy_price) > MIN_PRICE_MOVE_FROM_LAST_TRADE
* stdev_factor) # APO below buy entry threshold, we should buy
        or
        (position < 0 and (apo <= 0 or open_pnl >
MIN_PROFIT_TO_CLOSE / stdev_factor)))): # short from +ve APO and
APO has gone negative or position is profitable, buy to close
position
    orders.append(+1) # mark the buy trade
    last_buy_price = close_price
    position += NUM_SHARES_PER_TRADE # increase position by the
size of this trade
    buy_sum_price_qty += (close_price * NUM_SHARES_PER_TRADE) #
update the vwap buy-price
    buy_sum_qty += NUM_SHARES_PER_TRADE
    traded_volume += NUM_SHARES_PER_TRADE
    print("Buy ", NUM_SHARES_PER_TRADE, " @ ", close_price,
"Position: ", position)
  else:
    # No trade since none of the conditions were met to buy or sell
```

```
orders.append(0)

positions.append(position)
```

6. Now, we will check that, after any potential orders have been sent out and trades have been made this round, we haven't breached any of our risk limits, starting with the Maximum Position Holding Time risk limit. Let's have a look at the following code:

```
# flat and starting a new position
if current_pos == 0:
  if position != 0:
    current_pos = position
    current_pos_start = len(positions)
  continue

# going from long position to flat or short position or
# going from short position to flat or long position
if current_pos * position <= 0:
  current_pos = position
  position_holding_time = len(positions) - current_pos_start
  current_pos_start = len(positions)

  if position_holding_time >
RISK_LIMIT_MAX_POSITION_HOLDING_TIME_DAYS:
    print('RiskViolation position_holding_time',
position_holding_time, ' >
RISK_LIMIT_MAX_POSITION_HOLDING_TIME_DAYS',
RISK_LIMIT_MAX_POSITION_HOLDING_TIME_DAYS)
    risk_violated = True
```

7. We will check that the new long/short position is within the Max Position risk limits, as shown in the following code:

```
if abs(position) > RISK_LIMIT_MAX_POSITION:
  print('RiskViolation position', position, ' >
RISK_LIMIT_MAX_POSITION', RISK_LIMIT_MAX_POSITION)
  risk_violated = True
```

8. Next, we also check that the updated traded volume doesn't violate the allocated Maximum Traded Volume risk limit:

```
if traded_volume > RISK_LIMIT_MAX_TRADED_VOLUME:
  print('RiskViolation traded_volume', traded_volume, ' >
RISK_LIMIT_MAX_TRADED_VOLUME', RISK_LIMIT_MAX_TRADED_VOLUME)
  risk_violated = True
```

9. Next, we will write some code that updates the PnLs, unchanged from before:

```
open_pnl = 0
if position > 0:
  if sell_sum_qty > 0:
    open_pnl = abs(sell_sum_qty) * (sell_sum_price_qty /
sell_sum_qty - buy_sum_price_qty / buy_sum_qty)
    open_pnl += abs(sell_sum_qty - position) * (close_price -
buy_sum_price_qty / buy_sum_qty)
  elif position < 0:
    if buy_sum_qty > 0:
      open_pnl = abs(buy_sum_qty) * (sell_sum_price_qty /
sell_sum_qty - buy_sum_price_qty / buy_sum_qty)
    open_pnl += abs(buy_sum_qty - position) * (sell_sum_price_qty /
sell_sum_qty - close_price)
  else:
    closed_pnl += (sell_sum_price_qty - buy_sum_price_qty)
    buy_sum_price_qty = 0
    buy_sum_qty = 0
    sell_sum_price_qty = 0
    sell_sum_qty = 0
    last_buy_price = 0
    last_sell_price = 0

print("OpenPnL: ", open_pnl, " ClosedPnL: ", closed_pnl, "
TotalPnL: ", (open_pnl + closed_pnl))
pnls.append(closed_pnl + open_pnl)
```

10. Now, we need to write the following code, which checks that the new Total PnL, which is the sum of realized and un-realized PnLs, is not in violation of either the Maximum allowed Weekly Stop Loss limit or the Maximum allowed Monthly Stop Loss limit:

```
if len(pnls) > 5:
  weekly_loss = pnls[-1] - pnls[-6]

  if weekly_loss < RISK_LIMIT_WEEKLY_STOP_LOSS:
    print('RiskViolation weekly_loss', weekly_loss, ' <
RISK_LIMIT_WEEKLY_STOP_LOSS', RISK_LIMIT_WEEKLY_STOP_LOSS)
    risk_violated = True

if len(pnls) > 20:
  monthly_loss = pnls[-1] - pnls[-21]

  if monthly_loss < RISK_LIMIT_MONTHLY_STOP_LOSS:
    print('RiskViolation monthly_loss', monthly_loss, ' <
RISK_LIMIT_MONTHLY_STOP_LOSS', RISK_LIMIT_MONTHLY_STOP_LOSS)
    risk_violated = True
```

Here, we have added a robust risk management system to our existing trading strategy that can be extended to any other trading strategies we intend on deploying to live trading markets in the future. This will protect live trading strategies from going rogue in production or behaving outside of our expected parameters, hence providing great risk control over our trading strategies.

Realistically adjusting risk

In the risk management system we built in the previous section, we used static risk limits that we used for the duration of the strategy's lifetime. In practice, however, this is never the case. When a new algorithmic trading strategy is built and deployed, it is first deployed with very low-risk limits—usually the least amount of risk possible. This is for a variety of reasons, the first one being to make tests and work out software implementation bugs, if there are any. The larger the amount of new code being deployed to live markets, the greater the risk. The other reason is to make sure strategy behavior is consistent with what is expected based on historical performance analysis. It is usually monitored very closely by multiple people to make sure nothing unexpected happens. Then, after a couple of days or weeks, when initial bugs have been worked out and strategy performance is in line with simulation performance, it is slowly scaled up to take more risks in order to generate more profits.

Conversely, after a strategy goes through a bad patch of losses, it is often reevaluated at reduced risk limits to check whether the trading strategy's performance has degraded from historical expectations and if it is no longer profitable to deploy it in live markets anymore. The obvious objective is to make as much money as possible, but achieving that requires not only a good risk check system but also a good system to adjust risk through different PnL profiles in the lifetime of the strategy.

A simple intuitive approach to adjusting risk in trading can be to start with low risk, increase the risk slightly after a good performance, and reduce the risk slightly after a poor performance. This is generally the approach that's followed by most participants: the challenges are to quantify good/poor performance in order to increase/decrease risk and to quantify the amount by which to increase/decrease risk.

Let's look at a practical implementation using our previous volatility adjusted mean reversion strategy with risk checks. We will increase the trade size and risk after a good month and reduce the trade size and risk after a bad month by a small increment. Let's get started:

1. First, we will define the limits of how small a trade size can be and what the maximum allowed trade size can be over the course of the strategy's lifetime. For this implementation, we allow no less than 1 share per trade and no more than 50 per trade. Every time we have a good/bad month, we will increase/decrease the trade size by 2 shares. We will start very small, as we discussed previously, and increment slowly if we continue to do well. Let's have a look at the code:

```
MIN_NUM_SHARES_PER_TRADE = 1
MAX_NUM_SHARES_PER_TRADE = 50
INCREMENT_NUM_SHARES_PER_TRADE = 2
num_shares_per_trade = MIN_NUM_SHARES_PER_TRADE # Beginning number
of shares to buy/sell on every trade
num_shares_history = [] # history of num-shares
abs_position_history = [] # history of absolute-position
```

2. Next, we will define similar minimum, maximum, and increment values for the different risk limits. As the strategy trade size evolves over time, the risk limits will also have to be adjusted to accommodate the increased trading size:

```
# Risk limits and increments to risk limits when we have good/bad
months
risk_limit_weekly_stop_loss = -6000
INCREMENT_RISK_LIMIT_WEEKLY_STOP_LOSS = -12000
risk_limit_monthly_stop_loss = -15000
INCREMENT_RISK_LIMIT_MONTHLY_STOP_LOSS = -30000
risk_limit_max_position = 5
INCREMENT_RISK_LIMIT_MAX_POSITION = 3
max_position_history = [] # history of max-trade-size
RISK_LIMIT_MAX_POSITION_HOLDING_TIME_DAYS = 120 * 5
risk_limit_max_trade_size = 5
INCREMENT_RISK_LIMIT_MAX_TRADE_SIZE = 2
max_trade_size_history = [] # history of max-trade-size

last_risk_change_index = 0
```

3. Now, let's look at the main loop trading section. We will only look at the sections that are different from the previous strategy, along with risk checks. Now, the minimum profit to close is no longer a constant but is a function of the number of shares per trade, which varies over time:

```
MIN_PROFIT_TO_CLOSE = num_shares_per_trade * 10
```

4. Let's have a look at the main trading section. It will require some changes so that it adapts to the changing trade sizes. Let's look at the sell trade logic first:

```
if (not risk_violated and
        ((apo > APO_VALUE_FOR_SELL_ENTRY * stdev_factor and
abs(close_price - last_sell_price) > MIN_PRICE_MOVE_FROM_LAST_TRADE
* stdev_factor) # APO above sell entry threshold, we should sell
        or
        (position > 0 and (apo >= 0 or open_pnl >
MIN_PROFIT_TO_CLOSE / stdev_factor)))): # long from -ve APO and APO
has gone positive or position is profitable, sell to close position
    orders.append(-1) # mark the sell trade
    last_sell_price = close_price
    if position == 0: # opening a new entry position
        position -= num_shares_per_trade # reduce position by the
size of this trade
        sell_sum_price_qty += (close_price * num_shares_per_trade) #
update vwap sell-price
        sell_sum_qty += num_shares_per_trade
        traded_volume += num_shares_per_trade
        print("Sell ", num_shares_per_trade, " @ ", close_price,
"Position: ", position)
    else: # closing an existing position
        sell_sum_price_qty += (close_price * abs(position)) # update
vwap sell-price
        sell_sum_qty += abs(position)
        traded_volume += abs(position)
        print("Sell ", abs(position), " @ ", close_price, "Position:
", position)
        position = 0 # reduce position by the size of this trade
```

Finally, let's look at the buy trade logic:

```
elif (not risk_violated and
        ((apo < APO_VALUE_FOR_BUY_ENTRY * stdev_factor and
abs(close_price - last_buy_price) > MIN_PRICE_MOVE_FROM_LAST_TRADE
* stdev_factor) # APO below buy entry threshold, we should buy
        or
        (position < 0 and (apo <= 0 or open_pnl >
MIN_PROFIT_TO_CLOSE / stdev_factor)))): # short from +ve APO and
APO has gone negative or position is profitable, buy to close
```

```
position
    orders.append(+1) # mark the buy trade
    last_buy_price = close_price
    if position == 0: # opening a new entry position
      position += num_shares_per_trade # increase position by the
size of this trade
      buy_sum_price_qty += (close_price * num_shares_per_trade) #
update the vwap buy-price
      buy_sum_qty += num_shares_per_trade
      traded_volume += num_shares_per_trade
      print("Buy ", num_shares_per_trade, " @ ", close_price,
"Position: ", position)
    else: # closing an existing position
      buy_sum_price_qty += (close_price * abs(position)) # update
the vwap buy-price
      buy_sum_qty += abs(position)
      traded_volume += abs(position)
      print("Buy ", abs(position), " @ ", close_price, "Position:
", position)
      position = 0 # increase position by the size of this trade
  else:
    # No trade since none of the conditions were met to buy or sell
    orders.append(0)

  positions.append(position)
```

5. After adjusting the PnLs, as shown in the preceding code, we will add an implementation to analyze monthly performance and increase trade size and risk limits if we had a good month and decrease trade size and risk limits if we had a bad month. First, we will look at the logic to increase the trading risk after a good month of performance:

```
if len(pnls) > 20:
  monthly_pnls = pnls[-1] - pnls[-20]

  if len(pnls) - last_risk_change_index > 20:
    if monthly_pnls > 0:
      num_shares_per_trade += INCREMENT_NUM_SHARES_PER_TRADE
      if num_shares_per_trade <= MAX_NUM_SHARES_PER_TRADE:
        print('Increasing trade-size and risk')
        risk_limit_weekly_stop_loss +=
INCREMENT_RISK_LIMIT_WEEKLY_STOP_LOSS
        risk_limit_monthly_stop_loss +=
INCREMENT_RISK_LIMIT_MONTHLY_STOP_LOSS
        risk_limit_max_position +=
INCREMENT_RISK_LIMIT_MAX_POSITION
        risk_limit_max_trade_size +=
```

```
INCREMENT_RISK_LIMIT_MAX_TRADE_SIZE
        else:
            num_shares_per_trade = MAX_NUM_SHARES_PER_TRADE
```

6. Now, let's look at some similar logic, but which reduces risk after a month of poor performance:

```
elif monthly_pnls < 0:
    num_shares_per_trade -= INCREMENT_NUM_SHARES_PER_TRADE
    if num_shares_per_trade >= MIN_NUM_SHARES_PER_TRADE:
        print('Decreasing trade-size and risk')
        risk_limit_weekly_stop_loss -=
INCREMENT_RISK_LIMIT_WEEKLY_STOP_LOSS
        risk_limit_monthly_stop_loss -=
INCREMENT_RISK_LIMIT_MONTHLY_STOP_LOSS
        risk_limit_max_position -=
INCREMENT_RISK_LIMIT_MAX_POSITION
        risk_limit_max_trade_size -=
INCREMENT_RISK_LIMIT_MAX_TRADE_SIZE
    else:
        num_shares_per_trade = MIN_NUM_SHARES_PER_TRADE

last_risk_change_index = len(pnls)
```

7. Now, we need to look at the code to track the risk exposure evolution over time:

```
# Track trade-sizes/positions and risk limits as they evolve over
time
num_shares_history.append(num_shares_per_trade)
abs_position_history.append(abs(position))
max_trade_size_history.append(risk_limit_max_trade_size)
max_position_history.append(risk_limit_max_position)
```

8. Finally, let's visualize the performance and the evolution of trade sizes and risk limits over time:

```
data = data.assign(NumShares=pd.Series(num_shares_history,
index=data.index))
data = data.assign(MaxTradeSize=pd.Series(max_trade_size_history,
index=data.index))
data = data.assign(AbsPosition=pd.Series(abs_position_history,
index=data.index))
data = data.assign(MaxPosition=pd.Series(max_position_history,
index=data.index))

data['NumShares'].plot(color='b', lw=3., legend=True)
data['MaxTradeSize'].plot(color='g', lw=1., legend=True)
plt.legend()
```

```
plt.show()

data['AbsPosition'].plot(color='b', lw=1., legend=True)
data['MaxPosition'].plot(color='g', lw=1., legend=True)
plt.legend()
plt.show()
```

The following plots are the output of the preceding code. Let's have a look at the visualizations that we are already familiar with:

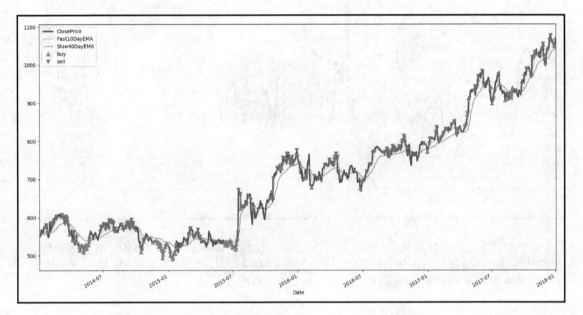

The plot that shows buy and sell trades overlaid on Google stock prices still stay consistent with what we've seen in the past, which shows that strategy behavior remains mostly unchanged as it goes through phases of risk increases and decreases:

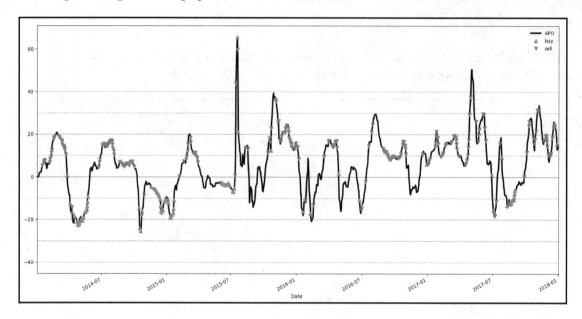

The buy and sell trades that are overlaid on APO signal value changes also stay consistent with the expected strategy behavior, which we're used to from our previous analysis of mean reversion trading strategy:

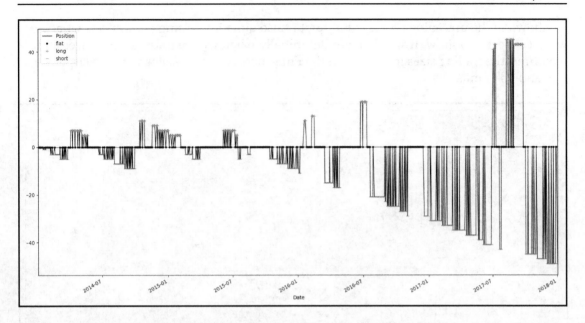

As shown in the preceding plot, the position plot is especially interesting because it shows how the magnitude of the positions increases over time. Initially, they are very small (less than 10 shares) and slowly increase over time as strategy performance stays consistently good and becomes quite large (more than 40 shares):

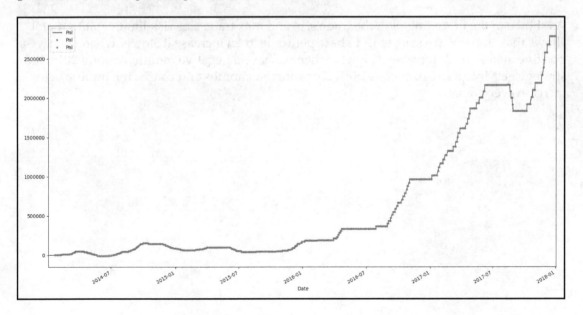

As shown in the preceding plot, the PnL plot is also quite interesting and reflects what we would expect it to show. It slowly increases initially when we are trading small sizes and over time, the trading sizes increase and the PnLs increase much faster with the larger trade size and risk limits:

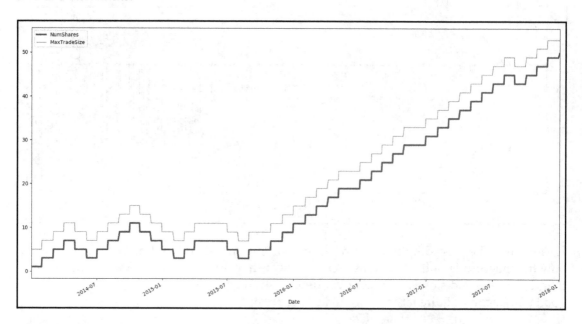

As shown in the preceding plot, the trade size and max trade size risk limit evolution plot shows that, initially, we start with 1 share per trade, then increase it slowly when we have a positive month, then decrease it slowly when we have a negative month. Around 2016, the strategy gets into a streak of consecutively profitable months and causes the trade size to increase every month:

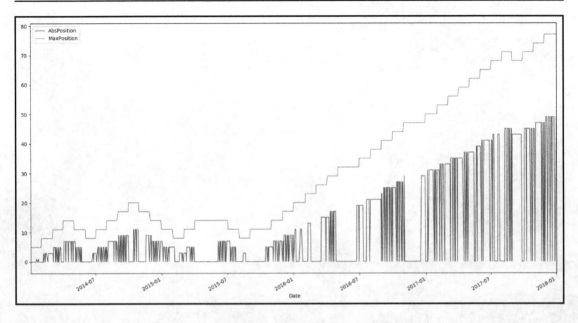

As shown in the preceding plot, the absolute positions that the strategy puts on, as well as the max position risk limit evolution plot, stay consistent with expectations, that is, starting low and then increasing as we get into a streak of consecutive good months.

Summary

In this chapter, you learned about the different types of risks and risk factors. Then, we went through the sources of risk and learned about quantifying the risks. Moving ahead, we also learned about how to measure and manage the risks (market risk, operational risk, and software implementation bugs) of algorithmic strategies. We incorporated a full production-ready risk management system into our previously built trading strategy, thus making them safe for deployment to live trading markets. Finally, we discussed and built a practical risk scaling system that starts with very low-risk exposure and dynamically manages the risk exposure over time as the strategy performance evolves.

In the next chapter, we will look at how the algorithm's trading interacts with the different factors in the trading arena. You will learn how to build a trading bot from scratch. Using the algorithm that we will build in the prior sections, you will know how to implement it, where to connect it, and how to handle it.

4

Section 4: Building a Trading System

In this section, you will learn how the trading algorithm we are building interacts with the different actors in the trading arena. You will learn how to build a trading bot from scratch. Using the algorithm constructed in the previous sections, you will learn how to implement it, where to connect it, and how to handle it.

This section comprises the following chapters:

- Chapter 7, *Building a Trading System in Python*
- Chapter 8, *Connecting to Trading Exchanges*
- Chapter 9, *Creating a Backtester in Python*

7
Building a Trading System in Python

In the initial chapters of this book, we learned how to create a trading strategy by analyzing historical data. In this chapter, we are going to study how to convert data analysis into real-time software that will connect to a real exchange to actually apply the theory that you've previously learned.

We will describe the functional components supporting the trading strategy based on the algorithm created in the previous chapters. We will be using Python to build a small trading system. We will use the algorithms to build a trading system capable of trading.

This chapter will cover the following topics:

- Understanding the trading system
- Building a trading system in Python
- Designing a limit order book

Understanding the trading system

A trading system will help you to automate your trading strategy. When you choose to build this kind of software, you need to take the following into consideration:

- **Asset class**: When you code, knowing which asset class will be used in your trading system will modify the data structure of this software. Each asset class is idiosyncratic and has its own set of features. US stocks are mainly traded on two exchanges (NY Stock Exchange and NASDAQ). There are about 6,000 companies (symbols) listed on these two exchanges. Unlike equities, **Foreign Exchange (FX)** has six major currency pairs, six minor currency pairs, and six more exotic currency pairs. We can add more currency pairs, but there will not be more than 100 currency pairs. However, there will be hundreds of market players (banks, brokers).

- **Trading strategy type (high frequency, long-term position)**: Depending upon the type of strategies, the design of the software architecture will be impacted. High-frequency trading strategies require sending orders very rapidly. A regular trading system for US equities will decide to send an order within microseconds. A system trading on the Chicago Mercantile Exchange (CME) could work within nanoseconds. Based on this observation, the technology will be critical in the choice of designing the software. If we just refer to the programming language, Python is not adapted to speed and we will preferably choose C++ or Java. If we want to take a long-term position such as many days, the speed allowing a trader to get a liquidity faster than others will not be important. A programming language such as Python will be fast enough to reach this goal.

- **The number of users (the number of trading strategies)**: When the number of traders increases, the number of trading strategies increases. This means that the number of orders is higher. Before sending an order to an exchange, we need to check the validity of the orders we are about to send: checking whether the overall position for a given instrument has not been reached. In trading world, we have more and more regulations moderating trading strategies. To follow that our trading strategy respect the regulation, we will test the compliance of the orders that we want to send. All these checks will add some calculation time. If we have too many orders, we will need to have all these verification done sequentially for one given instrument. If the software is not fast enough, it will slow down the orders to go out. So having more users will require a faster trading system.

These parameters modify the conception of the trading system you are going to build. It is essential to have a clear description of the requirements when you build a trading system.

Because the goal of a trading system is to support your trading ideas. The trading system will collect the information that your trading strategy needs and be in charge of sending orders and receiving responses from the market regarding this order. The main functionalities will be to collect the data (most of the time this will be price updates). If the trading strategy needs to get some quantitative data involving earnings, fed announcements (more generally news), these news will also trigger orders. When the trading strategy decide the direction of the position. the trading system will send orders accordingly . The trading system will also decide which specific exchange will be the best to get the order filled for the requested price and for the requested volume.

Gateways

A trading system collects price updates and sends orders on your behalf. In order to get to that, you need to code all the steps that you would do if you were trading without any trading system. If you would like to make money by buying low and selling high, you will need to choose the product you will use to trade. Once you select this product, you want to receive the order from the other traders. The other traders will provide you their intention (their orders) to trade a financial asset by indicating the side, the price and the quantity. As soon as you receive enough orders for the product that you want to trade, you can choose the trader you are going to make a deal with. You will make your decision based on the price of this asset. If you want to resell this asset later one, it will be important to buy it for a low price. When you agree with a price, you will indicate the other trader that you will want to buy for the advertised price. When the deal is done, you now own this product. You will proceed the same way when you want to sell it at a higher price. We formalize this way of trading using functional units:

- **Data handling**: Collecting price updates coming from the venues you will choose to trade with (exchanges, ECNs, dark pools). This component (called a **gateway** in the following diagram) is one of the most critical of the trading system. The task of this component is to get the book for a given instrument from an exchange to the trading system. This component will be linked to the network and it will get connected to exchanges receiving and sending streams to communicate with it.

The following diagram represents the location of the gateways in the trading system. They are the input and the output of the trading system:

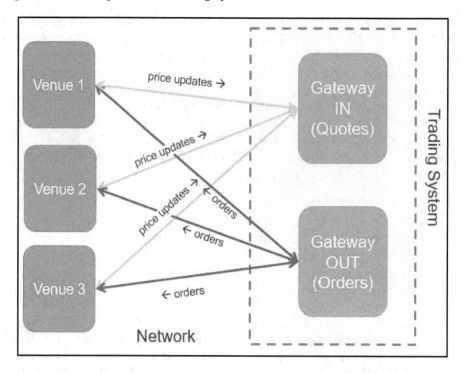

The diagram shows the following:

- The venues represent traders, exchanges, ecns, and dark pools.
- The getaways and venues can be linked by different ways (they are represented using arrows).
- We can use a wire, wireless network, internet, microwave, or fibers. All these different network media have different characteristics in terms of speed, data loss, and bandwidth.
- We can observe the arrows are bidirectional for the price updates and the orders. There is a protocol to ask for price updates.
- The gateway will initiate a network connection with the venue, authenticate itself, and subscribe to a given instrument to start receiving price updates (we will explain this part in more detail later).

- The gateway taking care of orders also receives and send messages. When an order is created, it is sent through the network to the venue.
- If the venue receives this order, an acknowledgment of this order will be sent. When this order has met a matching order, a trade will be sent to the trading system.

Order book management

The main task of data handling is to replicate the limit order book from the venues into your trading system. To combine all the different books you receive, the **book builder** will be in charge of gathering the prices and sorting them for your strategies.

In the following diagram, the price updates are converted by the gateway then transferred to the book builder. The book builder will use the books received by the gateways from the venues and it will gather and sort all the price updates:

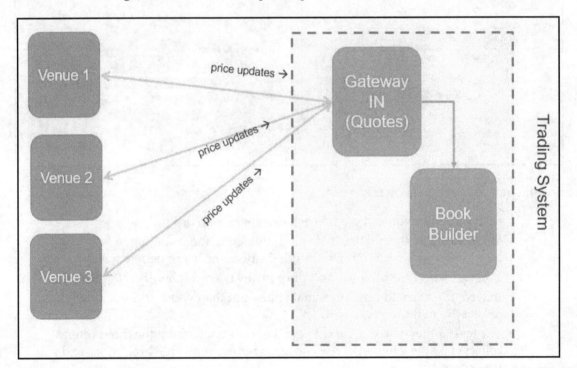

In the following diagram, we use an example of an **order book** for a given financial product. Since we have three venues, we observe three different books:

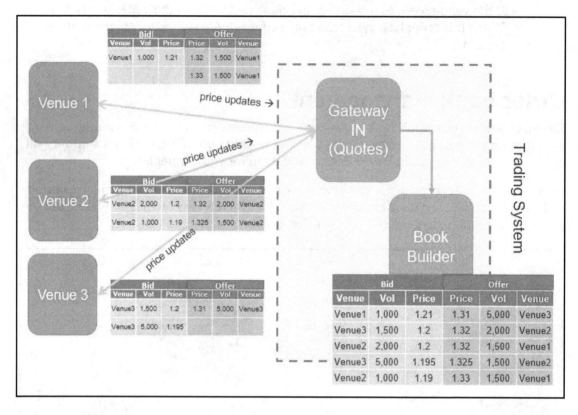

The diagram shows the following:

- In these books, you can see for each row there is an order.
- For instance, in the bid list of Venue 1, there is a trader willing to buy 1,000 shares for $1.21. On the other side is the list of people willing to sell.
- You can expect the offer (or ask) price to always be higher than the bid price.
- Indeed, if you could buy for a smaller amount than you could sell, it would be too easy to make money.
- The task of the book builder is to get the three books from the three venues collected by the gateways. The book builder regroups the three books and sort the orders.

Strategy

The trading strategy is the brain of the system. This is where your algorithm representing your trading idea will be implemented. Let's have a look at the diagram:

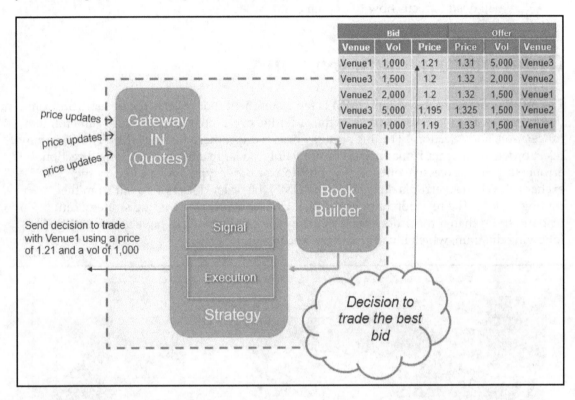

The diagram shows the following:

- The trading strategy is divided into two main components: **signal** and **execution**. In this book, the numerous strategies we saw in the first part can be called signal.
- The signals represent the indication of getting a long or a short position. For instance, in the dual moving average crossover momentum strategy, when the two average lines were crossing, a signal to go long or go short was generated.
- The signal component of this strategy only focuses on generating signals. However, having the intention (a signal) does not guarantee you to get the liquidity you are interested in. For instance, in high-frequency trading, it is highly likely your orders will be rejected because of the speed of your trading system.

- The execution part of the strategy will take care of handling response from the market. This part decides what to do for any responses from the market. For instance, what should happen when the order is rejected? You should continue trying to get an equivalent liquidity, another price. That's an important part you will need to focus how to implement.

Order management system

The **order management system** (OMS) is the component that collects the orders sent from the strategies. The OMS keeps track of the order life cycle (creation, execution, amendment, cancelation, and rejection). Trading strategy orders are gathered in the OMS. The OMS may reject orders if an order is malformed or not valid (too large a quantity, wrong direction, erroneous prices, excessive outstanding position, or order type not handled by the exchange). When an error is detected in the OMS, the order does not go out from the trading system. The rejection happens earlier. Consequently, the trading strategy can respond faster than if the order was rejected by the exchange. Let's have a look at the following diagram, which illustrates these features of the OMS:

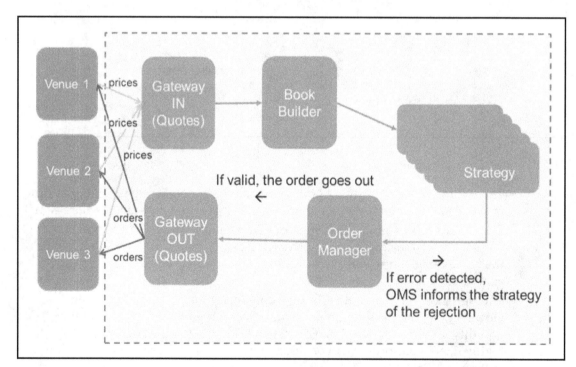

Critical components

Gateways, a book builder, strategies, and an OMS are the critical components of any trading system. They gather the essential functions you need to start trading. We measure the performance of a trading system in terms of speed by adding the processing time of all the critical components. We start a timer when a price update gets into the entrance of the trading system and we stop the timer when the order triggered by this price update goes out from the system. This time is called the **tick-to-trade** or **tick-to-order**.

In the most recent systems, this time is in the order of microseconds (around 10 microseconds). When optimized with special hardware and software programming, this time can even be reduced to nanoseconds (around 300 nanoseconds). Because we choose to use Python to implement our trading system, the tick-to-trade of this Python system will be in the order of milliseconds.

Non-critical components

The non-critical components are the components not directly linked with the decision to send an order. They modify parameters, report data, and gather data. For instance, when you design a strategy, you will have a set of parameters that you need to adjust in real time. You need a component capable of conveying the information to the trading strategy component. For that, we will have a component called **command and control**.

Command and control

Command and control is an interface between traders and the trading system. It can be a command-line system or a user interface receiving the commands from the traders and sending the messages to the appropriate components. Let's have a look at the following diagram:

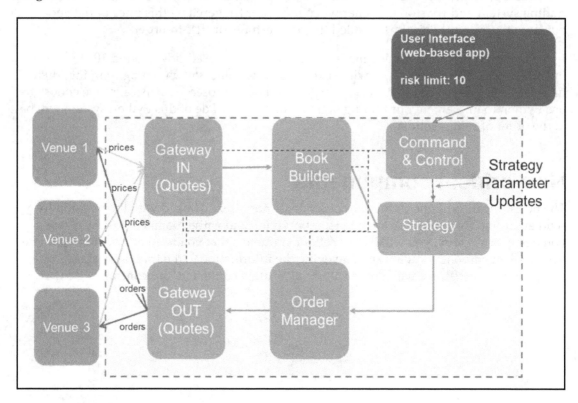

As shown in the diagram, if we need to update the trading strategy parameters, the trader can use a text field on a web-based application to specify the risk tolerance the trading strategy can take. The number (corresponding to the tolerance limit) will be sent to the appropriate trading strategy.

Services

Additional components may be added to the trading system. We will talk about the following components (it is not an exhaustive list):

- **Position server**: This keeps track of all the trades. It updates the positions for all the traded financial assets. For instance, if a trade is made for 100,000 EUR/USD at a price of $1.2, the notional position will be $120,000. If a trading system component needs the position amount for EUR/USD, it will subscribe the position server for getting position updates. The order manager or the trading strategy may want to know this information before allowing an order to go out. If we want to limit the position to $200,000 for a given asset, another order to get 100,000 EUR/USD will be rejected.

- **Logging system**: This gathers all the logs from the components and will write a file or modify a database. A logging system helps with debugging, figuring out causes of issues, and also just reports.

- **Viewers** (read-only user interface view): These display the views for trading (positions, orders, trades, task monitoring, and so on).

- **Control viewers** (interactive user interface): These provide a way to modify parameters and start/stop components of the trading system.

- **News server**: This gathers news from many news companies (such as Bloomberg, Reuters, and Ravenpack) and provides this news in real time or on demand to the trading system.

Building a trading system in Python

In this section, we will describe how to create a trading system from scratch. We will use Python to code this trading system but the approach is general enough to be transferred to other languages. We will talk about the design and the best software engineering practice. The system we will create will have the bare minimum components to trade and you may want to extend it after this first initial implementation.

Python is an object-oriented language. We will encapsulate the main functionalities of the trading system into Python objects. We will have these components communicate through channels. We will simplify the functional components by limiting this first implementation to five main components. We will code these five components into five different files. We will associate unit tests to all these components:

- 1-py: We will reproduce the behavior of liquidity providers. In this example, it sends price updates (orders).
- 2-py: To simplify the design, we are removing the gateway and we will plug the liquidity provider directly to the order book manager. This component will be in charge of building a book.
- 3-py: This file contains the trading strategy code.
- 4-py: This contains the code for the order manager.
- 5-py: This replicates the behavior of a market:

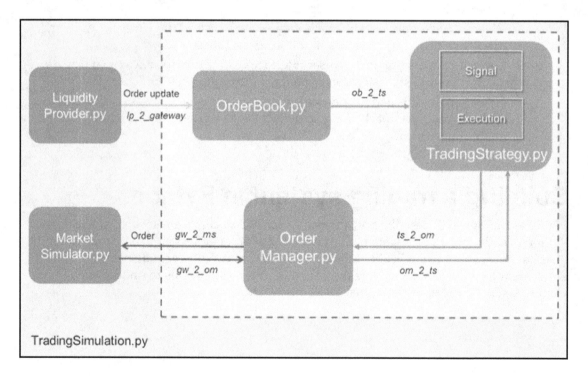

We observe from the preceding diagram that there are links between all the components. Every link is a unidirectional communication channel. In Python, the data structure we choose is a deque from the collections package.

We use two methods of the deque data structure:

- – `push`: This inserts an element into the channel.
- – `popleft`: This removes an element from the channel.

We will first describe the implementation of all these components one by one. We will describe the public methods that will be used to use them. When you start designing a class, you first need to know what this class is supposed to do. You will design the testing environment that will be able verify the component behavior.

The orders and the order updates will be represented by a simple Python dictionary. Let's have a look at the code:

```python
ord = {
    'id': self.order_id,
    'price': price,
    'quantity': quantity,
    'side': side,
    'action': action
}
```

LiquidityProvider class

The `LiquidityProvider` class is the simplest of all the others. The goal of this component is to generate liquidities. Since we randomly generate liquidities, we just need to test whether the first liquidity that is sent by the `LiquidityProvider` class is well formed. We will create the `generate_random_order` function, which will randomly pick a side, a price, a quantity, and an action associated to this order. We will have three kinds of actions: create a new order, amend an order, and cancel an order. Since we are going to create a full trading system, we will also want to test the full system by inserting the order manually. Hence, this `LiquidityProvider` component will have a way to insert manual orders into the system.

The following code describes the `LiquidityProvider` class. We will use a pseudo random generator initialized by a seed. When you run your code several times, a seed will allow you to make the random number deterministic.

The `generate_random_order` function uses the `lookup_orders` function to determine whether the next order that will be generated already exists:

1. In the code, we will create the `LiquidityProvider` class. The goal of this class is to act as a liquidity provider or an exchange. It will send price updates to the trading system. It will use the `lp_2_gateway` channel to send the price updates:

```python
from random import randrange
from random import sample, seed

class LiquidityProvider:
    def __init__(self, lp_2_gateway=None):
        self.orders = []
        self.order_id = 0
        seed(0)
        self.lp_2_gateway = lp_2_gateway
```

2. Here, we create a utility function to look up orders in the list of orders:

```python
def lookup_orders(self,id):
    count=0
    for o in self.orders:
        if o['id'] ==  id:
            return o, count
        count+=1
    return None, None
```

3. The `insert_manual_order` function will insert orders manually into the trading system. As shown, this function will be used for unit testing some components:

```python
def insert_manual_order(self,order):
    if self.lp_2_gateway is None:
        print('simulation mode')
        return order
    self.lp_2_gateway.append(order.copy())
```

The `generate_random_order` function will generate orders randomly. There will be three types of orders:

- New (we will create a new order ID)
- Modify (we will use the order ID of an order that was created and we will change the quantity)
- Delete (we will use the order ID and we will delete the order)

4. Each time we create a new order, we will need to increment the order ID. We will use the `lookup_orders` function as shown in the following code to check whether the order has already been created:

```python
def generate_random_order(self):
    price=randrange(8,12)
    quantity=randrange(1,10)*100
    side=sample(['buy','sell'],1)[0]
    order_id=randrange(0,self.order_id+1)
    o=self.lookup_orders(order_id)

    new_order=False
    if o is None:
        action='new'
        new_order=True
    else:
        action=sample(['modify','delete'],1)[0]

    ord = {
        'id': self.order_id,
        'price': price,
        'quantity': quantity,
        'side': side,
        'action': action
    }

    if not new_order:
        self.order_id+=1
        self.orders.append(ord)

    if not self.lp_2_gateway:
        print('simulation mode')
        return ord
    self.lp_2_gateway.append(ord.copy())
```

5. We test whether the `LiquidityProvider` class works correctly by using unit testing. Python has the `unittest` module . As shown, we will create the `TestMarketSimulator` class, inheriting from `TestCase`:

```python
import unittest
from chapter7.LiquidityProvider import LiquidityProvider


class TestMarketSimulator(unittest.TestCase):
    def setUp(self):
        self.liquidity_provider = LiquidityProvider()
```

```
    def test_add_liquidity(self):
        self.liquidity_provider.generate_random_order()
    self.assertEqual(self.liquidity_provider.orders[0]['id'],0)
    self.assertEqual(self.liquidity_provider.orders[0]['side'], 'buy')
    self.assertEqual(self.liquidity_provider.orders[0]['quantity'],
    700)
    self.assertEqual(self.liquidity_provider.orders[0]['price'], 11)
    OrderBook class
```

As shown, we have coded the `test_add_liquidity` function:

- This function tests whether the random generation of a liquidity functions by comparing values generated by this function to expected values.
- We used the functions belonging to this `TestCase` class to make a test fail if the returned values are not the expected ones.
- This code will generate an order and test the order characteristics. If one field value is not the expected one, the unit test will fail.

Strategy class

This class represents the trading strategy based on top of the book changes. This trading strategy will create an order when the top of the book is crossed. This means when there is a potential arbitrage situation. When the bid value is higher than the ask value, we can send an order to buy and sell at the same time and make money out of these two transactions.

This class is divided into two parts:

- **Signal part**: This part handles the trading signal. In this example, a signal will be triggered when the top of the book is crossed.
- **Execution part**: This part handles the execution of the orders. It will be responsible of managing the order life cycle.

The following are the steps for the strategy class:

1. As shown in the following code, we will create the `TradingStrategy` class. This class will have three parameters. They are references to the three communication channels. One is taking the book events form the order book, the two others are made to send orders and receive order updates from the market:

```
class TradingStrategy:
    def __init__(self, ob_2_ts, ts_2_om, om_2_ts):
        self.orders = []
        self.order_id = 0
```

```
        self.position = 0
        self.pnl = 0
        self.cash = 10000
        self.current_bid = 0
        self.current_offer = 0
        self.ob_2_ts = ob_2_ts
        self.ts_2_om = ts_2_om
        self.om_2_ts = om_2_ts
```

2. We will code two functions to handle the book events from the order book as shown in the code; `handle_input_from_bb` checks whether there are book events in deque `ob_2_ts` and will call the `handle_book_event` function:

```python
def handle_input_from_bb(self, book_event=None):
    if self.ob_2_ts is None:
        print('simulation mode')
        self.handle_book_event(book_event)
    else:
        if len(self.ob_2_ts)>0:
            be=self.handle_book_event(self.ob_2_ts.popleft())
            self.handle_book_event(be)

def handle_book_event(self, book_event):
    if book_event is not None:
        self.current_bid = book_event['bid_price']
        self.current_offer = book_event['offer_price']

    if self.signal(book_event):
        self.create_orders(book_event
                    , min(book_event['bid_quantity'],
                        book_event['offer_quantity']))
    self.execution()
```

The `handle_book_event` function calls the function signal to check whether there is a signal to send an order.

3. In this case, the signal verifies whether the bid price is higher than the ask price. If this condition is verified, this function returns `True`. The `handle_book_event` function in the code will create an order by calling the `create_orders` function:

```python
def signal(self, book_event):
    if book_event is not None:
        if book_event["bid_price"]>\
            book_event["offer_price"]:
            if book_event["bid_price"]>0 and\
                book_event["offer_price"]>0:
```

```
                    return True
            else:
                    return False
        else:
            return False
```

4. The `create_orders` function from the code creates two orders. When we have an arbitrage situation, we must trade fast. Therefore, the two orders must be created simultaneously. This function increments the order ID for any created orders. This order ID will be local to the trading strategy:

```python
def create_orders(self,book_event,quantity):
    self.order_id+=1
    ord = {
        'id': self.order_id,
        'price': book_event['bid_price'],
        'quantity': quantity,
        'side': 'sell',
        'action': 'to_be_sent'
    }
    self.orders.append(ord.copy())

    price=book_event['offer_price']
    side='buy'
    self.order_id+=1
    ord = {
        'id': self.order_id,
        'price': book_event['offer_price'],
        'quantity': quantity,
        'side': 'buy',
        'action': 'to_be_sent'
    }
    self.orders.append(ord.copy())
```

The function execution will take care of processing orders in their whole order life cycle. For instance, when an order is created, its status is *new*. Once the order has been sent to the market, the market will respond by acknowledging the order or reject the order. If the other is rejected, this function will remove the order from the list of outstanding orders.

5. When an order is filled, it means this order has been executed. Once an order is filled, the strategy must update the position and the PnL with the help of the code:

```python
def execution(self):
    orders_to_be_removed=[]
    for index, order in enumerate(self.orders):
```

```
        if order['action'] == 'to_be_sent':
            # Send order
            order['status'] = 'new'
            order['action'] = 'no_action'
            if self.ts_2_om is None:
                print('Simulation mode')
            else:
                self.ts_2_om.append(order.copy())
        if order['status'] == 'rejected':
            orders_to_be_removed.append(index)
        if order['status'] == 'filled':
            orders_to_be_removed.append(index)
            pos = order['quantity'] if order['side'] == 'buy' else
-order['quantity']
            self.position+=pos
            self.pnl-=pos * order['price']
            self.cash -= pos * order['price']
    for order_index in sorted(orders_to_be_removed,reverse=True):
        del (self.orders[order_index])
```

6. The `handle_response_from_om` and `handle_market_response` functions will collect the information from the order manager (collecting information from the market) as shown in the following code:

```
def handle_response_from_om(self):
    if self.om_2_ts is not None:
        self.handle_market_response(self.om_2_ts.popleft())
    else:
        print('simulation mode')

def handle_market_response(self, order_execution):
    order,_=self.lookup_orders(order_execution['id'])
    if order is None:
        print('error not found')
        return
    order['status']=order_execution['status']
    self.execution()
```

7. The `lookup_orders` function in the following code checks whether an order exists in the data structure gathering all the orders and return this order:

```
def lookup_orders(self,id):
    count=0
    for o in self.orders:
        if o['id'] ==  id:
            return o, count
        count+=1
    return None, None
```

Testing the trading strategy is critical. You need to check whether the trading strategy will place the correct orders. The `test_receive_top_of_book` test case verifies whether the book event is correctly handled by the trading strategy. The `test_rejected_order` and `test_filled_order` test cases verify whether a response from the market is correctly handled.

8. The code will create a `setUp` function, being called each time we run a test. We will create `TradingStrategy` each time we invoke a test. This way of doing it increases the reuse of the same code:

```python
import unittest
from chapter7.TradingStrategy import TradingStrategy

class TestMarketSimulator(unittest.TestCase):
    def setUp(self):
        self.trading_strategy= TradingStrategy()
```

The first unit test that we perform for a trading strategy is to validate that the book event sent by the book is received correctly.

9. We will create a book event manually and we will use the `handle_book_event` function. We are going to validate the fact that the trading strategy behaves the way it is supposed to by checking whether the orders produced were expected. Let's have a look at the code:

```python
def test_receive_top_of_book(self):
    book_event = {
        "bid_price" : 12,
        "bid_quantity" : 100,
        "offer_price" : 11,
        "offer_quantity" : 150
    }
    self.trading_strategy.handle_book_event(book_event)
    self.assertEqual(len(self.trading_strategy.orders), 2)
    self.assertEqual(self.trading_strategy.orders[0]['side'],
'sell')
    self.assertEqual(self.trading_strategy.orders[1]['side'],
'buy')
    self.assertEqual(self.trading_strategy.orders[0]['price'],
12)
    self.assertEqual(self.trading_strategy.orders[1]['price'],
11)
    self.assertEqual(self.trading_strategy.orders[0]['quantity'], 100)
    self.assertEqual(self.trading_strategy.orders[1]['quantity'], 100)
    self.assertEqual(self.trading_strategy.orders[0]['action'],
'no_action')
```

```
self.assertEqual(self.trading_strategy.orders[1]['action'],
'no_action')
```

The second test performed is to verify whether the trading strategy receives the market response coming from the order manager.

10. We will create a market response indicating a rejection of a given order. We will also check whether the trading strategy removes this order from the list of orders belonging to the trading strategy:

```python
def test_rejected_order(self):
    self.test_receive_top_of_book()
    order_execution = {
        'id': 1,
        'price': 12,
        'quantity': 100,
        'side': 'sell',
        'status' : 'rejected'
    }
    self.trading_strategy.handle_market_response(order_execution)
    self.assertEqual(self.trading_strategy.orders[0]['side'], 'buy')
    self.assertEqual(self.trading_strategy.orders[0]['price'], 11)
    self.assertEqual(self.trading_strategy.orders[0]['quantity'], 100)
    self.assertEqual(self.trading_strategy.orders[0]['status'], 'new')
```

11. The last part, we need to test the behavior of the trading strategy when the order is filled. We will need to update the position, the pn1, and the cash that we have to invest as shown in the following code:

```python
def test_filled_order(self):
    self.test_receive_top_of_book()
    order_execution = {
        'id': 1,
        'price': 11,
        'quantity': 100,
        'side': 'sell',
        'status' : 'filled'
    }
    self.trading_strategy.handle_market_response(order_execution)
    self.assertEqual(len(self.trading_strategy.orders),1)

    order_execution = {
        'id': 2,
        'price': 12,
        'quantity': 100,
        'side': 'buy',
        'status' : 'filled'
```

```
        }
        self.trading_strategy.handle_market_response(order_execution)
        self.assertEqual(self.trading_strategy.position, 0)
        self.assertEqual(self.trading_strategy.cash, 10100)
        self.assertEqual(self.trading_strategy.pnl, 100)
```

Next, we will look at working with the OrderManager class.

OrderManager class

The purpose of the order manager is to gather the orders from all the trading strategies and to communicate this order with the market. It will check the validity of the orders and can also keep track of the overall positions and PnL. It can be a safeguard against mistakes introduced in trading strategies.

This component is the interface between the trading strategies and the market. It will be the only component using two inputs and two outputs. The constructor of this class will take four arguments representing these channels:

```
class OrderManager:
    def __init__(self,ts_2_om = None,  om_2_ts = None,
                     om_2_gw=None, gw_2_om=None):
        self.orders=[]
        self.order_id=0
        self.ts_2_om = ts_2_om
        self.om_2_gw = om_2_gw
        self.gw_2_om = gw_2_om
        self.om_2_ts = om_2_ts
```

The four following functions will help with reading data from the channels and it will call the proper functions.

The handle_input_from_ts function checks whether the ts_2_om channel has been created. If the channel has not been created, it means that we will use the class for unit testing only. To get new orders into the OrderManager system, we check whether the size of the ts_2_om channel is higher than 0. If there is an order in the channel, we remove this order and we call the handle_order_from_tradinig_stategy function:

```
def handle_input_from_ts(self):
    if self.ts_2_om is not None:
        if len(self.ts_2_om)>0:
self.handle_order_from_trading_strategy(self.ts_2_om.popleft())
    else:
        print('simulation mode')
```

The `handle_order_from_trading_strategy` function handles the new order coming from the trading strategies. For now, the `OrderManager` class will just get a copy of the order and store this order into a list of orders:

```
def handle_order_from_trading_strategy(self,order):
    if self.check_order_valid(order):
        order=self.create_new_order(order).copy()
        self.orders.append(order)
        if self.om_2_gw is None:
            print('simulation mode')
        else:
            self.om_2_gw.append(order.copy())
```

Once we take care of the order side, we are going to take care of the market response. For this, we will use the same method we used for the two prior functions. The `handle_input_from_market` function checks whether the `gw_2_om` channel exists. If that's the case, the function reads the market response object coming from the market and calls the `handle_order_from_gateway` function:

```
def handle_input_from_market(self):
    if self.gw_2_om is not None:
        if len(self.gw_2_om)>0:
            self.handle_order_from_gateway(self.gw_2_om.popleft())
    else:
        print('simulation mode')
```

The `handle_order_from_gateway` function will look up in the list of orders created by the `handle_order_from_trading_strategy` function. If the market response corresponds to an order in the list, it means that this market response is valid. We will be able to change the state of this order. If the market response doesn't find a specific order, it means that there is a problem in the exchange between the trading system and the market. We will need to raise an error:

```
def handle_order_from_gateway(self,order_update):
    order=self.lookup_order_by_id(order_update['id'])
    if order is not None:
        order['status']=order_update['status']
        if self.om_2_ts is not None:
            self.om_2_ts.append(order.copy())
        else:
            print('simulation mode')
        self.clean_traded_orders()
    else:
        print('order not found')
```

The `check_order_valid` function will perform regular checks on an order. In this example, we will check that the quantity and price are not negative. You may consider adding more code and to check the position, PnL, or anything you consider important for your trading strategy:

```python
def check_order_valid(self,order):
    if order['quantity'] < 0:
        return False
    if order['price'] < 0:
        return False
    return True
```

The `create_new_order`, `lookup_order_by_id`, and `clean_traded_orders` functions will create an order based on the order sent by the trading strategy, which has a unique order ID. Indeed, each trading strategy can have its own local order ID. It is important that the orders we send to the market have an unique order ID. The second function will help with looking up the order from the list of outstanding orders. The last function will clean the orders that have been rejected, filled, or canceled.

The `create_new_order` function will create a dictionary to store the order characteristics:

```python
def create_new_order(self,order):
    self.order_id += 1
    neworder = {
        'id': self.order_id,
        'price': order['price'],
        'quantity': order['quantity'],
        'side': order['side'],
        'status': 'new',
        'action': 'New'
    }
    return neworder
```

The `lookup_order_by_id` function will return a reference to the order by looking up by order ID:

```python
def lookup_order_by_id(self,id):
    for i in range(len(self.orders)):
        if self.orders[i]['id']==id:
            return self.orders[i]
    return None
```

The `clean_traded_orders` function will remove from the list of orders all the orders that have been filled:

```python
def clean_traded_orders(self):
    order_offsets=[]
```

```
    for k in range(len(self.orders)):
        if self.orders[k]['status'] == 'filled':
            order_offsets.append(k)
    if len(order_offsets):
        for k in sorted(order_offsets, reverse=True):
            del (self.orders[k])
```

Since the `OrderManager` component is critical for the safety of your trading, we need to have exhaustive unit testing to ensure that no strategy will damage your gain, and prevent you from incurring losses:

```
import unittest
from chapter7.OrderManager import OrderManager

class TestOrderBook(unittest.TestCase):

    def setUp(self):
        self.order_manager = OrderManager()
```

The `test_receive_order_from_trading_strategy` test verifies whether an order is correctly received by the order manager. First, we create an order, `order1`, and we call the `handle_order_from_trading_strategy` function. Since the trading strategy creates two orders (stored in the channel `ts_2_om`), we call the `test_receive_order_from_trading_strategy` function twice. The order manager will then generate two orders. In this example, since we only have one strategy, when the orders are created by the order manager, they will have the same order IDs as the trading strategy created:

```
    def test_receive_order_from_trading_strategy(self):
        order1 = {
            'id': 10,
            'price': 219,
            'quantity': 10,
            'side': 'bid',
        }
        self.order_manager.handle_order_from_trading_strategy(order1)
        self.assertEqual(len(self.order_manager.orders), 1)
        self.order_manager.handle_order_from_trading_strategy(order1)
        self.assertEqual(len(self.order_manager.orders), 2)
        self.assertEqual(self.order_manager.orders[0]['id'], 1)
        self.assertEqual(self.order_manager.orders[1]['id'], 2)
```

To prevent a malformed order from being sent to the market, the `test_receive_order_from_trading_strategy_error` test checks whether an order created with a negative price is rejected:

```python
def test_receive_order_from_trading_strategy_error(self):
    order1 = {
        'id': 10,
        'price': -219,
        'quantity': 10,
        'side': 'bid',
    }
    self.order_manager.handle_order_from_trading_strategy(order1)
    self.assertEqual(len(self.order_manager.orders),0)
```

The following test, `test_receive_from_gateway_filled`, confirms a market response has been propagated by the order manager:

```python
def test_receive_from_gateway_filled(self):
    self.test_receive_order_from_trading_strategy()
    orderexecution1 = {
        'id': 2,
        'price': 13,
        'quantity': 10,
        'side': 'bid',
        'status' : 'filled'
    }
    self.order_manager.handle_order_from_gateway(orderexecution1)
    self.assertEqual(len(self.order_manager.orders), 1)

def test_receive_from_gateway_acked(self):
    self.test_receive_order_from_trading_strategy()
    orderexecution1 = {
        'id': 2,
        'price': 13,
        'quantity': 10,
        'side': 'bid',
        'status' : 'acked'
    }
    self.order_manager.handle_order_from_gateway(orderexecution1)
    self.assertEqual(len(self.order_manager.orders), 2)
    self.assertEqual(self.order_manager.orders[1]['status'], 'acked')
```

MarketSimulator class

The MarketSimulator class is central in validating your trading strategy. You will use this class to fix the market assumptions. For instance, you can indicate the rejection rate and which type of orders can be accepted, and you can set the trading rules belonging to the exchange you are targeting. In our example, the market simulator acknowledges and fills all new orders.

When creating this class, the constructor will have two channels. One will get input from the order manager and the other will give the response back to the order manager:

```python
class MarketSimulator:
    def __init__(self, om_2_gw=None, gw_2_om=None):
        self.orders = []
        self.om_2_gw = om_2_gw
        self.gw_2_om = gw_2_om
```

The lookup_orders function will help to look up outstanding orders:

```python
def lookup_orders(self,order):
    count=0
    for o in self.orders:
        if o['id'] ==  order['id']:
            return o, count
        count+=1
    return None, None
```

The handle_order_from_gw function will collect the order from the gateway (the order manager) through the om_2_gw channel:

```python
def handle_order_from_gw(self):
    if self.om_2_gw is not None:
        if len(self.om_2_gw)>0:
            self.handle_order(self.om_2_gw.popleft())
    else:
        print('simulation mode')
```

The trading rule that we use in the handle_order function will accept any new orders. If an order already has the same order ID, the order will be dropped. If the order manager cancels or amends an order, the order is automatically canceled and amended. The logic you will code in this function will be adapted to your trading:

```python
def handle_order(self, order):
    o,offset=self.lookup_orders(order)
    if o is None:
        if order['action'] == 'New':
```

```
                order['status'] = 'accepted'
                self.orders.append(order)
                if self.gw_2_om is not None:
                    self.gw_2_om.append(order.copy())
                else:
                    print('simulation mode')
                return
            elif order['action'] == 'Cancel' or order['action'] ==
'Amend':
                print('Order id - not found - Rejection')
                if self.gw_2_om is not None:
                    self.gw_2_om.append(order.copy())
                else:
                    print('simulation mode')
                return
        elif o is not None:
            if order['action'] == 'New':
                print('Duplicate order id - Rejection')
                return
            elif order['action'] == 'Cancel':
                o['status']='cancelled'
                if self.gw_2_om is not None:
                    self.gw_2_om.append(o.copy())
                else:
                    print('simulation mode')
                del (self.orders[offset])
                print('Order cancelled')
            elif order['action'] == 'Amend':
                o['status'] = 'accepted'
                if self.gw_2_om is not None:
                    self.gw_2_om.append(o.copy())
                else:
                    print('simulation mode')
                print('Order amended')

    def fill_all_orders(self):
        orders_to_be_removed = []
        for index, order in enumerate(self.orders):
            order['status'] = 'filled'
            orders_to_be_removed.append(index)
            if self.gw_2_om is not None:
                self.gw_2_om.append(order.copy())
            else:
                print('simulation mode')
        for i in sorted(orders_to_be_removed, reverse=True):
            del(self.orders[i])
```

The unit test will ensure that the trading rules are verified:

```python
import unittest
from chapter7.MarketSimulator import MarketSimulator


class TestMarketSimulator(unittest.TestCase):

    def setUp(self):
        self.market_simulator = MarketSimulator()

    def test_accept_order(self):
        self.market_simulator
        order1 = {
            'id': 10,
            'price': 219,
            'quantity': 10,
            'side': 'bid',
            'action' : 'New'
        }
        self.market_simulator.handle_order(order1)
        self.assertEqual(len(self.market_simulator.orders),1)
        self.assertEqual(self.market_simulator.orders[0]['status'],
'accepted')

    def test_accept_order(self):
        self.market_simulator
        order1 = {
            'id': 10,
            'price': 219,
            'quantity': 10,
            'side': 'bid',
            'action' : 'Amend'
        }
        self.market_simulator.handle_order(order1)
        self.assertEqual(len(self.market_simulator.orders),0)
```

TestTradingSimulation class

The goal of the TestTradingSimulation class is to create the full trading system by gathering all the prior critical components together.

This class checks whether, for a given input, we have the expected output. Additionally, we will test whether the PnL of the trading strategy has been updated accordingly.

We will first need to create all the deques representing the communication channels within the trading systems:

```python
import unittest
from chapter7.LiquidityProvider import LiquidityProvider
from chapter7.TradingStrategy import TradingStrategy
from chapter7.MarketSimulator import MarketSimulator
from chapter7.OrderManager import OrderManager
from chapter7.OrderBook import OrderBook
from collections import deque

class TestTradingSimulation(unittest.TestCase):
    def setUp(self):
        self.lp_2_gateway=deque()
        self.ob_2_ts = deque()
        self.ts_2_om = deque()
        self.ms_2_om = deque()
        self.om_2_ts = deque()
        self.gw_2_om = deque()
        self.om_2_gw = deque()
```

We instantiate all the critical components of the trading system:

```python
        self.lp=LiquidityProvider(self.lp_2_gateway)
        self.ob=OrderBook(self.lp_2_gateway, self.ob_2_ts)
        self.ts=TradingStrategy(self.ob_2_ts,self.ts_2_om,self.om_2_ts)
        self.ms=MarketSimulator(self.om_2_gw,self.gw_2_om)
        self.om=OrderManager(self.ts_2_om,
    self.om_2_ts,self.om_2_gw,self.gw_2_om)
```

We test whether. by adding two liquidities having a bid higher than the offer, we will create two orders to arbitrage these two liquidities. We will check whether the components function correctly by checking what they push to their respective channels. Finally, since we will buy 10 liquidities at a price of 218 and we sell at a price of 219, the PnL should be 10:

```python
    def test_add_liquidity(self):
        # Order sent from the exchange to the trading system
        order1 = {
            'id': 1,
            'price': 219,
            'quantity': 10,
            'side': 'bid',
            'action': 'new'
        }
        self.lp.insert_manual_order(order1)
        self.assertEqual(len(self.lp_2_gateway),1)
```

```
self.ob.handle_order_from_gateway()
self.assertEqual(len(self.ob_2_ts), 1)
self.ts.handle_input_from_bb()
self.assertEqual(len(self.ts_2_om), 0)
order2 = {
    'id': 2,
    'price': 218,
    'quantity': 10,
    'side': 'ask',
    'action': 'new'
}
self.lp.insert_manual_order(order2.copy())
self.assertEqual(len(self.lp_2_gateway),1)
self.ob.handle_order_from_gateway()
self.assertEqual(len(self.ob_2_ts), 1)
self.ts.handle_input_from_bb()
self.assertEqual(len(self.ts_2_om), 2)
self.om.handle_input_from_ts()
self.assertEqual(len(self.ts_2_om), 1)
self.assertEqual(len(self.om_2_gw), 1)
self.om.handle_input_from_ts()
self.assertEqual(len(self.ts_2_om), 0)
self.assertEqual(len(self.om_2_gw), 2)
self.ms.handle_order_from_gw()
self.assertEqual(len(self.gw_2_om), 1)
self.ms.handle_order_from_gw()
self.assertEqual(len(self.gw_2_om), 2)
self.om.handle_input_from_market()
self.om.handle_input_from_market()
self.assertEqual(len(self.om_2_ts), 2)
self.ts.handle_response_from_om()
self.assertEqual(self.ts.get_pnl(),0)
self.ms.fill_all_orders()
self.assertEqual(len(self.gw_2_om), 2)
self.om.handle_input_from_market()
self.om.handle_input_from_market()
self.assertEqual(len(self.om_2_ts), 3)
self.ts.handle_response_from_om()
self.assertEqual(len(self.om_2_ts), 2)
self.ts.handle_response_from_om()
self.assertEqual(len(self.om_2_ts), 1)
self.ts.handle_response_from_om()
self.assertEqual(len(self.om_2_ts), 0)
self.assertEqual(self.ts.get_pnl(),10)
```

Designing a limit order book

A limit order book is a component that gathers all the orders and sorts them in a way that facilitates the work of the trading strategy. The order book is used by exchanges to maintain sell and buy orders. When we trade, we need to get the book of the exchange to know which prices are the best or just to have a view on the market. Because the exchange is located on another machine, we will need to use the network to communicate changes on the exchange book. For that, we have two methods:

- The first method is to send the whole book. You will realize that this method would be very slow, especially when the exchanges is as large as NYSE or NASDAQ. This solution is not scalable.
- The second method is to first send the whole book (like the first method), but then instead of sending the whole book each time there is an update, we just send the update. This update will be the order (from the other traders placing orders on the exchange). They will arrive by time increments as small as microseconds.

The trading strategy needs to make a decision very rapidly (buying, selling, or holding stocks). Since the book provides the required information to the trading strategies to make the decision, it needs to be fast. An order book is, in reality, a book for the orders coming from buyers and a book for the orders from sellers. The highest bid and the lowest offer prices will have priority. In a situation where there is more than one bid with the same price competing for the best price, the time stamp will be used to sort out which one should be sold. The timestamp that is the earliest will be executed first.

The operations we will need to handle for the life cycle of the orders are the following:

- **Insertion**: An insertion will add an order to the book. This operation should be fast. The algorithm and data structure chosen for this operation are critical, because we need to have the book of bids and offers sorted at any time. We will have to privilege a data structure allowing a complexity of $O(1)$ or $O(\log n)$ to insert a new order.
- **Amendment/modification**: An amendment will look up the order in the book by using the order ID. This operation should also be with the same complexity as the insertion.
- **Cancelation**: A cancelation will allow an order to be removed from the book by using the order ID.

As you can understand, the choice of data structure and the algorithm associated with this data structure will change the performance a lot. If you are building a high-frequency trading system, you will need to choose accordingly. Since we are using Python and we are not implementing a high-frequency trading system, we will then use a list to simplify the coding part. This list will represent the orders and this list will be sorted for both sides (for the book of bids and for the book of offers).

We will build an `OrderBook` class; this class will collect orders from `LiquidityProvider` and sort the orders and create book events. The book events in a trading system are preset events and these events can be anything a trader thinks it is worth knowing. For instance, in this implementation, we choose to generate a book event each time there is a change on the top of the book (any changes in the first level of the book will create an event):

1. We choose to code `OrderBook` by having a list for *asks* and *bids*. The constructor has two optional arguments, which are the two channels to receive orders and send book events:

```python
class OrderBook:
    def __init__(self, gt_2_ob = None, ob_to_ts = None):
        self.list_asks = []
        self.list_bids = []
        self.gw_2_ob=gt_2_ob
        self.ob_to_ts = ob_to_ts
        self.current_bid = None
        self.current_ask = None
```

2. We will write a function, `handle_order_from_gateway`, which will receive the orders from the liquidity provider. Let's have a look at the code:

```python
def handle_order_from_gateway(self, order = None):
    if self.gw_2_ob is None:
        print('simulation mode')
        self.handle_order(order)
    elif len(self.gw_2_ob)>0:
        order_from_gw=self.gw_2_ob.popleft()
        self.handle_order(order_from_gw)
```

3. Next, as shown, we will write a function to check whether the `gw_2_ob` channel has been defined. If the channel has been instantiated, `handle_order_from_gateway` will pop the order from the top of deque `gw_2_ob` and will call the `handle_order` function to process the order for a given action:

```python
def handle_order(self,o):
    if o['action']=='new':
        self.handle_new(o)
    elif o['action']=='modify':
        self.handle_modify(o)
    elif o['action']=='delete':
        self.handle_delete(o)
    else:
        print('Error-Cannot handle this action')

    return self.check_generate_top_of_book_event()
```

In the code, `handle_order` calls either `handle_modify`, `handle_delete`, or `handle_new`.

The `handle_modify` function modifies the order from the book by using the order given as an argument of this function.

The `handle_delete` function removes an order from the book by using the order given as an argument of this function. The `handle_new` function adds an order to the appropriate list, `self.list_bids` and `self.list_asks` .

The code shows the implementation of the insertion of a new order. In this code, we check the order side. Depending on the side, we will choose the list of the bids or the list of asks:

```python
if o['side']=='bid':
    self.list_bids.append(o)
    self.list_bids.sort(key=lambda x: x['price'],reverse=True)
elif o['side']=='ask':
    self.list_asks.append(o)
    self.list_asks.sort(key=lambda x: x['price'])
```

4. As shown in the code, we will then implement the `handle_modify` function to manage the amendment. This function searches in the list of orders if the order exists. If that's the case, we will modify the quantity by the new quantity. This operation will be possible only if we reduce the quantity of the order:

```python
def handle_modify(self,o):
    order=self.find_order_in_a_list(o)
    if order['quantity'] > o['quantity']:
        order['quantity'] = o['quantity']
    else:
        print('incorrect size')
    return None
```

5. The `handle_delete` function will manage the order cancelation. As shown in the code, we will remove the orders from the list of orders by checking whether the order exists with the order ID:

```python
def handle_delete(self,o):
    lookup_list = self.get_list(o)
    order = self.find_order_in_a_list(o,lookup_list)
    if order is not None:
        lookup_list.remove(order)
    return None
```

The following two functions will help with finding an order by using the order ID.

6. The `get_list` function in the code will help to find the side (which order book) contains the order:

```python
def get_list(self,o):
    if 'side' in o:
        if o['side']=='bid':
            lookup_list = self.list_bids
        elif o['side'] == 'ask':
            lookup_list = self.list_asks
        else:
            print('incorrect side')
            return None
        return lookup_list
    else:
        for order in self.list_bids:
            if order['id']==o['id']:
                return self.list_bids
        for order in self.list_asks:
            if order['id'] == o['id']:
```

```
            return self.list_asks
        return None
```

7. The `find_order_in_a_list` function will return a reference to the order if this order exists:

```
def find_order_in_a_list(self,o,lookup_list = None):
    if lookup_list is None:
        lookup_list = self.get_list(o)
    if lookup_list is not None:
        for order in lookup_list:
            if order['id'] == o['id']:
                return order
        print('order not found id=%d' % (o['id']))
    return None
```

The following two functions will help with creating the book events. The book events as defined in the `check_generate_top_of_book_event` function will be created by having the top of the book changed.

8. As shown, the `create_book_event` function creates a dictionary representing a book event. In this example, a book event will be given to the trading strategy to indicate what change was made at the top of the book level:

```
def create_book_event(self,bid,offer):
    book_event = {
        "bid_price": bid['price'] if bid else -1,
        "bid_quantity": bid['quantity'] if bid else -1,
        "offer_price": offer['price'] if offer else -1,
        "offer_quantity": offer['quantity'] if offer else -1
    }
    return book_event
```

9. As shown, the `check_generate_top_of_book_event` function will create a book event when the top of the book has changed. When the price or the quantity for the best bid or offer has changed, we will inform the trading strategies that there is a change at the top of the book:

```
def check_generate_top_of_book_event(self):
    tob_changed = False
    if not self.list_bids:
        if self.current_bid is not None:
            tob_changed = True
            # if top of book change generate an event
        if not self.current_bid:
            if self.current_bid != self.list_bids[0]:
                tob_changed=True
```

```
                self.current_bid=self.list_bids[0] \
                            if self.list_bids else None

        if not self.current_ask:
            if not self.list_asks:
                if self.current_ask is not None:
                    tob_changed = True
                elif self.current_ask != self.list_asks[0]:
                    tob_changed = True
                    self.current_ask = self.list_asks[0] \
                            if self.list_asks else None


        if tob_changed:
    be=self.create_book_event(self.current_bid,self.current_ask)
        if self.ob_to_ts is not None:
            self.ob_to_ts.append(be)
        else:
            return be
```

When we test the order book, we need to test the following functionalities:

- Adding a new order
- Modifying a new order
- Deleting an order
- Creating a book event

This code will start creating the unit test for the Order Book. We will use the function setUp called for every test cases and create an reference to the Order Book for all the test cases.

```
import unittest
 from chapter7.OrderBook import OrderBook

class TestOrderBook(unittest.TestCase):

    def setUp(self):
        self.reforderbook = OrderBook()
```

10. We will create a function to verify if the order insertion works. The book must have the list of asks and the list of bids sorted:

```python
def test_handlenew(self):
    order1 = {
        'id': 1,
        'price': 219,
        'quantity': 10,
        'side': 'bid',
        'action': 'new'
    }

    ob_for_aapl = self.reforderbook
    ob_for_aapl.handle_order(order1)
    order2 = order1.copy()
    order2['id'] = 2
    order2['price'] = 220
    ob_for_aapl.handle_order(order2)
    order3 = order1.copy()
    order3['price'] = 223
    order3['id'] = 3
    ob_for_aapl.handle_order(order3)
    order4 = order1.copy()
    order4['side'] = 'ask'
    order4['price'] = 220
    order4['id'] = 4
    ob_for_aapl.handle_order(order4)
    order5 = order4.copy()
    order5['price'] = 223
    order5['id'] = 5
    ob_for_aapl.handle_order(order5)
    order6 = order4.copy()
    order6['price'] = 221
    order6['id'] = 6
    ob_for_aapl.handle_order(order6)

    self.assertEqual(ob_for_aapl.list_bids[0]['id'],3)
    self.assertEqual(ob_for_aapl.list_bids[1]['id'], 2)
    self.assertEqual(ob_for_aapl.list_bids[2]['id'], 1)
    self.assertEqual(ob_for_aapl.list_asks[0]['id'],4)
    self.assertEqual(ob_for_aapl.list_asks[1]['id'], 6)
    self.assertEqual(ob_for_aapl.list_asks[2]['id'], 5)
```

11. Next, we will write the following function to test whether the amendment works. We fill the book by using the prior function, then we amend the order by changing the quantity:

```python
def test_handleamend(self):
    self.test_handlenew()
    order1 = {
        'id': 1,
        'quantity': 5,
        'action': 'modify'
    }
    self.reforderbook.handle_order(order1)

    self.assertEqual(self.reforderbook.list_bids[2]['id'], 1)
    self.assertEqual(self.reforderbook.list_bids[2]['quantity'], 5)
```

12. The last function in the code involves book management that removes order from the book by the order ID. In this test case, we fill the book with the prior function and we remove the order:

```python
def test_handledelete(self):
    self.test_handlenew()
    order1 = {
        'id': 1,
        'action': 'delete'
    }
    self.assertEqual(len(self.reforderbook.list_bids), 3)
    self.reforderbook.handle_order(order1)
    self.assertEqual(len(self.reforderbook.list_bids), 2)
```

13. The book event is created when there is a change at the top of the book. We will write the following function to test the creation of the book event after the top of the book changes:

```python
def test_generate_book_event(self):
    order1 = {
        'id': 1,
        'price': 219,
        'quantity': 10,
        'side': 'bid',
        'action': 'new'

    }
    ob_for_aapl = self.reforderbook
    self.assertEqual(ob_for_aapl.handle_order(order1),
                    {'bid_price': 219, 'bid_quantity': 10,
```

```
                                    'offer_price': -1, 'offer_quantity': -1})
            order2 = order1.copy()
            order2['id'] = 2
            order2['price'] = 220
            order2['side'] = 'ask'
            self.assertEqual(ob_for_aapl.handle_order(order2),
            {'bid_price': 219, 'bid_quantity': 10,
             'offer_price': 220, 'offer_quantity': 10})

    if __name__ == '__main__':
        unittest.main()
```

In this section, we studied how to build a limit order book. This was a naive implementation. The complexity to add an order is in the order of *O(N)* and for each insertion, we use a sorting algorithm with a complexity of *O(N log N)*. In order to get a book working faster for order insertion, order lookup, we should use more advanced data structures, as described in *Algorithm Analysis, Packt Publishing*. Because we need to sort the order by price, we need to use an ordered data structure, such as trees. We will change the complexity of insertion to *O(log N)*. Concurrently, we will fix the lookup time to retrieve the best price.

Summary

In this chapter, we learned how to build a Python trading system. The trading system we built presents the critical components that you will need to start trading in real time. Depending on the trading strategy you implement, you will add some services and you will modify the behavior of these components. As mentioned at the beginning of this chapter, the number of traders, the type of strategies, and the types of asset classes will affect the design of the trading system. Learning how to design a trading system takes years and it is very common to become expert in a trading system for a given strategy, given asset class and given number of users. But it is uncommon to become expert in all trading system types because of their complexity. We built the minimum functionalities that a trading system must have. To be fully functional, we need to learn how to get this component connected to a trading system.

In the next chapter, we will focus on explaining all the details related to connection with exchanges.

8
Connecting to Trading Exchanges

At this point, we have a good understanding of how to write a trading system and writing the code for all the critical components. We went into detail about book building, creating trading signals, and getting a market response.

In this chapter, we will introduce the component that's in charge of communicating with the outside world and the gateway. We will look at the different functionalities of this component and describe the different types of protocols that we will encounter. Finally, we will implement a gateway that will connect to a real liquidity provider.

In this chapter, we will cover the following topics:

- Making a trading system trade with exchanges
- Reviewing the Communication API
- Receiving price updates
- Sending orders and receiving market responses

Making a trading system trade with exchanges

As we saw in `Chapter 7`, *Building a Trading System in Python*, a trading system is a piece of software that is capable of collecting financial data and sending orders to the market. This trading system has many functional components that are in charge of handling trading and risks, as well as monitoring the trading process that happens on one or many exchanges. When you code a trading strategy, it will become a component of the trading system. You will need input price information and your trading strategy as output. This will send trading indications. To complete this flow, we require gateways since they are the main components.

The following diagram shows the functional components of a trading system, the gateway's interface, and the outside world with the trading system. The gateways collect prices and market responses and send orders. Its main role is to initiate a connection and to convert the data that's sent from the outside world into the data structure that will be used in the trading system:

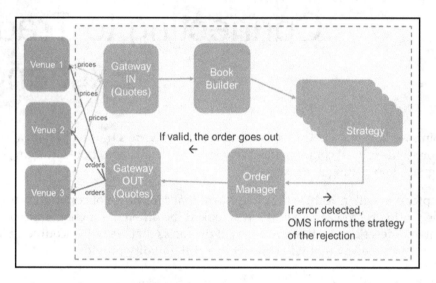

The following is shown in the preceding diagram:

- When you implement your trading strategy, this trading strategy will be on your machine. The exchange will be located on another machine.
- Since these two machines are on different sites, they need to communicate through a network.
- Depending on the location of the system, the ways that are used to communicate can be different.
- If the trading system is collocated (the machines are located in the same facility), a single wire will be used, which will reduce the network latency.
- If we use a cloud solution, the internet could be another method of communication. In that case, the communication will be much slower than a direct connect one.

Take a look at the following diagram, which depicts the communication taking place between the gateways:

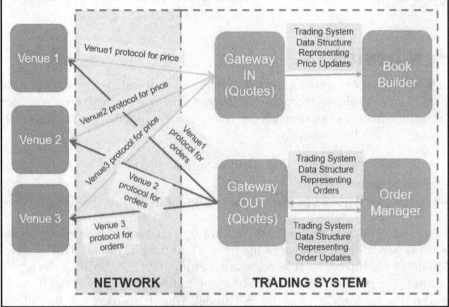

The following is shown in the preceding diagram:

- When we look closer at the communication that's handled by the gateways, we can observe that the venues can have different protocols.
- The gateways will need to be able to process numerous protocols so that they can convert them into trading system data structures.

Reviewing the Communication API

Network protocols define the rules of communication between machines. They define how these machines will be recognized on the network and how they will interact. In trading finance, we use the UDP and TCP over the IP protocol. Additionally, we use a software protocol that will define how to communicate with an order and get a price update. The Communication API will set the rules of communication at the software level. The Communication API is given by the entity that you would like to trade with. This document contains all the messages that you will use to receive prices and send orders.

You can find examples of trading API documents at `https://en.wikipedia.org/wiki/List_of_electronic_trading_protocols`.

Before diving into the trading API, we will need to explain the basics of networking.

Network basics

The network is in charge of making the computers communicate with each other. Networks need a physical layer to share information. Choosing the correct media (communication layer) is critical for the network to reach a given speed or reliability, or even security. In trading finance, we use the following:

- **Wire**: Electrical currents that are limited in bandwidth
- **Fiber**: More bandwidth
- **Microwave**: An easy-to-install, large bandwidth, but can be impacted by storms

The media will vary, depending on the type of trading strategy you're using. Choosing the correct media is part of the first layer of the network in the ISO model. This layer is called the physical layer. On top of this one, there are six more layers describing the type of communication. The protocol that we will be using in trading finance is the IP protocol. This is a part of the network layer of the ISO model. This IP protocol sets the rules for routing network packets in the network. The last layer that we will talk about is the transport layer. The two most well-known protocols in finance are TCP and UDP. These two protocols are very different. TCP works by establishing communication between two machines. All the messages that were sent first will arrive first. UDP doesn't have any mechanism to establish whether the network packets have been received by the network.

All the exchanges will choose their own protocol by using either TCP or UDP. In the next section, we will talk about the content that's sent through the network.

Trading protocols

To have two entities communicate with each other, they need to talk the same language. In networking, we use a protocol. In trading, this protocol is used for any venue. Some venues can have numerous protocols. Even if they are different, the steps that these protocols go through to establish a connection and start trading are similar:

1. They start by initiating a logon describing who the trading initiator is, who the recipient is, and how the communication remains alive.

2. Then, they inquire about what they expect from the different entities, for example, trading or subscribing price updates.
3. After, that they receive orders and price updates.
4. Then, they maintain communication by sending heartbeats.
5. Finally, they close communication.

The protocol we will be using in this chapter is called the **Financial Information eXchange** (**FIX**) protocol. It was created in 1992 for international real-time exchanges to handle securities between Fidelity Investments and Salomon Brothers. It expanded to **foreign exchange** (**FX**), **fixed income** (**FI**), derivatives, and clearing. This protocol is a string-based protocol, which means humans can read it. It is platform-independent, is an open protocol, and has many versions. The most widely used versions are versions 4.2, 4.4, 5, and 1. There are two types of messages:

- The administrative messages, which do not carry any financial data
- The application messages, which are used to get price updates and orders

The content of these messages is like a Python dictionary: it is a list of key-value pairs. The keys are predefined tags; every tag is a number that corresponds to a specific feature. Associated with these tags are the values, which can be numerical or string values. Let's take a look at an example:

- Let's say that the tag corresponding to the price of an order has the value 44 if we want to send an order with a price of $1.23. Therefore, in the order message, we will have 44=1.23.
- All the pairs are character-1 separated. This means that if we add the quantity (tag 38) of 100,000 to our prior example to create an order, we will have 44=1.23|38=100000. The| symbol represents the character-1.
- All the messages start with a prefix, that is, 8=FIX.X.Y. This prefix indicates the fix version numbers. X and Y represent the numbers of the version.
- They all terminate when 10=nn corresponds to the checksum.
- The checksum is the sum of all the binary values in the message. It helps us identify transmission problems.

The following is an example of an FIX message:

```
8=FIX.4.2|9=76|35=A|34=1|49=DONALD|52=20160617-23:11:55.884|56=VENUE1|98=0|
108=30|141=Y|10=134
```

The preceding FIX message has the following mandatory fields:

- A tag of 8, which is associated with the value 4.2. This corresponds to the FIX version number.
- A version number lower than FIX4.4: 8(BeginString), 9(BodyLength), and 35(MsgType).
- A version number higher than FIX4.4: 8(BeginString), 9(BodyLength), 35(MsgType), 49(SnderCompID), and 56(TargetCompID).
- The message type is defined by the tag 35.
- The body length tag, 9, corresponds to the character count starting at tag 35 all the way to tag 10.
- The 10 field is the checksum. The value is calculated by summing up the decimal value of the ASCII representation of all the bytes up to, but not including, the checksum field (which is the last field), and returns the value modulo 256.

FIX communication protocols

A trading system must use two connections to be able to trade: one connection to receive the price updates, and another one for the orders. The FIX protocol conforms to that requirement by having different messages for the following connections.

Price updates

Trading systems need prices for the liquidities that traders choose to trade. For that, it initiates a connection to the exchange to subscribe to liquidity updates.

The following diagram describes the communication between the initiator, which is the trading system, and the acceptor, which is the exchange:

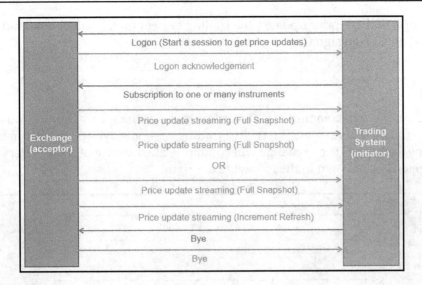

The following diagram represents the FIX messages that are exchanged between the acceptor and the initiator:

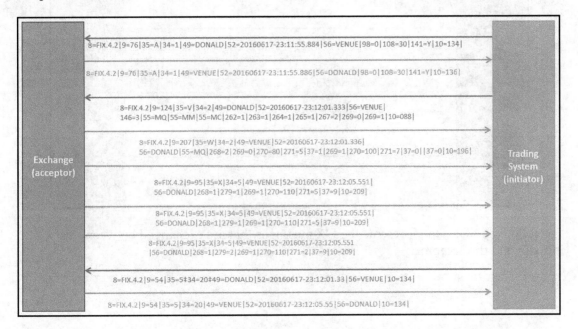

Upon reception of these price updates, the trading system updates the books and will place orders based on a given signal.

Orders

The trading system will communicate the orders to the exchange by opening a trading session with the exchange. While this active trading session stays open, order messages will be sent to the exchange. The exchange will communicate the state of these orders by using FIX messages. This is shown in the following diagram:

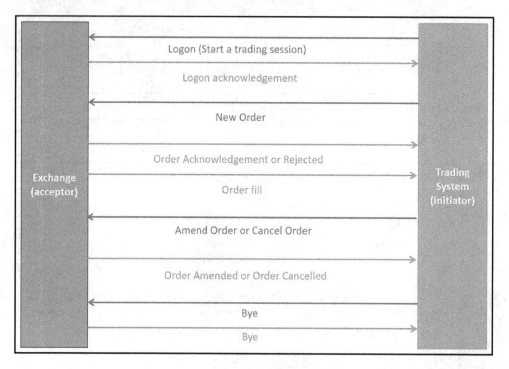

The following diagram represents the FIX messages that are exchanged between the initiator and the acceptor:

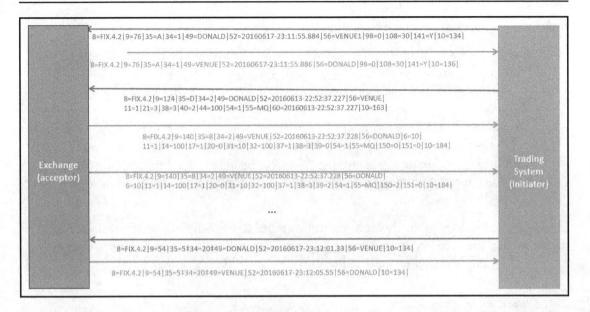

Receiving price updates

When we implement an FIX parser and an FIX composer, we know how tedious and time-consuming this process is. If you choose to implement these parts from scratch, you will need to take care of the network connections, the parsing operations, and the part creating the FIX messages. Because we want to focus on creating a trading system that's capable of working quickly, we will want to use a library where all the functions have already been implemented. There are many commercial FIX libraries available, including NYFIX, Aegisfot – Aethna, Reuters – Traid, and Financial Fusion – Trade Force. The one we will use is called the `quickfix` library.

This library can be downloaded from `http://www.quickfixengine.org/`.

This library was created in 2000 and is supported by Java, C++, and Python.

The libraries simplify the developer's role by using callbacks. A callback is a computer engineering term and something that we will be using if we have a task that could take some time to finish. In naive code (code without callbacks), we wait for the end of the execution of this task.

If we use a callback system, the following takes place:

- We start a task and then proceed to the other tasks while this task keeps running.
- Once that task has finished, it will call a function to leave the program to handle the result of this task. Let's assume that we have a trading system with many tasks.
- If one of them is to receive price updates from exchanges, we just use a callback that's triggered once a price update has been received and parsed by the system.
- Once the callback has been called, we will be able to read the specific fields we need in order to proceed with the rest of our system by using this new price update.

The `quickfix` library gives the developer the ability to implement specific tasks for any messages that are received by the trading system. The following code describes the general structure of a piece of Python code using the `quickfix` library:

```python
import sys
import time
import quickfix as fix
import quickfix42 as fix42

class Application(fix.Application):
    def onCreate(self, sessionID): return
    def onLogon(self, sessionID):
            self.sessionID = sessionID
            print ("Successful Logon to session '%s'." %
sessionID.toString())
            return
    def onLogout(self, sessionID): return
    def toAdmin(self, sessionID, message):return
    def fromAdmin(self, sessionID, message):return
    def toApp(self, sessionID, message):
        print "Sent the following message: %s" % message.toString()
        return
    def fromApp(self, message, sessionID):
        print "Received the following message: %s" % message.toString()
        return
```

The code imports the `quickfix` library and creates a
class called `Application` that's derived from the `fix.Application` object. Let's go
through this now:

- The `onLogon` and `onLogout` functions are callback functions that are called
  when a logon/logout message (35=A) has been received and parsed by the
  system. The argument of the `onLogon` function is the session ID. It is received
  when a connection has been successfully established between the acceptor and
  the initiator.
- The `onCreate` function is called when a new session is created to initialize a
  trading session.
- The `toAdmin` and `toApp` functions are used to modify the messages that are sent
  to the acceptor.
- The `fromAdmin` and `fromApp` functions are called when we receive a message
  from the acceptor.
- The incoming code is the minimal code you need to have an FIX application in
  Python.

Each FIX application has its own `config` file. By reading the documentation on the
`quickfix` library, you will learn how to configure the application. We are going to
comment on a simple configuration example. The `quickfix` configuration file is divided
into several parts. The DEFAULT part configures the main app attributes:

- The connection type: *Initiator* or *acceptor*
- The reconnection time: 60 seconds (in this config file)
- `SenderCompIT`: The identification of the initiator

The SESSION part describes the FIX message format. In this example, the FIX version that's
being used is version 4.1. `TargetCompID` corresponding to the identification of the acceptor
is ARCA. The heartbeat interval is set in this file. This sets a heartbeat that checks whether
the acceptor is still alive and has been sent. The network connection is established by using
a socket. This socket is created based on the IP address (`SocketConnectHost`) and the port
(`SocketConnectPort`).

We use a dictionary that defines all the mandatory and optional tags for all the message
types:

```
# default settings for sessions
[DEFAULT]
ConnectionType=initiator
ReconnectInterval=60
SenderCompID=TW
```

```
# session definition

[SESSION]
# inherit ConnectionType, ReconnectInterval and SenderCompID from default
BeginString=FIX.4.1
TargetCompID=ARCA
StartTime=12:30:00
EndTime=23:30:00
HeartBtInt=20
SocketConnectPort=9823
SocketConnectHost=123.123.123.123
DataDictionary=somewhere/FIX41.xml
```

For the upcoming code example, we will use some free open source software code from GitHub. It can be found at `https://github.com/gloryofrobots/fixsim`. This code is a good example of Python code for initiators and acceptors in terms of the price update and order side of things.

Initiator code example

The initiator starts communication with the exchange. An initiator will take care of getting the price updates, while another initiator will take care of the order.

Price updates

The role of the initiator is to start a connection with the acceptor. When the connection is established, the initiator will subscribe to the acceptor and request price updates. The first function we will review is the function to subscribe. This function will be called once the connection is established.

The `subscribe` function will be called after fixed intervals. When this function is called, we need to check whether there is an active session. It will build the market data request by iterating through the list of symbols. Let's have a look at the following code block:

```
8=FIX.4.4|9=78|35=V|146=1|55=USD/RUB|460=4|167=FOR|262=2|263=1|264=0|265=0|
267=2|269=0|269=0|10=222|
```

As we can see, the message will have a message type of 35=V. The tags and their corresponding fields and values have been listed in the following table:

Tag	Field	Value
8	BeginString	FIX.4.4
9	BodyLength	78
35	MsgType	V
146	NoRelatedSym	1
55	Symbol	USD/RUB
460	Product	4
167	SecurityType	FOR
262	MDReqID	2
263	SubscriptionRequestType	1
264	MarketDepth	0

265	MDUpdateType	0
267	NoMDEntryTypes	2
269	MDEntryType	0
269	MDEntryType	1
10	CheckSum	222

We can see the following in the preceding table:

- For each symbol (the ticker you would like to trade), this function will create a new market data request message.
- Each market data request must have a unique identifier (Market Data Request ID, that is, MDReqID) that's associated with a given symbol. In the following example, we use USD/RUB:

```python
def subscribe(self):
    if self.marketSession is None:
        self.logger.info("FIXSIM-CLIENT Market session is none,
skip subscribing")
        return

    for subscription in self.subscriptions:
        message = self.fixVersion.MarketDataRequest()
        message.setField(quickfix.MDReqID(self.idGen.reqID()))
message.setField(quickfix.SubscriptionRequestType(quickfix.Subscrip
tionRequestType_SNAPSHOT_PLUS_UPDATES))
message.setField(quickfix.MDUpdateType(quickfix.MDUpdateType_FULL_R
EFRESH))
        message.setField(quickfix.MarketDepth(0))
        message.setField(quickfix.MDReqID(self.idGen.reqID()))

        relatedSym =
self.fixVersion.MarketDataRequest.NoRelatedSym()
```

```
        relatedSym.setField(quickfix.Product(quickfix.Product_CURRENCY))
        relatedSym.setField(quickfix.SecurityType(quickfix.SecurityType_FOR
EIGN_EXCHANGE_CONTRACT))
            relatedSym.setField(quickfix.Symbol(subscription.symbol))
            message.addGroup(relatedSym)

            group = self.fixVersion.MarketDataRequest.NoMDEntryTypes()
        group.setField(quickfix.MDEntryType(quickfix.MDEntryType_BID))
            message.addGroup(group)
        group.setField(quickfix.MDEntryType(quickfix.MDEntryType_OFFER))
            message.addGroup(group)

            self.sendToTarget(message, self.marketSession)
```

We can see the following in the preceding code:

- Once we subscribe to all the desired symbols (in this example, currency pairs), the acceptor will start sending market updates.
- The `onMarketDataSnapshotFullRefresh` function will receive the full snapshot of every price update coming into the system.

The type of message that's received by the price update gateway is as follows:

```
8=FIX.4.4|9=429|35=W|34=1781|49=FIXSIM-SERVER-
MKD|52=20190909-19:31:48.011|56=FIXSIM-CLIENT-
MKD|55=EUR/USD|262=74|268=4|269=0|270=6.512|15=EUR|271=2000|276=A|299=a23de
46d-6309-4783-
a880-80d6a02c6140|269=0|270=5.1|15=EUR|271=5000|276=A|299=1f551637-20e5-4d8
b-85d9-1870fd49e7e7|269=1|270=6.512|15=EUR|271=2000|276=A|299=445cb24b-8f94
-47dc-9132-75f4c09ba216|269=1|270=9.49999999999999|15=EUR|271=5000|276=A|29
9=3ba6f03c-131d-4227-b4fb-bd377249f50f|10=001|
```

This function is a callback. It is called when a Full Snapshot message is received and parsed. The `message` parameter will contain the message. Let's have a look at the code:

```python
def onMarketDataSnapshotFullRefresh(self, message, sessionID):

    fix_symbol = quickfix.Symbol()
    message.getField(fix_symbol)
    symbol = fix_symbol.getValue()

    group = self.fixVersion.MarketDataSnapshotFullRefresh.NoMDEntries()
    fix_no_entries = quickfix.NoMDEntries()
    message.getField(fix_no_entries)
    no_entries = fix_no_entries.getValue()

    for i in range(1, no_entries + 1):
```

```
message.getGroup(i, group)
price = quickfix.MDEntryPx()
size = quickfix.MDEntrySize()
currency = quickfix.Currency()
quote_id = quickfix.QuoteEntryID()

group.getField(quote_id)
group.getField(currency)
group.getField(price)
group.getField(size)

quote = Quote()
quote.price = price.getValue()
quote.size = size.getValue()
quote.currency = currency.getValue()
quote.id = quote_id.getValue()

fix_entry_type = quickfix.MDEntryType()
group.getField(fix_entry_type)
entry_type = fix_entry_type.getValue()
```

As we can see, we can access the field by using the `getField` method.

Sending orders and receiving a market response

The main goal of a trading system is to send orders and receive market responses regarding these orders. In this section, we will cover how to send an order and how to get an update on these orders.

The role of the initiator is to initiate a connection with the acceptor. When the connection is established, the trading session is enabled. From this very moment, the trading system can send orders to the exchange. The order will have the following type of message:

```
8=FIX.4.4|9=155|35=D|11=3440|15=USD|21=2|38=20000|40=D|44=55.945|54=1|55=US
D/RUB|59=3|60=20190909-19:35:27|64=SP|107=SPOT|117=b3fc02d3-373e-4632-80a0-
e50c2119310e|167=FOR|10=150|
```

The initiator creates the orders by using the message type 35=D (representing a single order). All the fields of these orders will be filled in by the function of the `quickfix` library. Let's have a look at the code:

```
def makeOrder(self, snapshot):
    self.logger.info("FIXSIM-CLIENT Snapshot received %s", str(snapshot))
    quote = snapshot.getRandomQuote()

    self.logger.info("FIXSIM-CLIENT make order for quote %s", str(quote))
    order = self.fixVersion.NewOrderSingle()
order.setField(quickfix.HandlInst(quickfix.HandlInst_AUTOMATED_EXECUTION_OR
DER_PUBLIC_BROKER_INTERVENTION_OK))
order.setField(quickfix.SecurityType(quickfix.SecurityType_FOREIGN_EXCHANGE
_CONTRACT))

    order.setField(quickfix.OrdType(quickfix.OrdType_PREVIOUSLY_QUOTED))
    order.setField(quickfix.ClOrdID(self.idGen.orderID()))
    order.setField(quickfix.QuoteID(quote.id))

    order.setField(quickfix.SecurityDesc("SPOT"))
    order.setField(quickfix.Symbol(snapshot.symbol))
    order.setField(quickfix.Currency(quote.currency))
    order.setField(quickfix.Side(quote.side))

    order.setField(quickfix.OrderQty(quote.size))
    order.setField(quickfix.FutSettDate("SP"))
    order.setField(quickfix.Price(quote.price))
    order.setField(quickfix.TransactTime())
order.setField(quickfix.TimeInForce(quickfix.TimeInForce_IMMEDIATE_OR_CANCE
L))
```

Once an order is received by an exchange, it will be handled and the exchange will reply to this order with a specific FIX message. The nature of this message is the execution report 35=8.

The message will acknowledge the order by using the execution report message 35=8, the `ExecType` tag 150=0, and `OrdStatus` 39=0:

```
8=FIX.4.4|9=204|35=8|34=4004|49=FIXSIM-
SERVER|52=20190909-19:35:27.085|56=FIXSIM-
CLIENT|6=55.945|11=3440|14=20000|15=USD|17=3440|31=55.945|32=20000|37=3440|
38=20000|39=0|44=55.945|54=1|55=USD/RUB|64=20190910|150=0|151=0|10=008|
```

The order will be filled and the server will send an execution report message indicating that 150=2 and 39=2 for a fill:

```
8=FIX.4.4|9=204|35=8|34=4005|49=FIXSIM-
SERVER|52=20190909-19:35:27.985|56=FIXSIM-
CLIENT|6=55.945|11=3440|14=20000|15=USD|17=3440|31=55.945|32=20000|37=3440|
38=20000|39=2|44=55.945|54=1|55=USD/RUB|64=20190910|150=2|151=0|10=008|
```

The onExecutionReport callback in the code will be called once these messages are received by the trading system:

```
def onExecutionReport(self, connectionHandler, msg):
    codec = connectionHandler.codec
    if codec.protocol.fixtags.ExecType in msg:
        if msg.getField(codec.protocol.fixtags.ExecType) == "0":
            side = Side(int(msg.getField(codec.protocol.fixtags.Side)))
            logging.debug("<--- [%s] %s: %s %s %s@%s" %
(codec.protocol.msgtype.msgTypeToName(msg.getField(codec.protocol.fixtags.M
sgType)), msg.getField(codec.protocol.fixtags.ClOrdID),
msg.getField(codec.protocol.fixtags.Symbol), side.name,
msg.getField(codec.protocol.fixtags.OrderQty),
msg.getField(codec.protocol.fixtags.Price)))
        elif msg.getField(codec.protocol.fixtags.ExecType) == "2":
            logging.info("Order Filled")
    else:
        logging.error("Received execution report without ExecType")
```

As shown in the preceding code, we have parsed the fields that we need to get the required information from the execution report message. We have also tested whether the order has been acknowledged or filled.

Acceptor code example

The role of the acceptor is to receive the connection from the initiator. As an automatic trader, you will rarely code this part. However, you will be improving your knowledge if you know how exchange handle messages are sent by the initiator.

There are two main functions that an acceptor will take care of:

- **Market data request handling**: This is the function that's called when the market data request is received by the server.
- **Order handling**: This is the function that's called when order messages are received.

Market Data request handling

Market Data request handling allows the acceptor (the exchange) to register the request from an initiator who's willing to trade a given symbol. Once this request is received, the acceptor starts streaming the price updates to the initiator. Let's have a look at the following code:

```
def onMarketDataRequest(self, message, sessionID):
 requestID = quickfix.MDReqID()
 try:
 message.getField(requestID)
 except Exception as e:
 raise quickfix.IncorrectTagValue(requestID)

 try:
 relatedSym = self.fixVersion.MarketDataRequest.NoRelatedSym()
 symbolFix = quickfix.Symbol()
 product = quickfix.Product()
 message.getGroup(1, relatedSym)
 relatedSym.getField(symbolFix)
 relatedSym.getField(product)
 if product.getValue() != quickfix.Product_CURRENCY:
 self.sendMarketDataReject(requestID, " product.getValue() !=
quickfix.Product_CURRENCY:", sessionID)
 return

 # bid
 entryType = self.fixVersion.MarketDataRequest.NoMDEntryTypes()
 message.getGroup(1, entryType)

 # ask
 message.getGroup(2, entryType)

 symbol = symbolFix.getValue()
 subscription = self.subscriptions.get(symbol)
 if subscription is None:
 self.sendMarketDataReject(requestID, "Unknown symbol: %s" % str(symbol),
sessionID)
 return

 subscription.addSession(sessionID)
 except Exception as e:
 print e,e.args
 self.sendMarketDataReject(requestID, str(e), sessionID)
```

As shown in the preceding code, the `onMarketDataRequest` callback that's handling the market data request does the following:

- **Gets the request ID**: The exchange will check whether the request ID has not already been processed.
- **Gets the symbol ID**: The symbol updates that are linked to this symbol will be sent to the initiator.
- **Gets the product**: The exchange checks whether the product that was requested is in the system. If the product isn't, a rejection message will be sent to the initiator.

Order

Order management is the main functionality of an initiator. An exchange must be capable of handling the following:

- **New order (35=D)**: This message is sent for a trading indication. This message can describe numerous types of orders, such as Limit, Fill or Kill, and Market order.
- **Cancel order (35=F)**: This message is sent to indicate that an order's been canceled.
- **Amend order (35=G)**: This message is sent to amend an order.

The `onNewOrderSingle` function is the function that handles the orders that are sent by the initiator. This function needs to get the principal order features:

- Symbol (the ticker symbol)
- Side (buy or sell)
- Type (market, limit, stop, stop limit, and so on)
- Quantity (the quantity to be traded)
- Price (the price to be traded)
- Client order ID (the unique identifier for an order)
- Quote ID (the quote identifier to be traded)

An exchange checks whether the order ID already exists. If it does, a rejection message should be sent to indicate that it isn't possible to create a new order with the same order ID. If the order is correctly received by the exchange, an execution report message will be sent to the initiator, indicating that the exchange has received the order.

In the GitHub fixsim code, the author chose to reject randomly incoming orders. When we will talk about backtesting later in this book, we will mention the different options we can introduce to model the market's behavior. Introducing a random rejection is one way of mimicking the market's behavior. If there is no rejection, the exchange will fill the order by sending an execution report 35=8 with an order status indicating that it's been filled.

The onNewOrderSingle function (callback) is divided into two parts. The first part collects the information from the *New Order* (35=D) message. The second part creates a response for the initiator. This response will be an *Execution Report* 35=8 message.

The code will create quickfix objects (symbol, side, ordType, and so on) and get the value from the tag values by using the getField function. The author of this code chooses to accept an order, but only if this order has been previously quoted. This means that the order will be based on a price update that has been received by our trading system:

```
def onNewOrderSingle(self, message, beginString, sessionID):
    symbol = quickfix.Symbol()
    side = quickfix.Side()
    ordType = quickfix.OrdType()
    orderQty = quickfix.OrderQty()
    price = quickfix.Price()
    clOrdID = quickfix.ClOrdID()
    quoteID = quickfix.QuoteID()
    currency = quickfix.Currency()

    message.getField(ordType)
    if ordType.getValue() != quickfix.OrdType_PREVIOUSLY_QUOTED:
        raise quickfix.IncorrectTagValue(ordType.getField())

    message.getField(symbol)
    message.getField(side)
    message.getField(orderQty)
    message.getField(price)
    message.getField(clOrdID)
    message.getField(quoteID)
    message.getField(currency)
```

The following code will create the *Execution Report* (35=8) message. The first line of this code creates an object execution report representing this message. The line after that will create the required headers for this message:

```
executionReport = quickfix.Message()
executionReport.getHeader().setField(beginString)
executionReport.getHeader().setField(quickfix.MsgType(quickfix.MsgType_Exec
utionReport))
executionReport.setField(quickfix.OrderID(self.idGen.orderID()))
executionReport.setField(quickfix.ExecID(self.idGen.execID()))
```

The following code takes care of building the code so that it simulates rejections. It will reject the code by taking a `reject_chance` (a percentage) into account:

```
try:
    reject_chance = random.choice(range(1, 101))
    if self.rejectRate > reject_chance:
        raise FixSimError("Rejected by cruel destiny %s" %
str((reject_chance, self.rejectRate)))
```

The following code will run some checks on the execution size and the price:

```
execPrice = price.getValue()
execSize = orderQty.getValue()
if execSize > quote.size:
    raise FixSimError("size to large for quote")

if abs(execPrice - quote.price) > 0.0000001:
    raise FixSimError("Trade price not equal to quote")
```

The code will finish by populating the required fields of the *Execution Report* message:

```
executionReport.setField(quickfix.SettlDate(self.getSettlementDate()))
        executionReport.setField(quickfix.Currency(subscription.currency))
executionReport.setField(quickfix.OrdStatus(quickfix.OrdStatus_FILLED))
        executionReport.setField(symbol)
        executionReport.setField(side)
        executionReport.setField(clOrdID)
        executionReport.setField(quickfix.Price(price.getValue()))
        executionReport.setField(quickfix.AvgPx(execPrice))
        executionReport.setField(quickfix.LastPx(execPrice))
        executionReport.setField(quickfix.LastShares(execSize))
        executionReport.setField(quickfix.CumQty(execSize))
        executionReport.setField(quickfix.OrderQty(execSize))
        executionReport.setField(quickfix.ExecType(quickfix.ExecType_FILL))
        executionReport.setField(quickfix.LeavesQty(0))
```

The following code will build the rejection message in case of an error. It is done in the same way as building the message to indicate that the order has been executed. We specify the *Rejected* value in the *Order Status* of the *Execution Report* message:

```
except Exception as e:
        self.logger.exception("FixServer:Close order error")
        executionReport.setField(quickfix.SettlDate(''))
        executionReport.setField(currency)
executionReport.setField(quickfix.OrdStatus(quickfix.OrdStatus_REJECTED))
        executionReport.setField(symbol)
        executionReport.setField(side)
        executionReport.setField(clOrdID)
        executionReport.setField(quickfix.Price(0))
        executionReport.setField(quickfix.AvgPx(0))
        executionReport.setField(quickfix.LastPx(0))
        executionReport.setField(quickfix.LastShares(0))
        executionReport.setField(quickfix.CumQty(0))
        executionReport.setField(quickfix.OrderQty(0))
executionReport.setField(quickfix.ExecType(quickfix.ExecType_REJECTED))
        executionReport.setField(quickfix.LeavesQty(0))
```

Finally, we will send the message back to the initiator:

```
self.sendToTarget(executionReport, sessionID)
```

This concludes the part of the code that's specific to the acceptor. The role of the acceptor can be more rich than the bare minimum code we implement. The main role of the acceptor is to match orders between traders. If we were implementing an exchange, we would need to create a matching engine (to match orders that can be filled). In this simple example, we chose to fill our orders regardless of the state of the market. The main goal was just to build a simulation mimicking the behavior of the market by filling and rejecting orders.

Other trading APIs

The FIX protocol has been used since 1992. By understanding FIX, which is a string-based protocol, you will be able to understand other protocols. Nasdaq uses the direct data feed, ITCH and the direct-trading OUCH protocol. These protocols are much faster than the FIX protocols because of their limit overhead. These protocols use a fixed offset to specify the tag values. For instance, instead of using 39=2, the OUCH protocol will use a value of 2 at an offset of 20.

The **New York Stock Exchange** (**NYSE**) uses UTP Direct, which is similar to the NASDAQ protocols. The cryptocurrency world uses HTTP requests while using the RESTful API or Websocket way of communicating. All of these protocols provide us with different ways to represent financial exchange information. They all have the same goal: price update and order handling.

Summary

In this chapter, we learned that trading system communication is key to trading. The trading system is in charge of collecting the required prices to make an informed decision. If this component is slow, it will make the trading decision slower. Gateways are technically more challenging than any of the other components because they need to deal with the communication. The communication implies that layers are handled perfectly on the computer level; that is, the computer architecture (network layer), operating system (system calls, the driver that talks to the network card, and so on), and the software itself. All of these layers must be optimized so that they have a fast trading system. Because of their level of technical complexity, it is unlikely that you will implement this communication if you have strategies for high-frequency trading. Instead, you will use a system that's been provided by experts in this domain. However, if your trading strategy is not time-sensitive, you will be able to use the information you gained from this chapter to implement communication with the exchange.

We also talked about the communication between your trading system and exchanges. We learned how to use the Python *quickfix* library to simplify the time of the communication system's implementation. We used some software alongside quickfix to simulate exchanges between the initiator and the acceptor. By doing this, we learned about the workflows of trading communication systems. We are now aware of how to create a trading system and how to make this system communicate with the outside world. The last thing we need is to have confidence that the strategy will perform well on this trading system.

In the next chapter, we will talk about another critical step when it comes to testing a trading strategy: backtesting.

Creating a Backtester in Python

9

By now, we know how to implement a trading strategy idea. We learned how to write the code to make it run in a trading system. The final step before going live with a trading strategy is backtesting. Whether you want to be more confident in the performance of your strategy or you want to show your managers how well your trading idea performs, you will have to use a backtester using a large amount of historical data.

In this chapter, you will learn how to create a backtester. You will improve your trading algorithm by running different scenarios with large amounts of data to validate the performance of your trading strategy. Once a model is implemented, it is necessary to test whether the trading robot behaves as expected in the trading infrastructure.

In this chapter, we will learn how backtesting works, and then we will talk about the assumptions you will need to consider when creating a backtester. Finally, we will provide a backtester example by using a momentum trading strategy.

In this chapter, we will cover the following topics:

- Learning how to build a backtester
- Learning how to choose the correct assumptions
- Evaluating what the value of time is
- Backtesting the dual-moving average trading strategy

Learning how to build a backtester

Backtesting is key in the creation of trading strategies. It assesses how profitable a trading strategy is by using historical data. It helps to optimize it by running simulations that generate results showing risk and profitability before risking any capital loss. If the backtesting returns good results (high profits with reasonable risk), it will encourage getting this strategy to go alive. If the results are not satisfactory, backtesters can help to find issues.

Trading strategies define rules for entry and exit into a portfolio of assets. Backtesting helps us to decide whether it is worth going live with these trading rules. It provides us with an idea of how a strategy might have performed in the past. The ultimate goal is to filter out bad strategy rules before we allocate any real capital.

Backesting can sound out a run of a trading strategy using past market data. Most of the time, we consider a backtester like a model of reality. We will make assumptions based on the experience. But if the model is not close enough to reality, the trading strategies will end up not performing as well, which will result in financial losses.

The first part we will cover in this chapter is getting the data. The data will be stored in many different forms and, depending on them, we will need to adapt our backtester.

Backtesters use data heavily. In trading, getting 1 terabyte of data a day is pretty common. It can take a few minutes for a hard disk to read this amount of data. If you are looking for a specific range of dates, or if you are looking for specific symbols. It will be very important to have a performance index for the dates, the symbols, or other attributes. The data in finance is a value associated to a particular time, called time series. Regular relational databases are not efficient at reading these time series. We will review a few ways to handle time series.

In-sample versus out-of-sample data

When building a statistical model, we use cross-validation to avoid overfitting. Cross-validation imposes a division of data into two or three different sets. One set will be used to create your model, while the other sets will be used to validate the model's accuracy. Because the model has not been created with the other datasets, we will have a better idea of its performance.

When testing a trading strategy with historical data, it is important to use a portion of data for testing. In a statistical model, we call training data the initial data to create the model. For a trading strategy, we will say that we are in the in-sample data. The testing data will be called out-of-sample data. As for cross-validation, it provides a way to test the performance of a trading strategy by resembling real-life trading as far as possible by testing on new data.

The following diagram represents how we divide the historical data into two different sets. We will build our trading strategy using the in-sample data. Then, we will use this model to validate our model with the out-of-sample data:

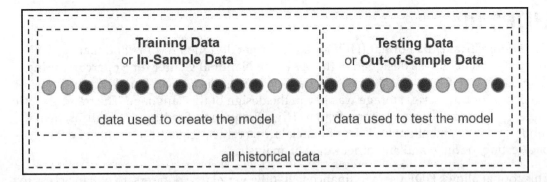

When we build a trading strategy, it is important to set aside between 70% and 80% to build the model. When the trading model is built, the performance of this model will be tested out of the out-of-sample data (20-30% of data).

Paper trading (forward testing)

Paper trading (also known as forward performance testing) is the final step of the testing phase. We include the trading strategy to the real-time environment of our system and we send fake orders. After a day of trading, we will have the logs of all the orders and compare them to what they were supposed to be. This step is useful because it allows us to test the strategy and use the entire trading system.

This phase is a way to do a last test of the trading strategy before investing real money. The benefits of this phase are the absence of any financial risk whatsoever, while the trading strategy creator can acquire confidence and practice in a stress-free environment while building new datasets that will be used for further analysis. Unfortunately, performance obtained by paper trading is not directly correlated to the market. It is difficult to ensure that an order can be fulfilled, or not, and at what price. Indeed, during a period of high market volatility, most orders can be rejected. Additionally, orders could be fulfilled at a worse price (negative slippage).

Naive data storage

One of the most intuitive ways to store data is to use flat file on the hard disk. The problem with this approach is that the hard disk will need to traverse a vast area to get to the part of a file corresponding to the data you would like to use for your backtesting. Having indexes can help enormously in looking up the correct segment to read.

HDF5 file

The **Hierarchical Data Format** (**HDF**) is a file format designed to store and manage large amounts of data. It was designed in the 90s at the **National Center for Supercomputing Applications** (**NCSA**), and then NASA decided to use this format. Portability and efficiency for time series storage was key in the design of this language. The trading world rapidly adopted this format, in particular, **High-Frequency Trading** (**HFT**) firms, hedge funds, and investment banks. These financial firms rely on gigantic amounts of data for backtesting, trading, and any other kinds of analysis.

This format allows HDF users in finance to handle very large datasets, to obtain access to a whole section or a subsection of the tick data. Additionally, since it is a free format, the number of open source tools is significant.

The hierarchical structure of the HDF5 shown uses two major types:

- **Datasets**: Multidimensional arrays of a given type
- **Groups:** Container of other groups and/or datasets

The following diagram shows the hierarchical structure of the HDF5:

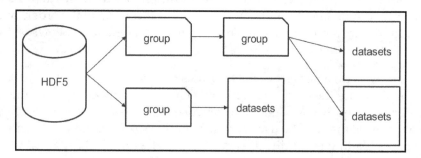

To get the dataset's content, we can access it like a regular file using the POSIX syntax /path/file. The metadata is also stored in groups and datasets. The HDF5 format uses B-trees to index datasets, which makes it a good storage format for time series, especially financial asset price series.

In the code, we will describe an example of how to use an HDF5 file in Python. We will use the load_financial_data function we used in this book to get the GOOG prices. We store the data frame in an HDF5 file called goog_data. Then, we use the h5py library to read this file and read the attributes of these files. We will print the data content of this files.

In this code will get the GOOG financial data. We store this data into the data frame goog_data:

```
!/bin/python3
import pandas as pd
import numpy as np
from pandas_datareader import data
import matplotlib.pyplot as plt
import h5py

def load_financial_data(start_date, end_date,output_file):
    try:
        df = pd.read_pickle(output_file)
        print('File data found...reading GOOG data')
    except FileNotFoundError:
        print('File not found...downloading the GOOG data')
        df = data.DataReader('GOOG', 'yahoo', start_date, end_date)
        df.to_pickle(output_file)
    return df

goog_data=load_financial_data(start_date='2001-01-01',
                    end_date = '2018-01-01',
                    output_file='goog_data.pkl')
```

In this part of the code we will store the data frame goog_data into the file goog_data.h5.

```
goog_data.to_hdf('goog_data.h5', 'goog_data',mode='w',format='table',data_co
lumns=True)
```

We will then load this file from the file goog_data.h5 and create a data frame goog_data_from_h5_file:

```
goog_data_from_h5_file = h5py.File('goog_data.h5')

print(goog_data_from_h5_file['goog_data']['table'])
print(goog_data_from_h5_file['goog_data']['table'][:])
for attributes in
goog_data_from_h5_file['goog_data']['table'].attrs.items():
    print(attributes)
```

Despite being portable and open source, the HDF5 file format has some important caveats:

- The likelihood of getting corrupted data is high. When the software handing the HDF5 file crashes, it is possible to lose all the data located in the same file.
- It has limited features. It is not possible to remove arrays.
- It offers low performance. There is no use of operating system caching.

Many financial companies still use this standardized file. It will remain on the market for a few years. Next, we will talk about the file storage alternative: databases.

Databases

Databases are made to store data. Financial data is time series data, and most databases do not handle time series data in the most efficient way. The biggest challenge associated with storing time series data is scalability. An important data stream comes rapidly. We have two main groups of databases: relational and non-relational databases.

Relational databases

Relational databases have tables that can be written and accessed in many different ways without having the need to reorganize the database structure. They usually use **Structured Query Language** (**SQL**). The most widely used databases are Microsoft SQL Server, PostgreSQL, MySQL, and Oracle.

Python has many libraries capable of using any of these databases. We will use PostGresSQL as an example. The PostGresSQL library, `Psycopg2`, is used by Python to handle any SQL queries:

1. We will use the GOOG data prices to create the database for GOOG data:

```
goog_data.head(10)
                      High          Low         Open         Close
Volume    Adj Close
Date
2014-01-02   555.263550   550.549194   554.125916   552.963501
3666400.0   552.963501
2014-01-03   554.856201   548.894958   553.897461   548.929749
3355000.0   548.929749
2014-01-06   555.814941   549.645081   552.908875   555.049927
3561600.0   555.049927
2014-01-07   566.162659   556.957520   558.865112   565.750366
5138400.0   565.750366
2014-01-08   569.953003   562.983337   569.297241   566.927673
4514100.0   566.927673
2014-01-09   568.413025   559.143311   568.025513   561.468201
4196000.0   561.468201
2014-01-10   565.859619   557.499023   565.859619   561.438354
4314700.0   561.438354
2014-01-13   569.749329   554.975403   559.595398   557.861633
4869100.0   557.861633
```

```
2014-01-14   571.781128   560.400146   565.298279   570.986267
4997400.0   570.986267
2014-01-15   573.768188   568.199402   572.769714   570.598816
3925700.0   570.598816
```

2. To create a table in SQL, we will use the following command. You will need to install PostGresSQL on your machine. Then, you will need to insert the following content:

```sql
CREATE TABLE "GOOG"
(
    dt timestamp without time zone NOT NULL,
    high numeric NOT NULL,
    low numeric NOT NULL,
    open numeric NOT NULL,
    close numeric NOT NULL,
    volume numeric NOT NULL,
    adj_close numeric NOT NULL
    CONSTRAINT "GOOG_pkey" PRIMARY KEY (dt)
);
```

This command will create a SQL table named GOOG. The primary key of this table will be the timestamp, dt.

3. As an example, we will run the following query to get the GOOG data from 2016-11-08 to 2016-11-09:

```sql
SQL = '''SELECT
    dt,high,low,open,close,volume, adj_close
FROM "GOOG"
WHERE dt BETWEEN '2016-11-08' AND '2016-11-09'
ORDER BY dt
LIMIT 100;'''
```

The Python code will be the following:

```python
import psycopg2
conn = psycopg2.connect(database='name_of_your_database')  # set
the appropriate credentials
cursor = conn.cursor()
def query_ticks():
    cursor.execute(SQL)
    data = cursor.fetchall()
    return data
```

The query_ticks function will return the GOOG data.

The main issue with a relational database is speed. They are not made to work with large amounts of data indexed by time. To speed up, we will need to use non-relational databases.

Non-relational databases

Non-relational databases are very widespread. Because the nature of the data is increasingly based on time series, this type of database has developed rapidly during the last decade. The best non-relational database for time series is called **KDB**. This database is designed to achieve performance with time series. There are many other competitors, including InfluxDB, MongoDB, Cassandra, TimescaleDB, OpenTSDB, and Graphite.

All of these databases have their pros and cons:

	Pros	Cons
KDB	High performance	Price; very difficult to use because of a non-SQL language
InfluxDB	Free, performant, quick start	Small community; poor performance analysis tool, no security
MongoDB	Faster than rational databases	No data joins; slow
Cassandra	Faster than rational databases	Unpredictable performance
TimescaleDB	SQL support	Performance
Graphite	Free, widespread support	Performance
OpenTSDB	Faster than rational databases	Small number of features

As shown in the table, it is difficult to choose an alternative to KDB. We will code an example of Python code using the KDB library, `pyq`. We will create an example similar to the one we created for PostGresSQL:

```
from pyq import q
 from datetime import date

# This is the part to be run on kdb
#googdata:([]dt:();high:();low:();open:();close:();volume:(),adj_close:())

 q.insert('googdata', (date(2014,01,2), 555.263550, 550.549194, 554.125916,
552.963501, 3666400.0, 552.963501))
 q.insert('googdata', (date(2014,01,3), 554.856201, 548.894958, 553.897461,
548.929749, 3355000.0, 548.929749))

 q.googdata.show()
                    High          Low          Open        Close       Volume
```

```
Adj Close
 Date
 2014-01-02   555.263550   550.549194   554.125916   552.963501   3666400.0
552.963501
 2014-01-03   554.856201   548.894958   553.897461   548.929749   3355000.0
548.929749

 # This is the part to be run on kdb
 # f:{[s]select from googdata where date=d}

 x=q.f('2014-01-02')
 print(x.show())

 2014-01-02   555.263550   550.549194   554.125916   552.963501   3666400.0
552.963501
```

This code ends this section on data storage. This part is critical in the design of your backtester since the running time of your backtesting will enable you to save time so as to be able to run many more backtests to validate your trading strategy. Following this section on different ways of storing financial data, we will introduce how a backtester works.

Learning how to choose the correct assumptions

Backtesting is a required step for deploying trading strategies. We use the historical data stored in databases to reproduce the behavior of the trading strategy. The fundamental assumption is that any methodology that functioned in the past is probably going to function in the future. Any strategies that performed ineffectively in the past are probably going to perform inadequately in the future. This section investigates what applications are utilized in backtesting, what sort of information is obtained, and how to utilize them.

A backtester can be a *for-loop* or *event-driven* backtester system. It is always important to consider how much time you will spend in order to achieve higher accuracy. It is impossible to obtain a model corresponding to reality; a backtester will just be a model of reality. However, there are rules to be followed in order to be as close as possible to the real market:

- **Training/testing data**: As with any models, you should not test your model with the data you use to create this model. You need to validate your data on unseen data to limit overfitting. When we use machine learning techniques, it is easy to overfit a model; that's why it is capital to use cross-validation to improve the accuracy of your model.

- **Survivorship-bias free data**: If your strategy is a long-term position strategy, it is important to use the survivorship-bias free data. This will prevent you from focusing on winners alone without considering the losers.
- **Look-ahead data**: When you build a strategy, you should not look ahead to make a trading decision. Sometimes, it is easy to make this mistake by using numbers calculated using the whole sample. This may be the case with an average that could potentially be calculated within all the data; data that you shouldn't have since you calculate the average using just the prices you get before placing an order.
- **Market change regime**: Modeling stock distribution parameters are not constant in time because the market changes regime.
- **Transaction costs**: It is important to consider the transaction costs of your trading. This is very easy to forget and not to make money on the real market.
- **Data quality/source**: Since there are many financial data sources, data composition differs a lot. For instance, when you use OHLC data from Google Finance, it is an aggregation of many exchange feeds. It will be difficult to obtain the same highs and lows with your trading system. Indeed, in order to have a match between your model and reality, the data you use must be as close as possible to the one you will use.
- **Money constraint**: Always consider that the amount of money you trade is not infinite. Additionally, if you use a credit/margin account, you will be limited by the position you take.
- **Average daily volume (ADV)**: The average number of shares traded over a day for a given ticker. The quantity of shares you choose to trade will be based on this number so as to avoid any impact on the market.
- **Benchmark testing**: In order to test the performance of your trading strategy, you will compare against another type of strategy or just against the return of some indexes. If you trade futures, do not test against the S&P 500. If you trade in airlines, you should check whether the airline industry as a whole performs better than your model.
- **Initial condition assumption**: In order to have a robust way of making money, you should not depend on the day you start your backtesting or the month. More generally, you should not assume that the initial condition is always the same.
- **Psychology**: Even if we are building a trading robot, when we trade for real, there is always a way to override what the algorithm is doing, even if, statistically speaking, based on the backtest, a trading strategy can have a large dropdown but, after a few days, this strategy can bring in a lot of profit if we maintain a given position. For a computer, there are no problems with taking that risk but, for a human, it is more difficult. Therefore, psychology can play a large role in the performance of a strategy.

On top of the prior rules, we will need to assume how we expect the market to behave. When you present a trading strategy to anyone, it is important to specify what these assumptions are.

One of the first assumption you need to consider is the fill ratio. When we place an order, depending on the type of strategies, the change of getting the order executed varies. If you trade with a high-frequency trading strategy, you may have 95% of the orders rejected. If you trade when there are important news on the market (such as FED announcements), you may have most of your orders rejected. Therefore, you will need to give a lot of thoughts on the fill ratio of your backtester.

Another important consideration is when you create a market making strategy. Unlike market trading strategies, a market making strategy does not remove liquidities from the market but add liquidities. Therefore it is important to create an assumption regarding when your order will be executed (or maybe it will not be executed). This assumption will add a condition to the backtester. We may get additional data. For instance, the trades which have been done in the market at a given time. This information will help us to decide whether a given market making order was supposed to be executed or not.

We can add additional latency assumptions. Indeed, since a trading system relies on many components. All the components have latencies and they also add latency when communicating. We can latency of any components of the trading systems, we can add network latency but also the latency to have an order executed, acknowledged.

The list of assumptions can be pretty long but it will be very important to show these assumptions to explain how likely your trading strategy will perform on the real market.

For-loop backtest systems

The for-loop backtester is a very simple infrastructure. It reads price updates line by line and calculates more metrics out of those prices (such as the moving average at the close). It then makes a decision on the trading direction. The profit and loss is calculated and displayed at the end of this backtester. The design is very simple and can quickly discern whether a trading idea is feasible.

An algorithm to picture how this kind of backtester works is shown here:

```
for each tick coming to the system (price update):
    create_metric_out_of_prices()
    buy_sell_or_hold_something()
    next_price()
```

Advantages

The for-loop backtester is very simple to comprehend. It can be easily implemented in any programming language. The main functionality of this type of backtester is to read a file and calculate new metrics based on price alone. Complexity and the need for calculating power are very low. Therefore, execution does not take too long and it is quick to obtain results regarding the performance of the trading strategies.

Disadvantages

The main weakness of the for-loop backtester is accuracy in relation to the market. It neglects transactions costs, transaction time, the bid and offer price, and volume. The likelihood of making a mistake by reading a value ahead of time is pretty high (look-ahead bias).

While the code of a for-loop backtester is easy to write, we should still use this type of backtester to eliminate low-performance strategies. If a strategy does not perform well with for-loop backtesters, this means that it will perform even worse on more realistic backtesters.

Since it is important to have a backtester that's as realistic as possible, we will learn how an event-driven backtester works in the following section.

Event-driven backtest systems

An event-driven backtester uses almost all the components of the trading system. Most of the time, this type of backtester encompass all the trading system components (such as the order manager system, the position manager, and the risk manager). Since more components are involved, the backtester is more realistic.

The event-driven backtester is close to the trading system we implemented in Chapter 7, *Building a Trading System in Python*. We left the code of the `TradingSimulation.py` file empty. In this section, we will see how to code that missing code.

We will have a loop calling all the components one by one. The components will read the input one after the other and will then generate events if needed. All these events will be inserted into a queue (we'll use the Python `deque` object). The events we encountered when we coded the trading system were the following:

- Tick events – When we read a new line of market data
- Book events – When the top of the book is modified

- Signal events – When it is possible to go long or short
- Order events – When orders are sent to the market
- Market response events – When the market response comes to the trading system

The pseudo code for an event-driven backtesting system is as follows:

```python
from chapter7.LiquidityProvider import LiquidityProvider
from chapter7.TradingStrategy import TradingStrategy
from chapter7.MarketSimulator import MarketSimulator
from chapter7.OrderManager import OrderManager
from chapter7.OrderBook import OrderBook
from collections import deque

def main():
    lp_2_gateway = deque()
    ob_2_ts = deque()
    ts_2_om = deque()
    ms_2_om = deque()
    om_2_ts = deque()
    gw_2_om = deque()
    om_2_gw = deque()

    lp = LiquidityProvider(lp_2_gateway)
    ob = OrderBook(lp_2_gateway, ob_2_ts)
    ts = TradingStrategy(ob_2_ts, ts_2_om, om_2_ts)
    ms = MarketSimulator(om_2_gw, gw_2_om)
    om = OrderManager(ts_2_om, om_2_ts, om_2_gw, gw_2_om)

    lp.read_tick_data_from_data_source()
    while len(lp_2_gateway)>0:
        ob.handle_order_from_gateway()
        ts.handle_input_from_bb()
        om.handle_input_from_ts()
        ms.handle_order_from_gw()
        om.handle_input_from_market()
        ts.handle_response_from_om()
        lp.read_tick_data_from_data_source()
if __name__ == '__main__':
    main()
```

We can see that all the components of the trading system are called. If we had a service checking the position, this service would be called.

Advantages

Because we use all the components, we will have a result that more closely corresponds to reality. One of the critical components is the market simulator (`MarketSimulator.py`). This component must have the same market assumptions. We can add the following parameters to the market simulator:

- Latency to send an acknowledgement
- Latency to send a fill
- An order filling condition
- A volatility filling condition
- A market making estimate

The advantages of the event-based backtester are as follows:

- Look-ahead bias elimination—since we receive events, we cannot look at the data ahead.
- Code encapsulation—because we use objects for the different parts of the trading system, we can just change the behavior of our trading system by changing the objects. The market simulation object is one such example.
- We can insert a position/risk management system and check whether we do not go against the limit.

Disadvantages

Even if the advantages are numerous, we need to consider that this type of event-based system is difficult to code. Indeed, if there are threads in the trading system, we will need to make this thread deterministic. For instance, let's assume the trading system takes care of timing out if an order doesn't get a response within 5 seconds. The best practice to code this functionality would be to have a thread counting 5 seconds and then timing out. If we use the thread in backtesting, the time shouldn't be the real time because when we read the tick, the time will be the simulated time.

Additionally, it requires a lot of handling, such as log management, unit testing, and version control. The execution of this system can be very slow.

Evaluating what the value of time is

As we saw in the previous parts of this chapter, backtester accuracy is critical when we build a trading strategy. The two main components creating discrepancies between the paper trading of your trading strategy and the actual performance are as follows:

- The market behavior that we face when the trading strategy goes live
- The trading system that you use to trade

We saw that the market impact can be medicated by making assumptions regarding the manner in which the market will respond. This part is very challenging because it is just based on assumptions. As regards the second cause of discrepancies, the trading system itself, we can find an easy solution. We will be able to use the trading system as it is to be the backtester. We will get all the main trading components together and we will have them communicate between one another as if they were in production.

When we use the time in production, we can get the time from the computer's clock. For instance, we can stamp a book event coming to the trading strategy by just getting the time from the function *now* coming from the `datetime` module in Python. By way of another example, suppose we place an order. Because it is unsure whether the market will respond to this order, we will use a timeout system. This timeout system will call a function after a given period of time if no acknowledgement has been received by the trading system from the market. To accomplish this operation, we usually spawn a thread counting the number of seconds up to the timeout time. When counting, if the state of the order has not changed to acknowledge the order, this thread will call a callback function, `onTimeOut`. This callback will have the role of handling what should occur when an order timed out on the market. If we want to mock the timeout system in the backtester, this is going to be more challenging. Because we cannot use the real-time clock of the machine to count to the timeout time, we will need to use a simulated clock during the whole process.

The following diagram shows how the backtester will work with the new simulated clock component handling the time. Each time a component needs to get the time, it will call a function, getTime. This function will return the simulated time (being the time of the last tick read by the LiquidityProvider class):

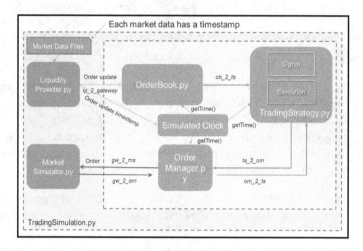

1. We will implement the **Simulated Clock** function (SimulatedRealClock class). Each time the trading system is started in backtest mode, we will use the SimulatedRealClock class with the simulated=True argument. If the trading system runs in real time to place orders on the market, the SimulatedRealClock class will be created without arguments or with the simulated=False argument, . When the time is given by a simulated time, the time will come from the order timestamps:

```python
from datetime import datetime

class SimulatedRealClock:
    def __init__(self, simulated=False):
        self.simulated = simulated
        self.simulated_time = None
    def process_order(self, order):
        self.simulated_time= \
            datetime.strptime(order['timestamp'], '%Y-%m-%d
%H:%M:%S.%f')
    def getTime(self):
        if not self.simulated:
            return datetime.now()
        else:
            return self.simulated_time
```

```
realtime=SimulatedRealClock()
print(realtime.getTime())
# It will return the date/time when you run this code
simulatedtime=SimulatedRealClock(simulated=True)
simulatedtime.process_order({'id' : 1, 'timestamp' : '2018-06-29
08:15:27.243860'})
print(simulatedtime.getTime())
# It will return 2018-06-29 08:15:27.243860
```

When coding a trading system, when you need the value of time, you will always need to use a reference to the `SimulatedRealClock` class and use the value returned by the `getTime` function.

2. In the following code, we will see the implementation of an order management system timing out 5 seconds after sending an order. We will first show you how to create a `TimeOut` class counting to the timeout value and calling a function when a timeout occurs. This `TimeOut` class is a thread. It means that the execution of this class will be concurrent to the main program. The arguments to build this class are the `SimulateRealClock` class, the time considered as the timeout time, and a function that will be called as a callback, `fun`. This class will run a loop as long as the current time is not older than the time to stop the countdown. If the time is higher and the `TimeOut` class has not been disabled, the `callback` function will be called. If the `TimeOut` class is disabled because the response to the order arrived in the system, the `callback` function will not be called. We can observe that we will compare the time to stop the timer with the current time by using the `getTime` function from the `SimulatedRealClock` class:

```
class TimeOut(threading.Thread):
    def __init__(self,sim_real_clock,time_to_stop,fun):
        super().__init__()
        self.time_to_stop=time_to_stop
        self.sim_real_clock=sim_real_clock
        self.callback=fun
        self.disabled=False
    def run(self):
        while not self.disabled and\
                self.sim_real_clock.getTime() < self.time_to_stop:
            sleep(1)
        if not self.disabled:
            self.callback()
```

3. The following OMS class that we will implement is just a small subset of what the order manager service can do. This OMS class will be in charge of sending an order. Each time an order is sent, a 5-second timeout will be created. This means that the onTimeOut function will be called if the OMS does not receive a response to the order placed on the market. We can observe that we build the TimeOut class by using the getTime function from the SimulatedRealClock class:

```python
class OMS:
    def __init__(self, sim_real_clock):
        self.sim_real_clock = sim_real_clock
        self.five_sec_order_time_out_management=\
            TimeOut(sim_real_clock,
                sim_real_clock.getTime()+timedelta(0,5),
                    self.onTimeOut)
    def send_order(self):
        self.five_sec_order_time_out_management.disabled = False
        self.five_sec_order_time_out_management.start()
        print('send order')
    def receive_market_reponse(self):
        self.five_sec_order_time_out_management.disabled = True
    def onTimeOut(self):
        print('Order Timeout Please Take Action')
```

When we run the following code to verify whether that works, we create two cases:

- **Case 1**: This will use the OMS in real time by using SimulatedRealClock in real-time mode.
- **Case 2**: This will use the OMS in simulated mode by using SimulatedRealClock in simulated mode.

4. In the following code, *Case 1* will trigger a timeout after 5 seconds, and *Case 2* will trigger a timeout when the simulated time is older than the time to trig the timeout:

```python
if __name__ == '__main__':
    print('case 1: real time')
    simulated_real_clock=SimulatedRealClock()
    oms=OMS(simulated_real_clock)
    oms.send_order()
    for i in range(10):
        print('do something else: %d' % (i))
        sleep(1)

    print('case 2: simulated time')
```

```
simulated_real_clock=SimulatedRealClock(simulated=True)
simulated_real_clock.\
    process_order({'id' : 1,\
                     'timestamp' : '2018-06-29 08:15:27.243860'})
oms = OMS(simulated_real_clock)
oms.send_order()
simulated_real_clock. \
    process_order({'id': 1, \
                     'timestamp': '2018-06-29 08:21:27.243860'})
```

When we use a backtester as a trading system, it is very important to use a class capable of handling simulation and real time. You will be able to achieve better accuracy by using the trading system and you will build better confidence in your trading strategy.

Backtesting the dual-moving average trading strategy

The dual-moving average trading strategy places a buy order when the short moving average crosses the long moving average in an upward direction and will place a sell order when the cross happens on the other side. This section will present the backtesting implementation of the dual-moving average strategy. We will present the implementation of a for-loop backtester and an event-based backtester.

For-loop backtester

1. As regards the implementation of this backtester, we will use the GOOG data by retrieving it with the same function we used previously, load_financial_data. We will follow the pseudo code that we proposed during the previous section:

   ```
   for each price update:
       create_metric_out_of_prices()
       buy_sell_or_hold_something()
       next_price();
   ```

   We will create a ForLookBackTester class. This class will handle, line by line, all the prices of the data frame. We will need to have two lists capturing the prices to calculate the two moving averages. We will store the history of profit and loss, cash, and holdings to draw a chart to see how much money we will make.

The `create_metrics_out_of_prices` function calculates the long moving average (100 days) and the short moving average (50 days). When the short window moving average is higher than the long window moving average, we will generate a long signal. The `buy_sell_or_hold_something` function will place orders. The buy order will be placed when there is a short position or no position. The sell order will be placed when there is a long position or no position. This function will keep track of the position, the holdings, and the profit.

These two functions will be sufficient for this for-loop backtester.

2. Now, let's import the following libraries as shown in this code:

```
#!/bin/python3
import pandas as pd
import numpy as np
from pandas_datareader import data
import matplotlib.pyplot as plt
import h5py
from collections import deque
```

3. Next, as shown, we will call the `load_financial_data` function previously defined in this book:

```
goog_data=load_financial_data(start_date='2001-01-01',
                end_date = '2018-01-01',
                output_file='goog_data.pkl')

# Python program to get average of a list
def average(lst):
    return sum(lst) / len(lst)
```

4. Let's now define the `ForLoopBackTester` class as shown. This class will have the data structure to support the strategy in the constructor. We will store the historic values for profit and loss, cash, positions, and holdings. We will also keep the real-time profit and loss, cash, position, and holding values:

```
class ForLoopBackTester:
    def __init__(self):
        self.small_window=deque()
        self.large_window=deque()
        self.list_position=[]
        self.list_cash=[]
        self.list_holdings = []
        self.list_total=[]

        self.long_signal=False
```

```
self.position=0
self.cash=10000
self.total=0
self.holdings=0
```

5. As shown in the code, we will write the `create_metric_out_of_prices` function to update the real-time metrics the trading strategy needs in order to make a decision:

```python
def create_metrics_out_of_prices(self,price_update):
    self.small_window.append(price_update['price'])
    self.large_window.append(price_update['price'])
    if len(self.small_window)>50:
        self.small_window.popleft()
    if len(self.large_window)>100:
        self.large_window.popleft()
    if len(self.small_window) == 50:
        if average(self.small_window) >\
            average(self.large_window):
            self.long_signal=True
        else:
            self.long_signal = False
        return True
    return False
```

6. The `buy_sell_or_hold_something` function will take care of placing the orders based on the calculation from the prior function:

```python
def buy_sell_or_hold_something(self,price_update):
    if self.long_signal and self.position<=0:
        print(str(price_update['date']) +
            " send buy order for 10 shares price=" +
str(price_update['price']))
        self.position += 10
        self.cash -= 10 * price_update['price']
    elif self.position>0 and not self.long_signal:
        print(str(price_update['date'])+
            " send sell order for 10 shares price=" +
str(price_update['price']))
        self.position -= 10
        self.cash -= -10 * price_update['price']

    self.holdings = self.position * price_update['price']
    self.total = (self.holdings + self.cash)
    print('%s total=%d, holding=%d, cash=%d' %
            (str(price_update['date']),self.total,
self.holdings, self.cash))
```

```
                    self.list_position.append(self.position)
                    self.list_cash.append(self.cash)
                    self.list_holdings.append(self.holdings)
                    self.list_total.append(self.holdings+self.cash)
```

7. We will feed this class by using the `goog_data` data frame as shown:

```
naive_backtester=ForLoopBackTester()
for line in zip(goog_data.index,goog_data['Adj Close']):
    date=line[0]
    price=line[1]
    price_information={'date' : date,
                       'price' : float(price)}
    is_tradable =
naive_backtester.create_metrics_out_of_prices(price_information)
    if is_tradable:
naive_backtester.buy_sell_or_hold_something(price_information)
```

When we run the code, we will obtain the following curve. This curve shows that this strategy makes around a 50% return with the range of years we are using for the backtest. This result is obtained by assuming a perfect fill ratio. Additionally, we don't have any mechanism preventing drawdown, or large positions. This is the most optimistic approach when we study the performance of trading strategies:

Achieving improved confidence in the way the strategy will perform in the market implies having a backtester that considers the characteristics of the trading system (more generally, the specificities of the company trading strategy where you work) and market assumptions. To make things more akin to scenarios encountered in real life, we will need to backtest the trading strategy by using most of the trading system components. Additionally, we will include the market assumptions in a market simulator.

In the following section, we will implement an event-based backtester handling the same GOOG data and we will be able to appreciate the differences.

Event-based backtester

The goal of the event-based backtester is to achieve better accuracy in the trading arena. We will consider the internals of the trading system by using the trading system we built in the last chapter and we will use the market simulator to simulate the external constraints of the market.

In this section, we will create an EventBasedBackTester class. This class will have a queue between all the components of the trading systems. Like when we wrote our first Python trading system, the role of these queues is to pass events between two components. For instance, the gateway will send the market data to the book through a queue. Each ticker (price update) will be considered an event. The event we implemented in the book will be triggered each time there is a change in the top of the order book. If there is a change in the top of the book, the book will pass a book event, indicating that there is a change in the book. This queue will be implemented using the deque from the collection library. All the trading object components will be linked to one another by these queues.

The input for our system will be the *Yahoo finance* data collected by the panda DataReader class. Because this data doesn't contain any orders, we will change the data with the process_data_from_yahoo function. This function will use a price and will convert this price to an order.

The order will be queued in the `lp_2_gateway` queue. Because we need to fake the fact that this order will disappear after each iteration, we will also delete the order. The `process_events` function will ensure that all the events generated by a tick have been processed by calling the `call_if_not_empty` function. This function has two arguments:

- **A queue**: This queue is checked if empty. If this queue is not empty, it will call the second argument.
- **A function**: This is the reference to the function that will be called when the queue is not empty.

We will now describe the steps we will take to build the event-based backtester.

1. In the following code, we will import the objects we created during Chapter 7, *Building a Trading System in Python*. We will use the trading system we built as a backtester:

```python
from chapter7.LiquidityProvider import LiquidityProvider
from chapter7.TradingStrategyDualMA import TradingStrategyDualMA
from chapter7.MarketSimulator import MarketSimulator
from chapter7.OrderManager import OrderManager
from chapter7.OrderBook import OrderBook
from collections import deque
import pandas as pd
import numpy as np
from pandas_datareader import data
import matplotlib.pyplot as plt
import h5py
```

2. To read all the elements from a deque, we will implement the `call_if_not_empty` function. This function will help to call a function as long as a deque is not empty:

```python
def call_if_not_empty(deq, fun):
    while (len(deq) > 0):
        fun()
```

3. In the code, we will implement the `EventBasedBackTester` class. The constructor of this class will build all the deque needed to have all the components communicate. We will also instantiate all the objects in the constructor of `EventBasedBackTester`:

```python
class EventBasedBackTester:
    def __init__(self):
        self.lp_2_gateway = deque()
        self.ob_2_ts = deque()
```

```
            self.ts_2_om = deque()
            self.ms_2_om = deque()
            self.om_2_ts = deque()
            self.gw_2_om = deque()
            self.om_2_gw = deque()
            self.lp = LiquidityProvider(self.lp_2_gateway)
            self.ob = OrderBook(self.lp_2_gateway, self.ob_2_ts)
            self.ts = TradingStrategyDualMA(self.ob_2_ts,\
   self.ts_2_om,\
            self.om_2_ts)
            self.ms = MarketSimulator(self.om_2_gw, self.gw_2_om)
            self.om = OrderManager(self.ts_2_om, self.om_2_ts,\
            self.om_2_gw, self.gw_2_om)
```

4. The `process_data_from_yahoo` function will convert the data created by the panda `DataReader` class to orders that the trading system can use in real time. In this code, we will create a new order that we will then delete just after:

```python
def process_data_from_yahoo(self,price):

    order_bid = {
        'id': 1,
        'price': price,
        'quantity': 1000,
        'side': 'bid',
        'action': 'new'
    }
    order_ask = {
        'id': 1,
        'price': price,
        'quantity': 1000,
        'side': 'ask',
        'action': 'new'
    }
    self.lp_2_gateway.append(order_ask)
    self.lp_2_gateway.append(order_bid)
    self.process_events()
    order_ask['action']='delete'
    order_bid['action'] = 'delete'
    self.lp_2_gateway.append(order_ask)
    self.lp_2_gateway.append(order_bid)
```

5. The `process_events` function will call all the components as long as we have new orders coming. Every component will be called as long as we didn't flush all the events in the deque:

```python
def process_events(self):
    while len(self.lp_2_gateway)>0:
        call_if_not_empty(self.lp_2_gateway,\
            self.ob.handle_order_from_gateway)
        call_if_not_empty(self.ob_2_ts, \
            self.ts.handle_input_from_bb)
        call_if_not_empty(self.ts_2_om, \
            self.om.handle_input_from_ts)
        call_if_not_empty(self.om_2_gw, \
            self.ms.handle_order_from_gw)
        call_if_not_empty(self.gw_2_om, \
            self.om.handle_input_from_market)
        call_if_not_empty(self.om_2_ts, \
            self.ts.handle_response_from_om)
```

6. The following code will instantiate the event-based backtester by creating the `eb` instance. Because we are going to load the same GOOG financial data, we will use the `load_financial_data` function. Then, we will create a for-loop backtester where will feed, one by one, the price updates to the event-based backtester:

```python
eb=EventBasedBackTester()


def load_financial_data(start_date, end_date,output_file):
    try:
        df = pd.read_pickle(output_file)
        print('File data found...reading GOOG data')
    except FileNotFoundError:
        print('File not found...downloading the GOOG data')
        df = data.DataReader('GOOG', 'yahoo', start_date,
end_date)
        df.to_pickle(output_file)
    return df

goog_data=load_financial_data(start_date='2001-01-01',
                    end_date = '2018-01-01',
                    output_file='goog_data.pkl')


for line in zip(goog_data.index,goog_data['Adj Close']):
    date=line[0]
    price=line[1]
```

```
price_information={'date' : date,
                   'price' : float(price)}
eb.process_data_from_yahoo(price_information['price'])
eb.process_events()
```

7. At the end of this code, we will display the curve representing the cash amount within the trading period:

```
plt.plot(eb.ts.list_total,label="Paper Trading using Event-Based
BackTester")
plt.plot(eb.ts.list_paper_total,label="Trading using Event-Based
BackTester")
plt.legend()
plt.show()
```

The new code that we introduce in this section is the code for the trading strategy. Our first trading strategy that we implemented in our trading system was an arbitrage strategy. This time, we will continue the example of the dual-moving average trading strategy.

This code shows that the logic of the trading strategy uses the same code as the for-loop backtester. The `create_metrics_out_of_prices` and `buy_sell_or_hold_something` functions are untouched. The main difference is regarding the *execution* part of the class. The execution takes care of the market response. We will be using a set of variables related to the paper trading mode to show the difference between actual and paper trading. Paper trading implies that every time the strategy sends an order, this order is filled at the price asked by the trading strategy. On the other side of the coin, the `handle_market_response` function will consider the response from the market to update the positions, holdings, and profit and loss.

8. We will code the `TradingStrategyDualMA` class inspired by the `TradingStrategy` class that we coded in Chapter 7, *Building a Trading System in Python*. This class will take care of keeping track of two series of values, the values for paper trading and the values for backtesting:

```
class TradingStrategyDualMA:
    def __init__(self, ob_2_ts, ts_2_om, om_2_ts):
        self.orders = []
        self.order_id = 0

        self.position = 0
        self.pnl = 0
        self.cash = 10000
        self.paper_position = 0
```

```
self.paper_pnl = 0
self.paper_cash = 10000
self.current_bid = 0
self.current_offer = 0
self.ob_2_ts = ob_2_ts
self.ts_2_om = ts_2_om
self.om_2_ts = om_2_ts
self.long_signal=False
self.total=0
self.holdings=0
self.small_window=deque()
self.large_window=deque()
self.list_position=[]
self.list_cash=[]
self.list_holdings = []
self.list_total=[]
self.list_paper_position = []
self.list_paper_cash = []
self.list_paper_holdings = []
self.list_paper_total = []
```

9. For each tick received, we will create a metric to make decisions. In this example, we use the dual-moving average trading strategy. Therefore, we will use two moving averages that we will build tick by tick. The `create_metric_out_of_prices` function calculates the short and long moving averages:

```
def create_metrics_out_of_prices(self,price_update):
    self.small_window.append(price_update)
    self.large_window.append(price_update)
    if len(self.small_window)>50:
        self.small_window.popleft()
    if len(self.large_window)>100:
        self.large_window.popleft()
    if len(self.small_window) == 50:
        if average(self.small_window) >\
            average(self.large_window):
                self.long_signal=True
        else:
            self.long_signal = False
        return True
    return False
```

10. The `buy_sell_or_hold_something` function will check whether we have a long signal or a short signal. Based on the signal, we will place an order and we will keep track of the paper trading position, cash, and profit and loss. This function will also record the value of the backtested values of position, cash, and profit and loss. We will keep track of these values to create a chart of our trading execution.

```python
def buy_sell_or_hold_something(self, book_event):
    if self.long_signal and self.paper_position<=0:
        self.create_order(book_event,book_event['bid_quantity'],'buy')
        self.paper_position += book_event['bid_quantity']
        self.paper_cash -= book_event['bid_quantity'] *
book_event['bid_price']
    elif self.paper_position>0 and not self.long_signal:
self.create_order(book_event,book_event['bid_quantity'],'sell')
        self.paper_position -= book_event['bid_quantity']
        self.paper_cash -= -book_event['bid_quantity'] *
book_event['bid_price']

    self.paper_holdings = self.paper_position *
book_event['bid_price']
    self.paper_total = (self.paper_holdings + self.paper_cash)

    self.list_paper_position.append(self.paper_position)
    self.list_paper_cash.append(self.paper_cash)
    self.list_paper_holdings.append(self.paper_holdings)
    self.list_paper_total.append(self.paper_holdings+self.paper_cash)

    self.list_position.append(self.position)
    self.holdings=self.position*book_event['bid_price']
    self.list_holdings.append(self.holdings)
    self.list_cash.append(self.cash)
    self.list_total.append(self.holdings+self.cash)
```

11. As shown, the `signal` function will call the two prior functions:

```python
def signal(self, book_event):
    if book_event['bid_quantity'] != -1 and \
        book_event['offer_quantity'] != -1:
        self.create_metrics_out_of_prices(book_event['bid_price'])
        self.buy_sell_or_hold_something(book_event)
```

12. The following function differs from the original function `execution` that we implemented in Chapter 7, *Building a Trading System in Python*. This one will keep track of the profit and loss, position, and the cash:

```python
def execution(self):
    orders_to_be_removed=[]
    for index, order in enumerate(self.orders):
        if order['action'] == 'to_be_sent':
            # Send order
            order['status'] = 'new'
            order['action'] = 'no_action'
            if self.ts_2_om is None:
                print('Simulation mode')
            else:
                self.ts_2_om.append(order.copy())
        if order['status'] == 'rejected' or
          order['status']=='cancelled':
            orders_to_be_removed.append(index)
        if order['status'] == 'filled':
            orders_to_be_removed.append(index)
            pos = order['quantity'] if order['side'] == 'buy' else
              -order['quantity']
            self.position+=pos
            self.holdings = self.position * order['price']
            self.pnl-=pos * order['price']
            self.cash -= pos * order['price']

    for order_index in sorted(orders_to_be_removed,reverse=True):
        del (self.orders[order_index])
```

13. As shown, the following function will handle the market response:

```python
def handle_market_response(self, order_execution):
    print(order_execution)
    order,_=self.lookup_orders(order_execution['id'])
    if order is None:
        print('error not found')
        return
    order['status']=order_execution['status']
    self.execution()
```

14. The following function will return the profit and loss of the strategy:

```python
def get_pnl(self):
    return self.pnl + self.position * (self.current_bid +
    self.current_offer)/2
```

When we run this example, we will obtain the following chart. We can observe that the curve is the same as the prior one. This means that the trading system that we created and the paper trading have the same reality:

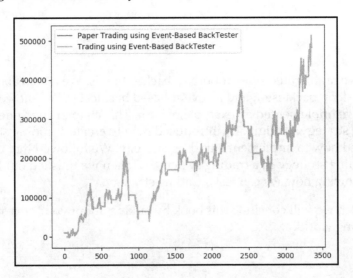

We will now modify the market assumptions by changing the fill ratio used by the market simulator. We are getting a fill ratio of 10%, and we can see that the profit and loss is profoundly impacted. Since most of our orders are not filled, we will not make money where the trading strategy was supposed to make money:

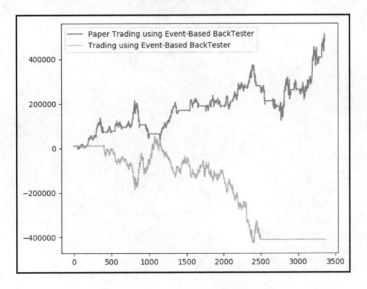

The chart reminds us of the importance of having a fast system. If we place an order, in most cases, the order is rejected. This will negatively impact the profit and loss of the trading strategy.

Summary

In this chapter, we highlighted how important backtesting is. We talked about two sorts of backtesters: a for-loop backtester, and an event-based backtester. We showed the two main differences and we implemented an example of both. This chapter concludes the creation path of a trading strategy. We initially introduced how to create a trading strategy idea, and then we explained how to implement a trading strategy. We followed that by explaining how to use a trading strategy in a trading system and then we finished our learning experience by showing how we can test a trading strategy.

In the next chapter, we will conclude this book by talking about your next steps in the algorithmic trading world.

Section 5: Challenges in Algorithmic Trading

This section covers the challenges faced after your algorithmic trading strategies have been deployed to the market. It provides examples of some of the common pitfalls faced by participants and offers potential solutions to them.

This section comprises the following chapter:

- Chapter 10, *Adapting to Market Participants and Conditions*

10
Adapting to Market Participants and Conditions

So far, we've gone over all the concepts and ideas involved in algorithmic trading. We went from introducing the different components and players of an algorithmic trading ecosystem to going over practical examples of trading signals, adding predictive analytics into algorithmic trading strategies, and actually building several commonly used basic, as well as sophisticated, trading strategies. We also developed ideas and a system to control risk and manage it over the evolution of a trading strategy. And finally, we went over the infrastructure components required to run these trading strategies as well as the simulator/backtesting research environment required to analyze trading strategy behavior. At this point in the book, you should be able to successfully develop a deep understanding of all the components and sophistication needed to build, improve, and safely deploy all components of an algorithmic trading strategy business stack.

The goal in this final section of the book is to begin to look beyond the deployment and operation of algorithmic trading strategies by considering things that can go wrong in live markets or slowly deteriorate as time passes, by trading signal edges vanish, and how new market participants are added, or more informed participants join the market and less informed participants leave. Financial markets and market participants are in a constant state of evolution, so algorithmic trading businesses that are able to evolve over time and in the face of changing market conditions, adapt to new conditions, and continue to be profitable, are the only ones that can survive long term. This is an extremely challenging problem to tackle, but in this chapter, we will go over the hurdles we typically encounter and offer some guidance on how to tackle them. We will discuss why strategies do not perform as expected when deployed in live trading markets – and show examples of how to address those issues in the strategies themselves or the underlying assumptions. We will also discuss why strategies that are performing well slowly deteriorate in performance, and then we'll look at some simple examples to explain how to address these.

In this chapter, we will cover the following topics:

- Strategy performance in backtester versus live markets
- Continued profitability in algorithmic trading

Strategy performance in backtester versus live markets

In this section, let's first tackle a very common problem encountered by a lot of algorithmic trading participants that lack sophistication in their backtesters/simulators. Since backtesters are a cornerstone in building, analyzing, and comparing algorithmic trading strategies irrespective of position holding times, if backtested results are not realized in live trading markets, it's difficult to get off the ground or continue trading. Typically, the shorter the position holding period and the larger the trading sizes, the greater the chance that simulation results are different from results actually achieved in live trading markets. Backtesters are often the most complex software component in a lot of **high frequency trading** (**HFT**) business because of the need to simulate very accurately. Also, the more complex or non-intuitive the trading model, the better the simulator needs to be, because it is often difficult to follow very fast automated trading using complex trading signals, predictions, and strategies in live markets given that they are not intuitive.

The basic problem boils down to trade prices and trade sizes for an algorithmic trading strategy not being identical in backtester and live markets. Since a trading strategy's performance is a direct function of the trade prices and the trade sizes it executes, it's not hard to see why this issue would cause differences in backtested results and live trading results, which we will refer to as simulation dislocations from live trading. Sometimes, the backtester is pessimistic in awarding executions to the trading strategy, or does so at worse prices than what is achieved in live trading. Such a backtester is pessimistic, and live trading results can be much better than backtested results.

Sometimes, the backtester is optimistic in awarding executions to the trading strategy, or does so at better prices than what is achieved in live trading. Such a backtester is optimistic and live trading results can be worse than backtested results. It is possible for the backtester to either be consistently pessimistic or consistently optimistic, or vary depending on the trading strategy type, market conditions, time of day, and so on. Backtesters that have a consistent bias are easier to deal with because, after a few live deployments, you can get an idea of, and quantify, the pessimism/optimism and use that to adjust expectations from historical results. Unfortunately, more often than not, backtesters have dislocations that cause differences in results that are not consistently biased, and which are much harder to quantify and account for. Let's have a look at the following plot, which represents the pessimistic backtester:

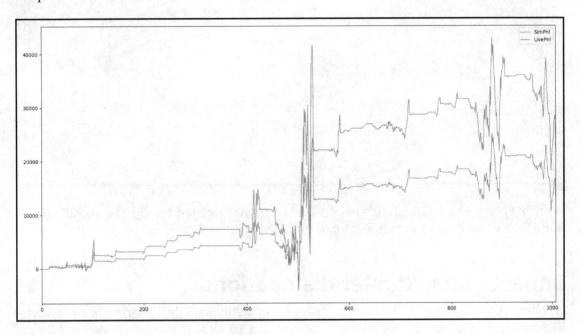

With a pessimistic backtester, live results deviate from simulated results but, overall, the trend is that live PnLs remain higher than simulated results. Now, let's have a look at the following plot, which represents the optimistic backtester:

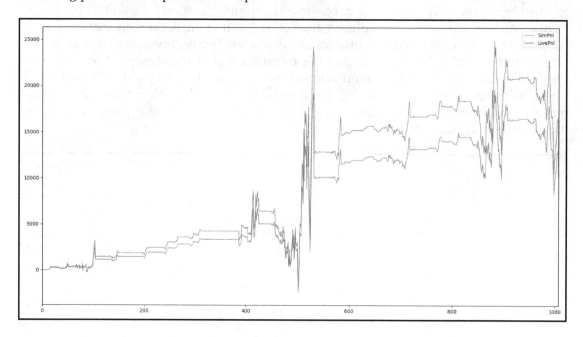

With an optimistic backtester, live results deviate from simulated results but, overall, the trend is that live PnLs remain lower than simulated results.

Impact of backtester dislocations

Not having a good backtester causes a variety of problems with the historical research and live deployment of algorithmic trading strategies. Let's look at these in more detail.

Signal validation

When we research and develop trading signals, we are able to compare predictions in price movements with actual price movements realized in the market based on historical data. This, of course, doesn't necessarily require a fully-fledged backtester, but does require a historical data playback software. This component, while less complex than a backtester, still has a decent amount of complexity to it and must be accurate in synchronizing different market data sources and playing market data back with accurate timestamps and event synchronization. If the market data played back in historical research platforms is not identical to what is received in live trading strategies, then the signal predictions and performance observed in historical research is not realized in live trading and can kill the profitability of a trading strategy.

Strategy validation

Strategy performance in backtester requires more complexity in the backtester than just the ability to properly synchronize and play back market data for multiple trading instruments over historically available market data, which is a requirement for signal validation that we discussed in the previous section. Here, we need to go one step further and build a backtester that can actually simulate the behavior and performance of a trading strategy over historical data as if it were trading in live markets by performing matching like an exchange would.

We covered all of this in the chapter on backtesting, and it should be clear how complex building a good backtester can be. When the backtester isn't very accurate, validating strategy behavior and performance is difficult since it is not possible to be confident of strategy performance based on the backtester results. This makes the design, development, improvement, and validation of trading strategies difficult and inaccurate.

Risk estimates

In the chapter on risk management, we use the backtester to quantify and measure the different risk measures in a trading strategy and trading strategy parameters to get a sense of what to expect before deploying to live markets. Again, this step requires an accurate backtester, and the lack of one will cause inaccuracies in measuring expected risk limits when strategies get deployed to live markets.

Risk management system

Similar to problems with quantifying and measuring risk estimates for a trading strategy in the absence of a very accurate backtester, it is also difficult to build an optimal risk-management system. Also, we saw in the chapter on risk management that we want to not only build a risk management system, but also a system of slowly increasing trading exposure and risk limits after good performance, and lower trading exposure and risk limits following a poor performance. Without a good backtester, this aspect of trading strategy development and deployment suffers and causes issues when deployed to live markets as it deviates from historical expectations.

Choice of strategies for deployment

When we have a pool of different possible trading strategies, different trading signal combinations, and different trading parameters, typically, we use the backester to build a portfolio of strategies to deploy to live markets in a way that minimizes risk for the entire portfolio. This step relies on having a good backtester, the lack of which causes live trading strategy portfolios to perform poorly and take more risk than historical simulations would have you believe.

Again, since a good backtester is at the core of this step, without it, live trading strategies and portfolios do not perform as expected. When backtesters vary in their deviations from live trading results for different trading strategies and different trading parameters, this problem can be even worse in the sense that not only do strategies that appear to be profitable in simulations not perform well in live markets, but we might also be missing out on strategies that appear to not be as profitable in simulations but actually might perform quite well if deployed to live markets because the backtester is pessimistic to those specific trading strategies or parameters.

Expected performance

It should be obvious that the major problem with a backtester that suffers from a lot of dislocations from live trading is that performance expectations derived from simulation results do not hold up in live trading. This throws off the signal validation, strategy validation, risk estimate, risk management, and risk adjustment strategies, but it also throws off risk-reward expectations. Since trading strategies do not live up to expected simulation performance, this can often result in the entire algorithmic trading business failing.

Causes of simulation dislocations

Now that we've covered all the issues that an inaccurate backtester can cause in terms of developing, optimizing, and deploying algorithmic trading strategies and algorithmic trading businesses, let's explore common causes of simulation dislocations.

Slippage

Slippage refers to the fact that expected trade prices from simulations, and actual trade prices as realized in live trading, can be different. This obviously can be detrimental to expected performance from algorithmic trading strategies because it is possible, and often likely, that trade prices in live markets are worse than what is expected from simulations. This can be due to historical market data playback issues, underlying assumptions about the latencies within the trading strategy, or the latencies between trading strategy and trading exchange, which we will explore shortly.

Another reason can be due to the market impact, where, with simulations, we try to trade larger sizes than can be traded in live markets without creating a market impact and inciting reactions from other market participants, such as removing available liquidity, which exacerbates trade prices in live markets as compared to simulations.

Fees

One major trading cost is trading fees, which are usually fees per traded share/future contract/options contract levied by the trading exchange and the broker. It is important to understand what these fees are and account for them in trading strategy performance analysis, otherwise it might lead to false estimates of expected risk versus reward.

It is important to consider the PnL per contract traded to make sure that the strategy covers trading fees and profits after fees, which is especially important for high-volume trading strategies such as HFT or market-making algorithmic trading strategies, which typically trade a lot of contracts and have lower PnL per contract-traded ratios than some other strategies.

Operational issues

When deploying algorithmic trading strategies to live markets, it is important to execute the strategy in live markets that are as close to simulation conditions as possible. The key objective is to try to realize the performance observed in backtesting/simulations in a live market. It is important to manually interrupt/intervene in live trading strategies as little as possible, because that can kill algorithmic trading strategies by interfering with, and deviating from, their expected simulated lifetime performance.

Operationally, it can be difficult to fight the temptation to interfere with live trading strategies and shut them down early if they are making money, or get scared and shut them down if they are losing money. For automated trading algorithms, which have been backtested extensively, manual intervention is a bad idea because simulated results can't be realized and they affect the expected versus realized profitability of a trading strategy.

Market data issues

Issues with playing back historical market data to trading strategies can become a problem if the market data that trading strategies observed in live trading is different from what is observed in simulations. This can be because of differences in the servers used for historical market data capture versus live trading, the way market data gets decoded in the historical archiver process versus live market data process, issues in how the data gets time stamped and stored, or even in the backtester that reads historical data and replays it to the trading strategy.

It is quite clear that if the market data time series is different in simulations versus live trading, then all aspects of algorithmic trading strategy suffer/deviate from historical expectations, and thus, the live trading performance doesn't live up to the simulation results.

Latency variance

In an algorithmic trading setup, there are many hops between when the market data first reaches the trading server and when the order flow in response to the new data reaches the trading exchange. First, the market data feed handler reads it and decodes it, the trading strategy then receives the normalized market data, and then the strategy itself updates the trading signals based on the new market data and sends new orders or modifications to existing orders. This order flow then gets picked up by the order gateway, converted to an exchange-order-entry protocol, and written to the TCP connection with the exchange.

The order finally gets to the exchange after incurring latency equal to the transmission latency from the trading server to the matching engine at the electronic trading exchange. Each one of these latencies needs to be accounted for in backtesting trading strategies, but it can often be a complicated problem. These latencies are most likely not static latency values, but vary depending on a lot of factors, such as trading signal and trading strategy software implementation, market conditions, and peak network traffic, and if these latencies are not properly modeled and accounted for in historical simulations, then live trading strategy performance can be quite different from expected historical simulation results, causing simulation dislocations, unexpected losses in live trading, and impaired trading strategy profitability, possibly to the point where the strategies cannot be run profitably.

Place-in-line estimates

Since electronic trading exchanges have different possible models for matching algorithms, such as FIFO and pro-rata, if a trading strategy's performance depends on having a good place in the line, that is, other market participants' sizes ahead of the strategy's orders at the same price level, then it is important to accurately simulate that. In general, if the backtester is too optimistic in estimating a trading strategy's order's priority in the limit order book as compared to the rest of the market participants, that is, it assumes our order is ahead of more market participants than it actually is in live markets, this leads to false and inflated expectations of trading strategy performance.

When such trading strategies are deployed to a live market, they often do not realize the expected simulated trading performance, which can hurt the trading strategy profitability. Modeling an accurate place in line is often a difficult problem and requires a lot of research and careful software development to get correct.

Market impact

Market impact refers to what happens when our trading strategy is deployed to live markets as compared to when it is not. This is basically to quantify and understand the reactions of other market participants in response to our order flow. Market impact is difficult to anticipate and simulate, and gets progressively worse the more the trading strategy is scaled up. While this is not a problem when algorithmic trading strategies are first deployed with very small risk exposure, it becomes an issue over time as they are scaled up.

Profitability does not increase linearly as risk is increased. Instead, the rate of increase of profitability slows down as size is increased but risk continues to increase, and that is due to market impact reasons. Eventually, strategies reach a size where large increases in risk still only marginally increase profitability, which is where the strategy has reached the limit of what it can be scaled up to. This is, of course, if we account for market impact when analyzing expected risk versus reward. Here, inaccuracies will always end up causing the trading strategy to take a lot more risk for very little extra profit and might end up causing a seemingly profitable trading strategy to massively underperform when deployed and scaled up in live markets.

Tweaking backtesting and strategies in response to live trading

Now that we've discussed the causes and impact of simulation dislocations from live trading performance, let's explore possible approaches/solutions to those problems if the algorithmic trading strategies deployed to live markets do not match th anticipated performance.

Historical market data accuracy

Something that should be obvious at this point is that the quality and quantity of the historical market data available is a key aspect in being able to build a profitable algorithmic trading business. For this reason, most market participants invest a lot of resources in building a market data capture and normalization process that is extremely accurate, and software implementation that is bug free and able to faithfully capture and replay live market data in historical mode to match exactly what algorithmic trading strategies will observe when they are deployed in live markets. Usually, if trading strategies are not performing in live markets as expected, this is the first place to start. By adding an extensive amount of instrumentation/recording to what market data update trading strategies observe, and comparing what is observed in simulations and live trading, it is relatively straightforward to find and fix underlying issues.

There may be issues in the historical market data recording setup, the live market data decoding and delivery setup, or both. Sometimes, latency sensitive trading strategies have a normalized market data format in live trading that is different from what is available in historical recording by streamlining market data information delivered to live trading strategies to be as compact and as fast as possible, in which case this can be another reason why live market data updates differ from historical market data updates. If issues are discovered in this step, first fix those issues in the historical and/or live market data protocol. Following that, the trading strategy results are recomputed, recalibrated if needed, and then redeployed to live markets to observe whether fixing these issues helps to reduce simulation dislocations.

Measuring and modeling latencies

After confirming that there are no outstanding market data issues, the next step is to look into the underlying latency assumptions in the backtester. In a modern algorithmic trading setup, there are many hops in between the exchange matching engine that generates market data and the trading strategy that receives the decoded and normalized market data, and then between the trading strategy that decides to send the order flow out to the exchange until it is actually received by the exchange matching engine. With modern improvements in server hardware, network switch, network card, and kernel bypass technologies, it is possible to record the timestamps between each of these hops very precisely in nanoseconds and then use those measurements to test the underlying latency assumptions/estimates used in the backtester.

In addition, modern electronic trading exchanges provide a lot of different timestamps that are also measured very precisely in the various hops within their own matching engine setup. These measurements include when an order request was received by the trading exchange, when it was picked up by the matching engine to be matched or added to the limit order book, when the private order notification and public market data update were generated, and when the corresponding network packets left the trading exchange infrastructure. Properly recording these timestamps provided by the exchange, using those measurements to gain insight into the conditions surrounding our orders getting matched, and calibrating the backtester on that basis, can help in addressing simulation dislocations. Each latency measurement between different hops is a distribution of possible values that vary by time, trading instrument, trading exchange, and trading strategy.

Typically, most simulators start with a static latency parameter for each one of these measurements, which is the mean or median of the distributions. If the variance for a specific latency measurement is very high, then a single static parameter no longer suffices and at that point one must use a more sophisticated latency modeling approach. One approach can be to use the mean latency as observed in live trading, but add an error term to the latency based on what is observed in live trading, while the more sophisticated approach is to implement features that can capture periods/conditions of higher or lower latencies and dynamically adjust those in the backtester. Some intuitive features would be to use the frequency of market data updates, frequency of trades, or the magnitude and momentum of price moves as a proxy for increased latency.

The idea behind this is that during periods of higher activity either due to busy market conditions and large price moves, or when lots of participants are sending a higher-than-normal amount of order flow to the exchange and, in turn, generating a larger-than-normal amount of market data, many of the latency measures are likely to be higher than normal and, in fact, be a function of increased market activity. This also makes sense because, during these periods, the trading exchange has to process more order flow, perform more matching per order flow, and generate and disseminate more market data for every order flow, so there are more delays due to processing times. Similarly, on the algorithmic trading strategy side, more market data means more time to read, decode, and normalize incoming market data updates, more time to update limit order books and update trading signals, more order flow generated to deal with the increased market activity, and more work done by the order gateway to deal with the increased order activity.

Modeling dynamic latencies is a difficult problem to solve in a backtester, and most sophisticated participants invest a lot of resources trying to get it right in addition to trying to build a trading infrastructure and trading strategies that have lower latency variance to begin with. To summarize this section, if simulation dislocations are associated with errors in latency assumptions/modeling, then the first step is to collect as many accurate measurements between each hop in the trading system and trading exchange as possible and build intelligence to faithfully reproduce those in historical simulations.

Improving backtesting sophistication

In the previous section, we looked at the importance of understanding and modeling latencies in an algorithmic trading setup correctly when backtesting trading strategies. If after carefully understanding, accounting for, and modeling latency variances in the algorithmic trading setup in historical simulations and redeploying the algorithmic trading strategy to live markets, we are still noticing simulation dislocations that are causing a deviation in strategy performance in live markets from what is expected, we can look into further backtesting sophistication.

Modern electronic exchangers provide a lot of information about every aspect of the matching process, beyond just providing accurate timestamps. There are a lot of transactions that take place during a matching event which, if not accounted for in a backtester, can cause a lot of simulation dislocations because they participate in matching events and can fundamentally change when a strategy can expect its orders to get executed. Non-conforming transactions such as self-match-prevention cancellations, stop-order releases during matching events, iceberg orders with hidden liquidity that over-execute or are replenished after being fully executed, matches during auction events, and implied/pro-rata matching considerations, can cause simulation dislocations if not correctly detected and accounted for in the simulator.

Different asset classes come with their own set of matching rules and complications. Dark pools, hidden liquidity, price improvements, hidden counter parties, and a lot of other factors can end up creating simulation dislocations and ultimately cause an algorithmic trading strategy to fail. Understanding all these rules, implementing them in software, and building accurate simulations on top of that is a very difficult problem to solve, but can often be the difference between success and failure in the algorithmic trading business.

Adjusting expected performance for backtester bias

We've looked at a lot of possible avenues for finding and fixing issues in the simulation and historical market data playback framework. If we are still observing differences in trading strategy performance in live markets as compared to simulations, then another possible solution to explore would be to adjust the expected performance results as obtained from simulations to account for the backtester bias.

As we discussed before, the backtester bias can be optimistic or pessimistic in nature and can be a constant bias or a bias that varies by trading strategy type, by strategy parameters, or by market conditions. If the bias can be isolated to be constant for a specific strategy type and strategy parameters, then it is able to collect simulation dislocation results from live trading results and organize them per strategy and per strategy parameter set. These expected dislocation values can then be used with the simulated results to estimate true live trading results. For example, if an algorithmic trading strategy with specific parameters always performs 20% worse in live trading as compared to simulation results because of simulation dislocations, we can account for that, reduce its simulated results by 20%, and re-evaluate it. We can take this estimation methodology one step further and try to model the magnitude of backtester optimism/pessimism as a function of traded volume and market conditions, such as how busy the market is or how much the prices changed.

In this manner, it is possible to build a system that takes simulated results for trading strategies and then takes live trading results for the same strategies and tries to quantify the simulation dislocations and provide estimates of true expected live trading performance. These methods of adjusting expected live trading performance are not ideal; they require feedback from running trading strategies in live trading, which might cause losses and, at the end of the day, is just an estimation. Ideally, we want a backtester capable of providing accurate simulation results, but since that is an extremely difficult and sometimes impossible task, this estimation method is a good middle ground for dealing with simulation dislocations and continuing to build up and manage an algorithmic trading business.

Analytics on live trading strategies

Another solution to dealing with live trading performance deviating from the expected simulation performance is to have sophisticated analytics on live trading strategies. This is another way of saying that instead of relying completely on backtesting performance and behavior, you can also invest in adding enough intelligence and sophistication directly to live trading strategies to reduce the likelihood of simulation dislocations derailing an algorithmic trading business. This, again, is an imperfect approach to solving the problem, but can be a good alternative to help with limitations and errors in backtesters. The idea is to deploy trading strategies to live markets with very small exposure, collect statistics on each strategy action, and properly instrument and collect statistics on why those decisions were made.

Then we resort to an extensive **Post Trade Analytics** (**PTA**) framework to dig through these strategy action records and classify winning and losing positions and statistics on strategy actions that led to these winning and losing positions. Often, performing this kind of PTA on trading performance from live trading can reveal a lot of insight about problems/limitations for that particular trading strategy. These insights can be used to guide the development and improvement of the algorithmic trading strategy and improve profitability over time. In many ways, this boils down to the approach of starting trading strategies at very small risk exposures with intuitive parameters and using feedback from live trading to improve the strategy's performance.

This is not a perfect approach, since it requires the trading strategies to be simple enough where they can be run under live trading conditions with easily understood parameters, in addition to the fact that we might have to run a trading strategy that is not profitable in live market conditions for a short time, while accruing losses that we don't want.

Continued profitability in algorithmic trading

In the first half of this chapter, we looked at what common issues you can expect when deploying algorithmic trading strategies that have been built and calibrated in simulations and appear to be profitable. We discussed the impact and common causes of simulation dislocation, which cause deviation in trading strategy performance when deployed to live trading markets. We then explored possible solutions to dealing with those problems and how to get algorithmic trading strategies off the ground and start scaling up safely to build a profitable algorithmic trading business. Now, let's look at the next steps after getting up and running with the algorithmic trading strategies in live trading markets. As we mentioned before, live trading markets are in a constant state of evolution, as participants enter and exit markets and adapt and change their trading strategies.

In addition to the market participants themselves, there are numerous global economic and political conditions that can influence price movements in global and/or local asset classes and trading instruments. It is not enough to just be able to set up an algorithmic trading business; it is also mandatory to be able to adapt to all of these possible changing conditions and market risk and continue to stay profitable. That is an extremely tough goal; over time, previously profitable and sophisticated market participants have had to shut down their trading businesses and exit the market, making algorithmic and quantitative trading one of the most challenging businesses out there. In this section, let's explore what causes winning trading strategies to die out after first being profitable.

We will explore solutions that can help us to maintain and improve trading strategy profitability after the initial deployment to live trading markets. Finally, we will wrap up this chapter by discussing adapting to changing market conditions and market participants, that is, dealing with the ever-evolving nature of the algorithmic trading business and how to work on building an algorithmic trading business that survives for a very long time.

Profit decay in algorithmic trading strategies

First, we need to understand what factors cause trading strategies that were initially profitable to slowly decay in profitability and eventually no longer be profitable at all. Having a good understanding of what possible factors can cause a currently profitable algorithmic trading business to deteriorate over time can help us put checks and re-evaluation mechanisms in place to detect these conditions and deal with them in time in order to maintain profitability of the algorithmic trading business. Now let's look at some of the factors involved in profit decay for algorithmic trading strategies.

Signal decay due to lack of optimization

The signals used in the trading strategy are obviously one of the key aspects that drive trading strategy performance. Trading signals come with a maintenance aspect that requires them to be constantly re-evaluated and re-adjusted to stay relevant/profitable. This is partially because trading signals with constant parameters cannot perform equally well through different market conditions and require some tweaking or adjustment as market conditions change.

Sophisticated market participants often have elaborate optimization/re-fitting setups meant to continuously adjust and adapt trading-signal parameters to deliver maximum trading performance and advantages. It is important to not just find trading signals that are performing well over recent days, but to also set up a systematic optimization pipeline to adapt trading signals to changing market conditions to keep them profitable.

Signal decay due to absence of leading participants

A lot of trading signals capture specific market participant behavior and predict future market price moves. A simple example would be trading signals that try to detect order flow coming from high-frequency trading participants and use that to get a sense of what portion of available liquidity is from very fast participants with the ability to add and remove liquidity at prices very fast, sometimes faster than other participants can react and trade against.

Another example would be trading signals trying to capture participant behavior in related markets, such as cash markets or options markets, to gain an advantage in other related markets, such as futures markets, for similar trading instruments. Sometimes, if a large amount of market participants that these trading signals capture and leverage exit the market, become more informed, or are able to disguise their intentions better, then these trading signals that depend on these participants no longer retain their predictive abilities and profitability. Since market participants and market conditions change all the time, signal decay due to absence of market participants is a very real and very common occurrence and something that all profitable market participants have to account for and deal with.

This involves having teams of quantitative researchers always searching for new predictive trading signals that are different from existing trading signals to counteract the possibility of currently profitable trading signal decay. The signal-parameter optimization aspects we covered in the previous section also help to alleviate this problem by using existing signals but with different parameters to get information from new participants, as information gleaned from existing participants decays over time.

Signal discovery by other participants

In the same way that we are continuously in the process of optimizing existing trading signal parameters as well as searching for new trading signals, all market participants are also searching for new trading signals. Often other market participants also discover the same trading signals that our trading strategies are using to be profitable. This can cause the market participants to react in a couple of different ways, one way would be to change their trading strategy's order flow to disguise their intent and make the trading signal no longer profitable for us.

Another reaction can be that these participants start using the same trading signal to run trading strategies very similar to our own, thus crowding the market with the same trading strategy and reducing our ability to scale up the trading strategy, leading to reduced profitability. It is also possible for the market participant to leverage better infrastructure or be better capitalized, and we can lose our trading edge completely and get squeezed out of the market. While there is no real way to ban other participants from discovering the same trading signals that are being used in our algorithmic trading strategies, the industry practices have evolved over time to reflect the extremely secretive nature of the business, where firms typically make it difficult for employees to go work for a competitor. This is done through **non-disclosure agreements** (NDAs), **non-compete agreements** (NCAs), and strictly monitoring the development and use of proprietary trading source code.

The other factor is the complexity of the trading signals. Typically, the simpler a trading signal is, the more likely it is to be discovered by multiple market participants. More complex trading signals are less likely to be discovered by competing market participants but also require a lot of research and effort to discover, implement, deploy, monetize, and maintain. To summarize this section, losing the trading edge when other participants discover the same signals that are working for us is a normal part of the business, but there is no direct solution to this problem, other than trying our best to keep discovering new trading signals ourselves to stay profitable.

Profit decay due to exit of losing participants

Trading is a zero-sum game; for some participants to make money, there must be less informed participants that lose money to the winning participants. The problem with this is that participants that are losing money either get smarter or faster and stop losing money, or they continue losing money and eventually exit the market altogether, which will hurt continued profitability of our trading strategies and can even get to a point where we cannot make any money at all. If our trading strategies are making money by trading against these less informed participants, and they either become better informed and stop losing money or they leave the market, either we lose our trading signal advantage that relied on their behavior, or the competition gains edge on us causing our trading strategies to go from being profitable to losing money. Intuitively, since no participant that is losing money continuously is likely to continue trading, it seems likely that this is a business that is eventually going to die out for everyone.

This doesn't happen in practice because large markets are composed of a very large number of participants with different trading strategies, different trading horizons, and different information. Also, participants exit the markets and new participants enter the markets every day, creating new opportunities for all participants to capitalize on. To summarize, since market participants are continuously evolving and new participants enter the market and existing participants leave the market, it is possible for us to lose those participants that provide the trading signals that we use in our trading strategies. To deal with this, we have to constantly search for new trading signals and diversify trading signals and strategies to capture more market participants' intentions and predict market price moves.

Profit decay due to discovery by other participants

We discussed the possibility of and the impact of other market participants discovering our trading signals and using the same signals that our trading strategies utilize to make money. Similar to other market participants discovering the same trading signals that our trading strategies use and hurting our profitability, it is possible for other market participants to discover our order flow and strategy behavior and then find ways to anticipate and leverage our trading strategy's order flow to trade against us in a way that causes our trading strategies to lose money.

Other ways other market participants can discover our order flow and anticipate market price moves in different asset classes or other trading instruments, perhaps for stat arb or pair-trading strategies or cross-asset strategies. This can lead to reduced profitability or it can worsen to a point where it is no longer feasible to continue running the specific algorithmic trading strategy. Sophisticated market participants often invest a lot of thought, design, and resources to make sure that the algorithmic trading strategy behavior does not immediately give away the strategy's behavior in a way that can be used by other market participants to hurt our trading profitability.

This often involves the use of GTC orders to build queue priority in FIFO markets, using icebergs to disguise the true liquidity behind orders, using stop orders to be triggered at specific prices ahead of time, using Fill and Kill or Immediate or Cancel orders to mask the true liquidity behind orders being sent to the exchange, and complicated order-execution strategies to hide the trading strategy's true intention. Obviously, trying to hide intentions from other market participants can be taken too far, as we saw in the case of Spoofing, which is an illegal algorithmic trading practice. In summary, to use sophisticated trading strategies in a very competitive and crowded market, the strategy implementation can often be a lot more complex than it needs to be for the purposes of mitigating information leak and reduced profitability.

Profit decay due to changes in underlying assumptions/relationships

All trading signals and trading strategies are built on top of certain underlying assumptions, such as assumptions about market participant behavior, and assumptions about interactions and relationships between different asset classes and different trading instruments. When we built basic trading strategies, we relied on the underlying assumptions that parameters such as 20 days and 40 days were correct for our trading instrument. With sophisticated trading strategies, such as volatility adjusted trading strategies, economic-release-based trading strategies, pair-trading strategies, and statistical arbitrage strategies, there are more underlying assumptions about the relationship between volatility measures and trading instruments, the relationship between economic releases and impact on economy, and price moves in trading instruments.

Pair-trading and statistical arbitrage trading strategies also make assumptions about the relationship between different trading instruments and how it evolves over time. As we discussed when we covered statistical arbitrage trading strategies, when these relationships break down, the strategies no longer continue to be profitable. When we build trading signals and algorithmic trading strategies, it's important to understand and be mindful of the underlying assumptions that the specific trading signals and the specific trading strategies depend on to be profitable. Market conditions and participants change all the time, hence it is possible that the assumptions that were true when these trading strategies were first built and deployed to live markets no longer hold true during certain times, or might not hold true moving forward.

When this happens, it is important to have the ability to detect, analyze, and understand what strategies will not perform as expected. It's also important to have a diverse set of trading signals and trading strategies. If we don't have enough diverse trading signals and strategies with non-overlapping underlying assumptions, it is possible that trading can get shut down completely. And if the assumptions are never true after that, it could be the end of the algorithmic trading strategy business. To summarize, the only way to deal with a situation where the trading strategies' underlying assumptions no longer hold is to have the ability to detect and understand such periods, and have a diverse set of trading signals and strategies capable of running through different kinds of market conditions and changing participants.

Seasonal profit decay

In the previous section, we talked about how algorithmic trading strategies have many underlying assumptions. Seasonality, which is a concept we covered in one of our chapters, is an assumption that dictates a trading strategy's profitability. For a lot of asset classes, their price moves, volatility, relationships with other asset classes, and expected behavior vary quite predictably. Trading signals and trading strategies need to account for these differences due to seasonal factors and adjust and adapt accordingly; without that, the profitability can vary over time and might not live up to the expected performance. Properly understanding the seasonality factors involved and the impact on the trading strategy performance is important when building and running a long-term algorithmic trading strategy business.

To avoid seasonal profit decay, sophisticated market participants have special trading signals and strategies in place to detect and adapt to seasonal market conditions and relationships between different contracts and trade profitably through all the different seasonal trends. Seasonal profit decay is a normal part of trading strategies that deal with asset classes and/or trading instruments that have seasonal trends in behavior and cross-asset relationships, and it is important to collect large amounts of data and build analytics to understand and manage seasonal trends to maximize profitability.

Adapting to market conditions and changing participants

Now that we've discussed all the different factors that cause the profitability of algorithmic trading strategies to decay over time, or because of changes in market participants' behavior or market conditions, in this section we will go over possible approaches and solutions to handling these conditions and maintaining the long-term profitability of algorithmic trading strategies.

Building a trading signals dictionary/database

In the previous section, we discussed the factors that causes profitable trading strategies to die, which include because the predictive power of trading signals died out over time, either due to lack of parameter optimizations, discovery by other market participants, violations of underlying assumptions, or seasonal trends. Before we explore optimizing trading signals and what that pipeline looks like, one component that is an important part of any quantitative research platform is called the trading signals dictionary/database. This component is a large database containing statistics of different trading signals and different trading signal parameter sets over years of data.

The statistics that this database contains are primarily ones to capture the predictive abilities of these signals over their prediction horizon. Some simple examples of such metrics can be the correlation of the trading signal value with the price movements in the trading instrument which this trading signal is meant for. Other statistics can be variance in the predictive power over days, that is, how consistent this trading signal is over a set amount of days to check whether it varies wildly over time.

In this database, there can be one entry per day or multiple entries per day for different time periods for every <signal, signal input instruments, signal parameters> tuple. As you can imagine, this database can grow to be very large. Sophisticated algorithmic trading participants often have database results going back several years for thousands of trading signal variants as well as complex systems to compute and add entries to this database with every additional day of market data recorded. The main advantage of having such a database is that, as market conditions change, it is very easy to query this database to understand and analyze which trading signal, signal input, and signal parameter sets do better than others in different market conditions. This helps us to analyze why certain signals might not be performing well in current market conditions, see which ones would have done better, and build new and diverse trading strategies based on those observations.

In a lot of ways, having access to a comprehensive trading signal dictionary/database allows us to quickly detect changing market conditions/participants by comparing the trading signal performance individually across training and testing history to see whether it is deviating from historical expectations. It also helps us to adapt to changing market conditions/participants by letting us quickly query the database for historical signal performance to see what other signals would have helped or worked better. It also answers the question of whether the same trading signal with same trading instrument input, but with different trading signal parameters, would have done better than the current parameter set being used in live trading.

Investing in setting up a research-platform component that can compute results across different trading signals, signal instrument input, signal parameters, signal prediction horizon, time periods over years of tick data, and then storing it in an organized manner can help you to understand and handle a lot of the factors that cause trading-signal-profit decay in algorithmic trading strategies deployed to live markets and facing changing market conditions.

Optimizing trading signals

In section, we discussed that trading signals with static input cannot deliver profitable results consistently, given that market conditions and market participants evolve over time. In the previous section, we saw how having a large quantitative system that can continuously compute and store results for different trading signals over time can help us to deal with this. Another component that should be part of a sophisticated algorithmic trading business' arsenal is a data-mining/optimization system capable of taking existing trading signals, building a very large number input instrument and parameter combinations, and then trying to optimize over that very large population of similar, but slightly different, trading signals of different prediction horizons over certain time periods and summarizing the results to find the best one. In essence, this is similar to the trading signals dictionary/database setup we discussed before, but the purpose here is to build and try variations of signals that the researcher does not need to provide manually and then find better variants than what they can come up with intuitively/manually.

This is often necessary to bridge the gap between what trading signals and parameters researchers believe should work intuitively and what is optimal and also helps us to discover trading signals, input, and parameter combinations that might otherwise be overlooked. This system can involve relatively straightforward methods, such as grid searching over permutations of different signals and parameter values, or can be quite advanced and involve optimization techniques, such as linear optimization, stochastic gradient descent, convex optimization, genetic algorithms, or maybe even non-linear optimization techniques. This is a very complex system that has many sub-components, such as a trading-signals and parameters-permutation generator, signal evaluator, quantitative measures of signal predictive abilities, signal performance summary algorithms, grid-searching methods, possibly advanced optimization implementations and components to analyze and visualize summary statistics for trading signal performance.

This is, however, an important optimization platform/system that will help prevent trading signal decay after being deployed to live trading markets, by letting us proactively adjust and adapt to changing market conditions and maintain profitability, and can often increase profitability over time by helping us to find better variants of trading signals than the ones we started with. Advanced market participants invest in massively scalable cloud/cluster computing systems to run these optimizations around the clock to look for better signals.

Optimizing prediction models

Most trading strategies in modern electronic trading exchanges employ more than a single trading signal, generally using at least a handful of trading signals, all the way up to hundreds of trading signals inside a single trading strategy. These trading signals interact with each other in numerous complex ways and it is often difficult to understand, analyze, and optimize these interactions. Sometimes these trading signals interact with each other through complex machine learning models, which makes it even more difficult to intuitively understand all the different interactions possible.

Similar to how we analyze trading signals over a larger search space using complex principles and methods from linear algebra, calculus, probability, and statistics, we also need a similar system for trading strategies. This system has to be capable of testing over a huge space of possible interactions between different trading signals and optimizing these interactions to find the optimal trading signal combination models. A lot of the possible techniques that can be used to optimize trading signals can also sometimes be directly used to optimize combinations of trading signals. However, the only thing to understand is that the size of the search space here is a function of how many trading signals are being combined in the final trading model.

Another consideration is the optimization method used to optimize the prediction model, which is a combination of individual trading signals. For complex methods with a lot of trading signals, this complexity can increase exponentially and become unsustainable very quickly. Sophisticated quantitative trading firms will use a combination of large cloud/cluster-computing systems, smart parallelization pipelines, and super-efficient optimization techniques to optimize their prediction models continuously with large datasets. Again, this is all in an effort to deal with changing market conditions and trading participants, and always have the optimal signals and signal combinations possible to maximize trading profitability.

Optimizing trading strategy parameters

Remember that a trading signal has input parameters that control its output/behavior. Similarly, prediction models, which are combinations of trading signals, have weights/coefficients/parameters that control how trading signals interact with each other. Finally, trading strategies also have many parameters that control how trading signals, predictive models, and execution models work together to send the order flow to the trading exchange in response to incoming market data, how positions are initiated and managed, and how the actual trading strategies behave. This is the final finished trading strategy that gets backtested and deployed to live trading markets.

Let's discuss this in the context of a trading strategy we're already quite familiar with. For example, in the trading strategies we saw in `Chapter 5`, *Sophisticated Algorithmic Strategies*, there were static parameters as well as volatility-adjusted dynamic parameters that controlled thresholds for buy/sell entries, thresholds to control over-trading, thresholds to lock in profits/losses, parameters that controlled position increase/decrease, and parameters/thresholds that controlled the strategy's trading behavior as a whole. As you can imagine, different trading strategy parameter sets can produce vastly different trading results in terms of PnLs and also in terms of risk exposure that the trading strategy is willing to take, even if the trading signals or predictive models themselves do not change.

Another way of thinking about this is that individual trading signals provide opinions about future market price moves, while predictive models combine many different trading signals with different opinions and produce a final opinion about future/expected market price moves. Finally, it is the trading strategy that takes these predictions and converts that into the outgoing order flow to be sent to the exchange to perform trades and manage positions and risk in a way that converts predicted price moves into actual dollars, which is the final objective of all algorithmic/quantitative trading strategies.

Trading strategy parameters are optimized using similar infrastructures, components, and methods to optimize trading signals and predictive models, the only difference is that here the optimization objectives are PnL and risk instead of predictive ability, which is used to evaluate trading signals and predictive models. Continuously evaluating and optimizing trading strategy parameters is another important step in adapting to changing market conditions/participants and staying consistently profitable.

Researching new trading signals

We've discussed in considerable detail the impact and causes of profit decay for existing trading signals and importance of continuously searching for new sources of trading edge/advantage in terms of researching and building new trading signals. As mentioned, a lot of market participants have entire teams of quantitative researchers implementing and validating new trading signals full-time to achieve this. Searching for new trading signals, or *alpha*, is an extremely difficult task, and is not a well-structured or well-known process.

Trading signal ideas are brainstormed from live trading analytics, by inspecting periods of losses, or by inspecting market data and interactions between market data, market participants, trading signals, and trading strategies during those times. Based on what is observed and understood from this inspection/analysis, new trading signals are conceptualized based on what *appears* like it would have helped avoid losing positions, decrease the magnitude of losing positions, help produce more winning positions, or increase the magnitude of winning positions. At this point, the new trading signal is just an idea with no quantitative research or proof to back it up. The next step is to implement the trading signal, then the values output by the trading signals are tweaked and validated to understand its predictive abilities similar to what we discussed in the section on trading signals database.

If the newly-developed trading signal seems to show some potential/predictive abilities, it passes the stage of prototyping and is forwarded to the trading signal optimization pipeline. Most trading signals never make it past the prototype stage, which is part of what makes developing new trading signals extremely challenging. That is often because what makes intuitive sense does not necessarily translate into useful/predictive trading signals. Or the newly-conceptualized trading signal turns out to be quite similar in predictive abilities to already-developed signals, in which case it is dropped since it doesn't offer any new predictive abilities. If it makes it to the optimizing step, then we find the best variants of the newly-developed trading signal and they are forwarded to the step of being added to predictive models. Here, it interacts with other pre-existing trading signals. It might take some time and many iterations before we find the correct method to combine the new trading signal with other predictive trading signals to find a final predictive model that is better than any other. After that step, the new trading signal is used in a final trading strategy with strategy parameters that undergo another round of evaluation and optimization before the final evaluation, where we try to determine whether the addition of the new trading signal improves the profitability of our trading strategies.

We saw how much time and resources need to be invested from brainstorming a new trading signal all the way to making it into a final trading strategy where it can improve profitability. It should be obvious that new trading signals have to pass many intermediate validation and optimization stages, compete with other pre-existing and well-known trading signals, and then interact with other trading signals in a way that improves PnLs by adding new value to the trading strategy's ability to trade profitability. In many ways, new trading signals have to go through a survival pipeline very similar to evolution and natural selection – only the best and fittest trading signals survive to make it to live trading strategies, and others die out. This is what makes developing new trading signals so difficult and a task with a very low probability of success. However, researching new trading signals is mandatory for all algorithmic trading business to compete and stay profitable, making the best *quants* the most sought-after employees in all algorithmic/quantitative trading businesses in the industry.

Expanding to new trading strategies

Similar to why it's important to continuously research and generate new trading signals to stay competitive and build an algorithmic trading business that stays profitable for a long period of time, effort must be made to build new trading strategies that add value to the trading strategies that currently exist and are being run in live markets. The idea here is that since trading strategy profitability is affected by a lot of factors, ranging from trading signal and trading strategy decay, improvements made by competing market participants and changes in market conditions that affect underlying assumptions for certain strategies may no longer hold true. In addition to continuously optimizing existing trading strategy signals and execution parameters, it's also necessary to invest resources in adding new, uncorrelated trading strategies that make money in the long run but perform differently. These new strategies should counteract the possibility that some trading strategies will go through periods of reduced profitability or diminishing profitability due to market conditions or seasonal aspects.

Similar to researching and building new trading signals that interact with other trading signals to add non-overlapping predictive powers, we need to build new trading strategies that interact with other pre-existing trading strategies to add non-overlapping sources of profit. It is important that newly-developed trading strategies make money during periods where other trading strategies might be losing money, and that newly-developed trading strategies don't also lose money when other trading strategies are losing money. This helps us to build up a diverse pool of trading strategies that rely on different trading signals, market conditions, market participants, relationships between trading instruments, and seasonal aspects. The key is to build a diverse pool of available trading strategies that can be deployed to live markets in parallel with the objective of having enough intelligent trading strategies running. This helps in dealing with changing market participants/conditions, which can be handled better under the assumption that since the trading strategies are based on different signals/conditions/assumptions, it is unlikely for all of them to decay simultaneously, thus reducing the probability of significant profit decay and of complete shut-down of the algorithmic trading business.

Trading strategies that we've covered in previous chapters that complement each other include trend-following strategies combined with mean-reversion strategies, since they often have opposing views on markets that are trending/breaking out. A slightly less intuitive pair would be pairs-trading and stat-arb trading strategies, since one relies on a co-linear relationship between different trading instruments holding and the other relies on a co-related lead-lag relationship holding between different trading instruments. For event-based trading strategies, it is better to deploy them simultaneously with their trend following as well as mean reversion bets. The more sophisticated market participants usually have combinations of all of these trading strategies with different trading signals and parameters deployed to different asset classes over multiple trading exchanges.

Thus, they maintain an extremely diverse range of trading exposure at all times. This helps to deal with issues of profit decay in trading signals and trading strategies, and optimize risk versus reward, but we will explore that more in the next section.

Portfolio optimization

In the previous section, we discussed the advantages of having a diverse set of trading strategies that rely on different trading signals. Here, each trading strategy is profitable by itself, but each one's performance is slightly different depending on market conditions, market participants, asset class, and time periods, which are, to a large extent, un-correlated to each other. To recap, the benefits are greater adaptability to changing market conditions/participants and a better risk-versus-reward profile for the entire portfolio. This is because all strategies do not lose money simultaneously, which would lead to very large drawdown across the entire portfolio of trading strategies deployed to live trading markets. Say we have a diverse set of trading strategies, how do we decide how much risk to allocate to each trading strategy? That is a field of study known as portfolio optimization, which has entire books dedicated to understanding the different methods involved.

Portfolio optimization is an advanced technique for algorithmic/quantitative trading, so we won't cover it in too much detail here. Portfolio optimization is the technique of combining different trading strategies with different risk-reward profiles together to form portfolios of trading strategies which, when run together, provide optimal risk-reward for the entire portfolio. By optimal risk-reward, we mean it delivers maximum returns while trying to minimize the amount of risk taken. Obviously, risk versus reward is inversely proportional, so we try to find the optimal reward for the amount of risk we are willing to take and then use the portfolio allocation that maximizes the total reward of the portfolio while respecting the maximum risk we are willing to take across the portfolio. Let's look at some common portfolio-optimization methods, and observe how allocation varies for different allocation methods.

Note that implementation details of different portfolio allocation techniques have been omitted here for brevity's sake, but if you are interested then you should check out `https://github.com/sghoshusc/stratandport` for a project that implements and compares these different methods. It uses mean-reversion, trend-following, stat-arb, and pairs-trading strategies applied to 12 different futures contracts and then builds optimal portfolios using the methods we've discussed here. It uses python3 with the `cvxopt` package to perform convex optimization for markowitz allocation and scikit learn for the regime predictive allocation and matplotlib for visualization purpose.

Uniform risk allocation

Uniform risk allocation is the easiest method of portfolio allocation/optimization to understand. It basically says we take the total amount of risk we are allowed to or willing to take across the entire portfolio, and distribute it equally among all available trading strategies. Intuitively, this is a good starting point or a baseline allocation method when we don't have a historical performance record for any of the trading strategy, since nothing has been deployed to live trading markets, but in practice this is rarely ever used.

PnL-based risk allocation

PnL-based risk allocation is probably the most intuitive portfolio allocation/optimization technique. It says to start all available trading strategies with an equal amount of risk when we have no live trading history. Then, as time goes on, we rebalance the portfolio-allocation amounts based on the average performance of each trading strategy.

Let's say we want to rebalance our portfolio of trading strategy every month. Then at the end of every month, we look at the average monthly PnLs of every trading strategy we have in our portfolio and for the next month, every trading strategy gets risk proportional to its average monthly performance, the best performers get the most risk and the worst performers get the least risk allocated to them. This makes intuitive sense and is often how a portfolio allocations are performed. It uses historical performance as a proxy for future performance, which obviously isn't always true but is a good start.

It, however, does not factor in that different trading strategies might be taking different kinds of risks, and a safer trading strategy might get less risk allocated to it in favor of more volatile trading strategies. This allocation method also does not take correlation of returns between different strategies into account while allocating risk to different trading strategies, which can end up causing very high volatility for the portfolio returns.

The interesting point here is that eventually the strategy with the best historical performance ends up with the majority of the risk allocation. Also, strategies that haven't been performing as well as their peers gradually have their risk cut down to a very small amount and often don't recover from there.

PnL-sharpe-based risk allocation

PnL-sharpe-based risk allocation is a step ahead of PnL-based risk allocation. It uses the average PnLs normalized by historic standard deviation of returns to penalize trading strategies that have large PnL swings, also known as very high volatility returns.

This allocation method solves the problem of avoiding the construction of a high-volatility portfolio. But it still does not account for the correlation of returns between different trading strategies, which can still end up causing us to construct a portfolio where the individual trading strategies have good risk-adjusted PnLs but the portfolio as a whole is highly volatile.

The trading strategy with the best performance still makes the most money, similar to what we saw in the individual PnL-based allocation. However the other trading strategies still get a decent portion of the total allocation amount. This is because when we factor for risk in our allocation method, even strategies that make a lot of money don't necessarily end up with large allocations because the volatility in their returns also increases with their PnLs.

Markowitz allocation

The Markowitz portfolio allocation is one of the most well-known portfolio-allocation approaches in modern algorithmic/quantitative trading and is based on modern portfolio theory. The idea here is to take the co-variance between the returns of all the trading strategies in our portfolio and account for that when allocating risk to individual trading strategies to minimize portfolio variance while maximizing portfolio returns. It is a convex optimization problem and has many well-known and well-understood techniques to solve. For a given level of portfolio variance, it can find the best allocation scheme to maximize portfolio returns by building what is known as an efficient frontier curve, which is the curve of optimal allocations for the trading strategies in the portfolio for different levels of risk. From there, as our risk appetite grows or shrinks, and as more strategy results are available as more trading days are seen, it is straightforward to rebalance the portfolio by using the readjusted efficient frontier.

For Markowitz allocation, we can state the following:

- Allocation seeks to maximize diversity of the different trading strategies in the portfolio, by ensuring that strategies with uncorrelated returns have risk allocated to them.
- While in other allocation methods, the risk allocation for strategies that have poor performance would have dropped close to 0, here even losing strategies have some allocation assigned to them. This is because the periods in which these losing strategies make money offsets periods where the rest of the portfolio loses money, thus minimizing overall portfolio variance.

Regime Predictive allocation

Regime Predictive allocation is a technique that has been used by some advanced participants in recent years and is still something that is actively being researched. This studies the performance of different trading strategies as a function of different economic indicators and then builds machine learning predictive models that can predict what kinds of trading strategies and what product groups are most likely to do well given current market conditions. To summarize, this allocation method uses economic indicators as input features to a model that predicts trading strategies' expected performance in the current market regime and then uses those predictions to balance allocations assigned to different trading strategies in the portfolio.

Note that this method is still able to allocate the largest risk to the best-performing strategy and reducing allocation on strategies that are performing poorly. This will make more sense when we compare it to all the different allocation methods covered in the following plot:

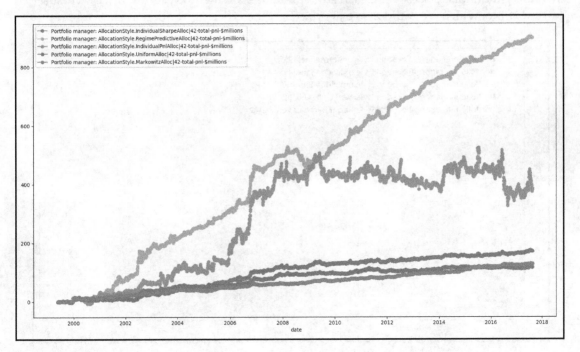

When we compare the different allocation methods next to each other, we can make a couple of observations. The first is that the Markowitz allocation method seems to be the one with the least variance and steadily rises up. The Uniform allocation method performs the worst. The Individual PnL-based allocation method actually has very good performance, with a cumulative PnL of around $400,000,000. However, visually we can observe that it has very large variance because the portfolio performance swings around a lot, which we intuitively expected because it doesn't factor for variance/risk in any way. The regime-based allocation method by far outperforms all other allocation methods with a cumulative PnL of around $900,000,000. The regime-based allocation method also seems like it has very low variance, thus achieving very good risk-adjusted performance for the portfolio.

Let's look at the different allocation methods portfolio performance by comparing daily average portfolio performance with daily standard deviation of portfolio performance in the plot. We do this to see where each strategy-allocation method lies on the risk versus reward curve, which we could also extend to find the efficient frontier, as shown here:

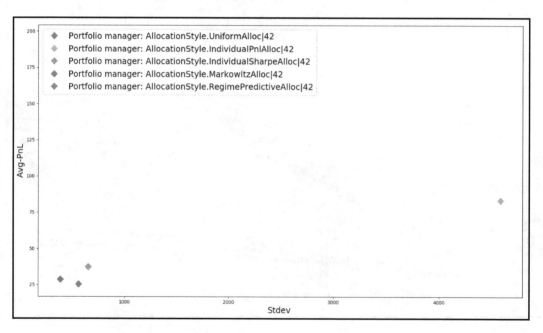

We can make the following observations from the preceding plot:

- The avg-daily-PnLs and daily-risk are in $1,000 units.
- We immediately see that Markowitz allocation has the minimum possible portfolio risk/variance with an avg-PnL of $25,000 and risk of $300,000.
- The Uniform risk allocation method has lowest portfolio avg-PnL of roughly $20,000 but higher risk of $500,000.
- The individual PnL allocation has a very large avg-PnL of $80,000 but with much higher risk of $4,700,000, which would likely make it unusable in practice.
- The Regime predictive allocation method has a very high avg-PnL of $180,000 and relatively low risk of $1,800,000, making it the best-available allocation method in practice, thus also validating why it's an active research area right now.

Incorporating technological advances

Now we approach the final section on best practices and the approaches to keeping up with competitive market participants and changing market conditions. As we've discussed, algorithmic/quantitative trading is largely a technology business and advances made in technology over the years have a large impact on the algorithmic trading business. Advances in technology is what allowed modern electronic trading in the first place, starting from outcry pits to mostly-automated and technology-assisted trading. Advances leading to faster trading servers, specialized network switches capable of higher throughput and lower switching latencies, advances made in network card technology and kernel bypass mechanisms, and even FPGA technology are important examples of this. This has caused the electronic trading business to evolve into a high-frequency, round-the-clock trading business where it is mostly automated trading bots trading against other automated trading bots.

Not only have there been hardware enhancements, but even software development practices have evolved over time. Now, large teams of talented software engineers have figured out how to build scalable and extremely low latency trading systems and trading strategies. This has been assisted by a combination of the evolution of both low-level and high-level programming languages, such as C, C++, and Java, along with improvements in compilers that can produce highly-optimized code; both have significantly improved the scalability and speed of what trading systems and trading strategies can be deployed to live trading markets.

A lot of market participants also now have access to microwave networks that can transmit data between locations much faster than physical fiber connections can, leading to latency-arbitrage opportunities. Time and time again, participants who have maintained their technological edge and kept up with the technological advancements made by their competition have been the ones to survive. Large algorithmic/HFT trading firms with superior technologies have even cornered the market on some trades and made it impossible for others to compete with them.

To summarize the main point of this section, algorithmic trading firms must continuously evolve their use of technology for their trading business to stay competitive. If other market participants gain access to breakthrough technologies, market participants who do not adapt will get wiped out.

Summary

This chapter explored what happens when algorithmic trading system and algorithmic trading strategies are deployed to live markets after months, and often years, of development and research. Many common issues with live trading strategies, such as not behaving or performing according to expectations, were discussed and we provided common causes and possible solutions or approaches to remedy these. This should help to prepare anyone looking to build and deploy algorithmic trading strategies to live markets, and equip them with the knowledge to improve trading strategy components when things don't go as expected.

Once the initial trading strategies are deployed and running in live markets as per expectations, we discussed the evolving nature of the algorithmic trading business and global markets in general. We covered a lot of different factors that cause profitable strategies to slowly decay due to a variety of reasons, both internal to the trading strategy itself and external in the form of other market participants and external conditions. We explored the different factors at play and the enormous amount of work that needs to be done on a continual basis to stay consistently profitable.

Final words

At this point, you have learned about all the components involved in a modern algorithmic trading business. You should be well-versed in all the different components involved in an end-to-end algorithmic trading setup between the trading exchange, as well as the interactions between the trading exchange and the different market participants. In addition, you should be able to understand how market participants interact with each other via the exchange matching engine and available market data.

We looked at all the different methods of incorporating intelligence into our trading signals using conventional technical analysis as well as advanced machine learning methods. We discussed the details of trading strategies and how they convert intelligence from trading signals into the order flow to manage positions and risk such that they are profitable, and then looked at some sophisticated trading strategies that incorporate a lot more intelligence available to them. We covered the extreme importance of strict risk management principles, building a risk management system, and how to adjust it over time with trading strategy performance.

We looked at all of the infrastructural components involved in a complete algorithmic trading setup. Don't forget that trading strategies sit on top of infrastructure components; hence, robust, fast, and reliable market data feed handlers, market data normalizers, and order gateways are a key aspect of a profitable algorithmic trading business and must not be overlooked.

We dedicated an entire chapter to understanding the inner workings of a backtester and explored all the challenges that come with building, maintaining, and tweaking it, another key element in quantitative automated data-driven trading strategies. Finally, you should now know what to expect when trading strategies are finally adopted by live markets and how to navigate that.

Remember, algorithmic trading is an extremely competitive and rewarding business and draws some of the brightest minds in the world. There are also risks involved in trading and it is in a constant state of evolution, so this journey will require a lot of dedication, hard work, analytical thinking, perseverance, and continuous innovation. We wish the you the best of luck as you embark on your journey into modern algorithmic trading!

Other Books You May Enjoy

If you enjoyed this book, you may be interested in these other books by Packt:

Mastering Python for Finance - Second Edition
James Ma Weiming

ISBN: 9781789346466

- Solve linear and nonlinear models representing various financial problems
- Perform principal component analysis on the DOW index and its components
- Analyze, predict, and forecast stationary and non-stationary time series processes
- Create an event-driven backtesting tool and measure your strategies
- Build a high-frequency algorithmic trading platform with Python
- Replicate the CBOT VIX index with SPX options for studying VIX-based strategies
- Perform regression-based and classification-based machine learning tasks for prediction
- Use TensorFlow and Keras in deep learning neural network architecture

Hands-On Machine Learning for Algorithmic Trading
Stefan Jansen

ISBN: 9781789346411

- Implement machine learning techniques to solve investment and trading problems
- Leverage market, fundamental, and alternative data to research alpha factors
- Design and fine-tune supervised, unsupervised, and reinforcement learning models
- Optimize portfolio risk and performance using pandas, NumPy, and scikit-learn
- Integrate machine learning models into a live trading strategy on Quantopian
- Evaluate strategies using reliable backtesting methodologies for time series
- Design and evaluate deep neural networks using Keras, PyTorch, and TensorFlow
- Work with reinforcement learning for trading strategies in the OpenAI Gym

Leave a review - let other readers know what you think

Please share your thoughts on this book with others by leaving a review on the site that you bought it from. If you purchased the book from Amazon, please leave us an honest review on this book's Amazon page. This is vital so that other potential readers can see and use your unbiased opinion to make purchasing decisions, we can understand what our customers think about our products, and our authors can see your feedback on the title that they have worked with Packt to create. It will only take a few minutes of your time, but is valuable to other potential customers, our authors, and Packt. Thank you!

Index

M

market conditions
  adapting to 353
market data feed handlers 19
market data request handling 292
Market Data request handling
  about 293
  product, obtaining 294
  request ID, obtaining 294
  symbol ID, obtaining 294
market data subscription 25
market participants
  changing 353
market risk 199, 200
market sectors 11, 12
MarketSimulator class 261, 263
Markowitz allocation 362
max drawdown 205, 206, 207
max-loss 203
mean reversion trading strategies
  absolute price oscillator (APO) trading signal,
    using 142, 145, 148, 149, 150, 151, 152
  dynamically, adjusting for changing volatility 152,
    153, 154, 156
  volatility, adjusting 142
measures of risk
  differentiating 202
  max drawdown 205, 206, 207
  maximum executions per period 213
  maximum trade size 216
  PnLs, variance 210, 212
  position holding time 209, 210
  position limits 207, 208
  Sharpe ratio 212
  stop-loss 203, 205
  volume limits 216
modern algorithmic trading 14, 15
momentum (MOM)
  about 72, 73
  implementing 73
momentum strategies
  advantages 110
  creating 110
  disadvantages 110

examples 111
moving average convergence divergence (MACD)
  about 59
  implementing 60, 63

N

naive data storage 301
National Center for Supercomputing Applications
    (NCSA) 302
New York Stock Exchange (NYSE) 298
non-compete agreements (NCAs) 349
non-critical components
  about 243
  command and control 244
  services 245
non-disclosure agreements (NDAs) 349
non-relational databases 306
notations 86, 87, 88

O

operations, limit order book
  amendment 266
  cancellation 266
  insertion 266
  modification 266
order book management 239, 240
order entry gateway 20
order handling 292
order management system (OMS) 242
order management
  about 294, 295, 296, 297
  amend order (35=G) 294
  cancel order (35=F) 294
  new order (35=D) 294
order types
  about 19
  Good Till Day (GTD) 19
  Immediate Or Cancel (IOC) 19
  stop orders 19
OrderManager class 256, 257, 259, 260
Ordinary Least Squares (OLS) 92, 93, 94, 95
other trading APIs 298
out-of-sample data
  versus in-sample data 300

U

V